HAYEK
— on —
LIBERTY

John Gray

BASIL BLACKWELL

© John Gray, 1984

First published in 1984 by Basil Blackwell Publishers Ltd.,
108 Cowley Road, Oxford OX4 1JF

Basil Blackwell Inc.
432 Park Avenue South, Suite 1505
New York, NY 10016, USA

British Library Cataloguing in Publication Data

Gray, John, 1948–
   Hayek on liberty.
   1. Hayek, F. A.
   I. Title
   192   HB101.H39

ISBN 0–85520–710–8

Typset by System 4 Associates, Gerrards Cross
Printed and bound in Great Britain by
The Camelot Press, Southampton

Contents

Preface and Acknowledgements   viii

1   HAYEK'S SYSTEM OF IDEAS: ITS ORIGINS AND SCOPE   1

The unity of Hayek's system of ideas and its philosophical
     character   1

Hayek's general philosophy: the Kantian heritage   4

Four influences on Hayek's sceptical Kantianism:
     Mach, Popper, Wittgenstein and Polanyi   8

Hayek's relations with the Austrian School of Economics
     and his account of the methodology of social science   16

Hayek on knowledge and the mind: implications for
     social theory   21

2   THE IDEA OF A SPONTANEOUS SOCIAL ORDER   27

Spontaneous order versus the constructivist fallacy   27

The central conception of spontaneous order and its
     applications to physical and social phenomena   31

The application of spontaneous order in economic life:
     the catallaxy   34

Cultural evolution and the natural selection of
     traditions   41

3 THE LAW OF LIBERTY 56

The origins and nature of law 56

Individual liberty under the rule of law 61

The rule of law and the myth of social justice 71

The juridical framework of spontaneous social order 76

4 ECONOMIC THEORY AND PUBLIC POLICY 79

Social science and public policy 79

Neoclassical equilibrium, the theory of capital and
the character of the business cycle 83

Hayek versus Keynes and Friedman on the rôle of
money in the real economy 88

Shackle's critique of Hayek 92

5 SOME CONTRASTS AND COMPARISONS 95

J. S. Mill 95

Herbert Spencer 103

Karl Popper 110

6 ASSESSMENT AND CRITICISM 116

The unity of Hayek's system of ideas 116

The status and content of the idea of spontaneous
order in society 118

Hayek's constitution of liberty: some criticisms
assessed 125

Conservatism and radicalism in Hayek's social
philosophy 129

The Hayekian research programme and the
prospects of social philosophy 134

Contents

BIOGRAPHICAL NOTE ON HAYEK   141

BIBLIOGRAPHY   143

Hayek's Works   145

Works About or Relevant to Hayek   181

Notes   210

Index   226

Preface and Acknowledgements

Though Hayek's central place in twentieth-century economic thought is uncontested, his general philosophy has yet to receive the sustained critical attention it merits. A major theme of this study is that Hayek's work composes a system of ideas, fully as ambitious as the systems of Mill and Marx, but far less vulnerable to criticism than theirs because it is grounded on a philosophically denfensible view of the scope and limits of human reason. A related claim made in this study is that we find in Hayek a restatement of classical liberalism in which it is purified of errors — specifically, the errors of abstract individualism and uncritical rationalism — which inform the work of even the greatest of the classical liberals and which Hayek has been able to correct by absorbing some of the deepest insights of conservative philosophy. For these two reasons alone, Hayek's work should command the critical interest of philosophers and social theorists as well as political economists.

More fundamentally, however, Hayek's work initiates a paradigm shift in social philosophy and launches a new research programme in social theory. In ways I will specify in detail in the body of this book, Hayek displaces the focus of social philosophy from the preoccupations which have led the analytical school into an impasse — preoccupations with the conceptual analysis of the main terms of political discourse and with the endless discussion of rival principles against a background of moral scepticism — to the areas of epistemology and philosophical psychology. His intuition is that a way of assessing different social systems more fruitful than the traditional method of appraising their moral content is to be found in illuminating the demands they make upon the powers of the mind and the uses they are able to make of human knowledge. His conclusion is that, once we have arrived at a realistic picture of the powers and limitations of the human mind, we see that many important social doctrines — those of socialism and interventionist liberalism, for example, — make impossible demands upon our knowledge. Even the liberalism of John Stuart Mill, for all its harping on the fallibility of our beliefs, embodies a naïvely rationalistic conception of the relations of the individual mind with its cultural inheritance of tradition. Hayek on liberty transcends the rationalistic fallacies which disfigure Mill's liberalism and gives us a defence of individual freedom without equal in modern thought. Hayek's work has every claim to occupy a distinguished place in the mainstream of contemporary philosophy.

This brief study has been assisted by a large number of people. Among those who have commented on the manuscript at various stages in its evolution, or with whom I have had extended discussions on Hayekian themes, I would like to thank particularly W. W. Bartley III (whose biography of Hayek will be a notable event in Hayek scholarship), Norman P. Barry, Samuel Brittan, James Buchanan, Tim Congdon, Walter Eltis, Milton Friedman, Sir H. J. Habbakuk, Donald Hay, Nevil Johnson, Israel Kirzner, Irving Kristol, Robert Nozick, J. C. Nyiri, Michael Oakeshott, Dr D. A. Rees, Murray Rothbard, G. L. S. Shackle and Jeremy Shearmur (whose important work on Hayek, shortly to be published in a book, has contributed a valuable reference point for my own, especially where our interpretations have differed widely). I wish to thank most warmly Professor Hayek himself, for the unstinting generosity and unfailing patience with which he has dealt with my innumerable (and often ill-formulated) questions and criticisms, and to Professor Hayek's secretary, Mrs C. Cubitt, for her assistance in revising the Bibliography.

I acknowledge permission to publish the following extracts: 'The Liberalism of Karl Popper' from *Government and Opposition*, Vol. II, no. 3 (Summer 1976), pp. 337–55 and 'Spencer on the Ethics of Liberty and the limits of State Interference' from *History of Political Thought*, Vol. III, no. 3 (Winter 1982), pp. 465–81.

I am grateful to the Principal and Fellows of my College for granting me two periods of sabbatical leave during which I was able to bring the book nearer completion. I wish to express my gratitude for the assistance given me in the early stages of my research by a small Research Grant in the Humanities awarded by the British Academy. Also, I wish to acknowledge a debt of gratitude to the Institute for Humane Studies in Menlo Park, California. Under the direction first of Kenneth S. Templeton Jr. and then Leonard P. Liggio, this excellent institution devoted to research and scholarship in the traditions of classical liberalism has since 1977 supported my studies of Hayek in many ways. With the invaluable support of Liberty Fund of Indianopolis the Institute enabled me to spend several summers in Menlo Park as a residential research scholar, pursuing my inquiries into Hayek in the context of colloquia on classical liberal thought operated by Liberty Fund. This book owes its origin to a monograph on 'F. A. Hayek and the Rebirth of Classical Liberalism' published by the Institute in its invaluable (but unhappily now defunct) journal *Literature of Liberty*. Without the interest shown in my work by Ken Templeton and Leonard Liggio, and the scholarly support given me at the Institute by John Cody and Walter Grinder, I am sure I would not have begun this book, still less finished it.

Finally, I would like to thank Carole Charlton in Oxford and Pat Ortega in Palo Alto for their work in deciphering my handwritten manuscript.

John Gray
Jesus College, Oxford

— 1 —

Hayek's system of ideas:
its origins and scope

THE UNITY OF HAYEK'S SYSTEM OF IDEAS AND
ITS PHILOSOPHICAL CHARACTER

As part of the reawakening of public and scholarly interest in
the intellectual tradition of classical liberalism, Hayek's
writings in a range of academic disciplines have been recalled
from a period of neglect during which it seemed to many that
they had been consigned to oblivion. It is not an exaggeration
to say that the re-emergence of classical liberalism and the
rediscovery of Hayek's writings are complementary aspects
of a single current of opinion. For, while Hayek's writings
address and illuminate some of the most formidable issues of
the age, and answer to many comtemporary anxieties, they
do so within the frame of thought constructed by the great
classical liberals. Hayek's work is in the tradition of classical
liberalism, not simply because his concerns are in many areas
those of Locke and Burke, Adam Smith and Kant, but also
because, like the theorists of liberalism s Golden Age in the
eighteenth century, Hayek seeks to raise up a system of ideas,
a structure of principles with the aid of which we can understand social and political life and subject it to reasoned
criticism. No-one who knows Hayek's work can doubt that
his attempt to restate liberal principles in a form appropriate
to the circumstances and temper of the twentieth century has

yielded a body of insights wholly comparable in profoundity and power with those of his forbears in the classical liberal tradition. In Hayek's work, the chief values of classical liberalism — the dignity of the human individual and the moral primacy of his freedom, the virtues of free markets and the necessity for limited government under the rule of law — are defended within an intellectual framework of uncompromising modernity. There can be no doubt that Hayek's reformulation of classical liberalism succeeds in building on the intellectual foundations inherited from the liberal period a body of thought as powerful as any that can be found within the classical liberal writers and far more resistant to criticism than was classical liberalism itself.

Even Hayek's most convinced critics would hesitate to deny these achievements of his work. At the same time, even among his friends and disciples, the sense of Hayek's work as composing a system of ideas is often missing. The reasons for this widespread failure to grasp the systematic character of Hayek's thought may seem obvious. His writings cross several major disciplines — theoretical economics, jurisprudence, philosophy, psychology and intellectual history among them — and they span over half a century. Again, though there has been some interest in recent years among philosophers and cultural historians in the milieu of thought of the last decades of Hapsburg Vienna, most economists and social theorists remain deeply ignorant of that milieu, and accordingly can have little understanding of the context of thought in which Hayek's outlook was nurtured. It seems to me, though, that the general failure of comprehension in regard to the character of Hayek's work as a system of ideas has other sources, distinct from the two I have just mentioned and having to do rather with the inherent structure of Hayek's outlook itself.

The chief aim of this study is to exhibit Hayek's contributions to the various disciplines of inquiry in which he has worked as constituting a system in virtue of their being informed and governed throughout by a distinctive philosophical outlook. Even Hayek's achievements in economic theory can be shown on the interpretation I advance to trade upon and put to work genuine and powerful insights in philosophy which Hayek achieved very early in his intellectual career. My interpretation has the novel aspect that it treats Hayek as a philosopher *sans phrase*, whose contributions to the social sciences (like those of J. S. Mill) express a natural application of his philosophical outlook. The comparison with Mill is here a close one, despite their many deep differences, in that in Hayek's case as in Mill's, his contributions to economics were preceded by an effort to establish a new position in the theory of knowledge in the most general sense. This has been concealed in Hayek's case because his profound and neglected study in epistemology and philosophical psychology, *The Sensory Order*, was published only in 1952, after Hayek's principal contributions to economics, whereas Mill's *System of Logic* (1843) is a temporal as well as a methodological forerunner of his *Principles of Political Economy* (1848). Though it was published only in the fifties, *The Sensory Order* was first sketched as a student paper by Hayek in 1920, and its argument was substantially complete by the early twenties. A careful investigation of its argument is indispensable to any adequate understanding of Hayek's work, not only because it remains his most extended explicit statement in general philosophy, but also because it reveals most clearly the intellectual influences at work in Hayek's writings. Most crucially, however, the view of knowledge it defends can be shown to be presupposed by many of the positions Hayek has adopted in economic theory and in social philosophy. The elusiveness and subtlety of Hayek's writings, on which many commentators have remarked, is in great part explained by their general failure to perceive the relevance of his work in the philosophies of knowledge and mind to the stands he has taken up in economic and social theory. This failure is regrettable and surprising: regrettable, in that it has reinforced the neglect which Hayek's work has suffered in contemporary intellectual life, and surprising in that his writings in the social sciences are studded with references to his more explicitly philosophical works, and, above all, to *The Sensory Order*.

Hayek's philosophical outlook is an extremely distinctive version of post-Kantian critical philosophy in which a number of more contemporary influences — the philosophies of Mach, Popper, Wittgenstein and Polanyi, most notably — have been synthesized into a coherent system. It would be a mistake, at the same time, to see Hayek's thought as essentially eclectic, a weaving together over decades of strands of reflection garnered from other writers, since all the evidence suggests that his conception of the mind and of the limits to our knowledge has been with him from the start, acquiring refinement and expansion in the course of his intellectual development but remaining unaltered in its most fundamental respects. The structure of his conception, and its persistence throughout the many influences under which he has temporarily come, has misled many of Hayek's interpreters into periodizing his intellectual career into distinct phases — a Misesian phase, perhaps, in which he supposedly embraced the philsophical outlook of his colleague in economics, L. von Mises, followed by a Popperian one which emerged from his meeting and friendship with Sir Karl Popper — but it is easy to show that such interpretations are wide of the mark. Hayek's thought retains the character of a coherent system rather than an eclectic construction, even if in the end it harbours conflicts which demand a revision of some of its elements.

HAYEK'S GENERAL PHILOSOPHY: THE KANTIAN HERITAGE

The entirety of Hayek's work — and, above all, his work in epistemology, psychology, ethics, and the theory of law — is informed by a distinctively Kantian approach. In its most fundamental aspect, Hayek's thought is Kantian in its denial of our capacity to know things as they are or the world as it is. It is in his denial that we can know things as they are, and in his insistence that the order we find in our experiences, including even our sensory experiences, is the product of the creative activity of our minds rather than a reality given to us by the world, that Hayek's Kantianism consists. It follows from this sceptical Kantian standpoint that the task of philosophy cannot be that of uncovering the necessary characters of things. The keynote of critical philosophy, after all, is the impossibility of our attaining any external or transcendental standpoint on human thought from which we could develop a conception of the world that is wholly uncontaminated by human experiences or interests. We find in Kant's own writings — above all the *Critique of Pure Reason* (1781) — a case against the possibility of speculative metaphysics which Hayek himself has always taken to be devastating and conclusive. It is a fundamental conviction of Hayek's, and one that he has in common with all those who stand in the tradition of post-Kantian critical philosophy, that we cannot so step out of our human point of view as to attain a presuppositionless perspective on the world as a whole and as it is in itself. The traditional aspiration of western philosophy — to develop a speculative metaphysics in terms of which human thought may be justified and reformed — must accordingly be abandoned. The task of philosophy, for Hayek as for Kant, is not the construction of any metaphysical system, but the investigation of the limits of reason. It is a reflexive rather than a constructive inquiry, since all criticism — in ethics as much as in science — must in the end be immanent criticism. In philosophy as in life, Hayek avers, we must take much for granted, or else we will never get started.

Hayek's uncompromisingly sceptical Kantianism is strongly evidenced in *The Sensory Order.* There Hayek disavows any concern as to 'how things really are in the world', affirming that '...a question like "what is X?" has meaning only within a given order, and...within this limit it must always refer to the relation of one particular event to other events belonging to the same order.'[1] Above all, the distinction between appearance and reality, which Hayek sees as best avoided in scientific discourse,[2] is not to be identified with the distinction between the mental or sensory order and the physical or material order. The aim of scientific investigation is not, then, for Hayek, the discovery behind the veil of appearance of the natures or essences of things in themselves, for, with Kant and against Aristotelian essentialism, he stigmatizes the notion of essence or absolute reality as useless or harmful in science and in philosophy. The aim of sience can only be the development of a system of categories or principles, in the end organized wholly deductively, which is adequate to the experience it seeks to order.[3]

Hayek is a Kantian, then, in disavowing in science or in philosophy any Aristotelian method of seeking the essences or natures of things. We cannot know how things are in the world, but only how our mind itself organizes the jumble of its experiences. He is Kantian, again, in repudiating the belief, common to empiricists and positivists such as David Hume and Ernst Mach, that there is available to us a ground of elementary sensory impressions, untainted by conceptual thought, which can serve as the foundation for the house of human knowledge. Against this empiricist dogma, Hayek is emphatic that everything in the sensory order is abstract, conceptual and theory-laden in character: 'It will be the central thesis of the theory to be outlined that it is not merely a part but the whole of sensory qualities which is...an "interpretation" based on the experience of the individual or the race. The conception of an original pure core of sensation which is merely modified by experience is an entirely unnecessary fiction.'[4] Again, he tells us that 'the elimination of the hypothetical "pure" or "primary" core of sensation, supposed not to be due to earlier experience, but either to involve some direct communication of properties of the external objects, or to constitute irreducible mental atoms or elements, disposes of various philosophical puzzles which arise from the lack of meaning of these hypotheses.'[5] The map or model we form of the world, in Hayek's view, is in no important respect grounded in a basis of sheer sense-data, themselves supposed to be incorrigible. Rather, the picture

we form of the world emerges straight from our interaction with the world, and it is always abstract in selecting
some among the infinite aspects which the world contains,
most of which we are bound to pass by as without interest
to us.

Hayek's Kantianism, so prominent in his theory of knowledge, is no less pronounced in his jurisprudence and in his
political philosophy. It is neglect of the influence on his
social theory of Kant's account of the law that has misled
some of Hayek's interpreters into construing him as a theorist
of rights in the tradition of John Locke (a tradition whose
most distinguished contemporary spokesman is found in
Robert Nozick). In fact Hayek's view of law and justice is
altogether Kantian in that it relinquishes any reference to
natural law — which forms the necessary matrix for any
account of natural rights — and treats moral rights, not as
themselves framing absolute constraints of justice on the
content of law, but rather as implications of the nature of
law itself when certain fundamental features of the human
circumstance are taken into account. As I shall try to make
clear in a later chapter, Hayek's theory of justice is not
rights-based, but procedural: we discover the demands of
justice by applying to the permanent conditions of human
life a Kantian test of universalizability. This is to say that, if
a rule or maxim is to be acceptable as just, its application
must be endorsed by rational agents across all relevantly
similar cases. Hayek's view of justice is little understood, in
part because it has often been assumed that the contrast
between a patterned account of justice such as that of John
Rawls (himself a theorist in a Kantian tradition) and the
entitlement-based theory of Robert Nozick in which moral
rights figure as fundamental constraints on all other values,
is a contrast which exhausts all plausible accounts. Hayek's
view of justice would have even been better understood, if
we had followed his own explicit guidance, and seen it as a
synthesis of Kant's requirement of universalizability in
practical reasoning with David Hume's account of the content

and basis of the rules of justice. One of the most intriguing features of Hayek's political philosophy is its attempt to mark out a *tertium quid* between the views of justice of Hume and Kant. His theory of knowledge may similarly be interpreted as aiming at a reconciliation of the apparently opposed insights of Popper and Wittgenstein. In all of his writings, however, the distinctively Kantian flavour is evident in his strategy of working with postulates or regulative ideas, epistemological and normative, which are as metaphysically neutral, and as uncommitted to specific conceptions of the good life, as he can reasonably make them. It is this minimalist or even formalist strategy of argument that most pervasively expresses Hayek's Kantian heritage.

FOUR INFLUENCES ON HAYEK'S SCEPTICAL KANTIANISM: MACH, POPPER, WITTGENSTEIN AND POLANYI

Hayek's theory of knowledge is Kantian, we have seen, in affirming that the order we find in the world is given to it by the organizing structure of our own mind and in claiming that even sensory experiences are suffused with the ordering concepts of the human mind. His view of the mind, then, is Kantian in that it accords a very great measure of creative power to the mind, which is neither a receptacle for the passive absorption of fugitive sensations, nor yet a mirror in which the world's necessities are reflected.

There are a number of influences on Hayek, however, which give his Kantianism a profoundly distinctive and original aspect. The first of these influences is the work of Ernst Mach (1836–1916), the positivist philosopher whose ideas dominated much of Austro-German intellectual life in the decades of Hayek's youth. Hayek's debts to Mach are not so much in the theory of knowledge, as in the attitude both take to certain traditional metaphysical questions. I have observed already that Hayek dissented radically from the Humean and Machian belief that human knowledge could be reconstructed on the basis of elementary sensory impressions, and throughout his writings Hayek has always repudiated as incoherent or unworkable the reductionist projects of phenomenalism in the theory of perception and behaviourism in the philosophy of mind. In these areas of philosophy, then, Hayek's work has been strongly antipathetic to distinctively positivistic ambitions for a unified science. At the same time, while never endorsing the dogma of the Vienna Circle that metaphysical utterances are literally nonsensical, Hayek has often voiced the view that many traditional metaphysical questions express 'phantom-problems'.

In both *The Sensory Order* and later in *The Constitution of Liberty*, Hayek affirms that the age-old controversy about the freedom of will embodies such a phantom-problem.[6] Hayek's 'compatibilist' standpoint in respect of freedom of the will — his belief that the casual determination of human actions is fully compatible with ascribing responsibility to human agents for what they do — is analogous with his stance on the mind—body question. In both controversies Hayek is concerned to deny any ultimate dualism in metaphysics or ontology, while at the same time insisting that a dualism in our practical thought and in scientific method is unavoidable for us. Thus he says of the relations of the mental and physical domains that 'While our theory leads us to deny any ultimate dualism of the forces governing the realms of the mind and that of the physical world respectively, it forces us at the same time to recognize that for practical purposes we shall always have to adopt a dualistic view.'[7] And Hayek concludes his study of the foundations of theoretical psychology in *The Sensory Order* with the claim that '*to us* mind must remain forever a realm of its own, which we can know only through directly experiencing it, but which we shall never be able to fully explain or to "reduce" to something else.'[8]

Hayek's thought has a Machian positivist aspect, then, not in the theories of mind or perception, but in its attitude to tradtional metaphysical questions, which is dissolutionist

and deflationary. There is yet another link with positivism.
Notwithstanding Hayek's opposition to any sort of reductionism, whether sensationalist or physicalist, he seems to be
a monist in ontology, averring that 'mind is thus the order
prevailing in a particular part of the physical universe — that
part of it which is ourselves.'[9] Hayek may seem here to be
qualifying or withdrawing from that stance of metaphysical
neutrality which in Machian spirit he commends, but this
appearance may be delusive. There is much to suggest that,
when Hayek denies any ultimate dualism in the nature of
things, he is not lapsing into an idiom of essences or natural
kinds, but simply observing — much in the fashion of the
American pragmatist philosopher, W. V. Quine — that nothing
in our experience compels us to adopt ideas of mental or
physical substance.[10] Though Hayek has not to my knowledge ever pronounced explicitly on the question, the whole
tenor of his thought inclines to a Quinean pragmatist view of
ontological commitments. In his sceptical and pragmatist
attitude to ultimate questions in metaphysics and ontology,
Hayek lines up with many positivists rather than with Kantian
critical philosophy — though positivists themselves sometimes
claim, with some justification, to be treading a Kantian path.

A second influence on Hayek's general philosophy which
gives it a distinctive temper is the thought of his friend, Karl
Popper (b. 1902). I mean here, not Popper's hypothetico-
deductive account of scientific method, which there is
evidence that Hayek held prior to his meeting with Popper,[11]
nor yet Popper's proposal (which Hayek was soon to accept)
that falsifiability rather than verifiability should be adopted
as a criterion of demarcation between the scientific and the
non-scientific. Again, Hayek has under Popper's influence
come to make an important distinction between types of
rationalism,[12] such that 'critical rationalism' is commended
and 'constructivistic rationalism' condemned, but this is
not what I have in mind. I refer rather to certain striking
affinities between Hayek's view of the growth of knowledge and that adumbrated in Popper's later writings on

'evolutionary epistemology'. As early as the manuscript which later became *The Sensory Order* (published in 1952, but composed in the twenties), Hayek made it clear that the principles of classification embodied in the nervous system were not for him fixed data; experience constantly forced reclassification on us. In his later writings, Hayek is explicit that the human mind is itself an evolutionary product and that its structure is therefore variable and not constant. The structural principles or fundamental categories which our minds contain ought not, then, to be interpreted in Cartesian fashion as universal and necessary axioms, reflecting the natural necessities of the world, but rather as constituting evolutionary adaptations of the human organism to the world that it inhabits.

The striking similarity between Popper's later views, and those expounded by Hayek in *The Sensory Order*, is shown by Popper's own application of the evolutionist standpoint in epistemology to the theory of perception:

...if we start from a critical commonsense realism...then we shall take man as one of the animals, and human knowledge as essentially almost as fallible as animal knowledge. We shall suppose the animal senses to have evolved from primitive beginnings; and we shall look therefore on our own senses, essentially, as part of a decoding mechanism — a mechanism which decodes, more or less successfully, the encoded information about the world which manages to reach us by sensory means.[13]

J. W. N. Watkins' comment on this view is as apposite in the respect of Hayek as it is of Popper:

Kant saw very clearly that the empiricist account of sense experience creates and cannot solve the problem of how the *manifold* and very various data which reach a man's mind from his various senses get unified into a coherent experience.

Kant's solution consisted, essentially, in leaving the old quasi-mechanistic account of sense-organs intact, and endowing the mind with a powerful set of organizing categories — free, universal and necessary — which unify and structure what would otherwise be a mad jumble.

Popper's evolutionist view modifies Kant's view at both ends: interpretative principles lose their fixed and necessary character, and sense organs lose their merely causal and mechanistic character.[14]

Hayek's account of sense perception anticipates Popper's later views in a most striking fashion, because, in both, sensation is conceived as a decoding mechanism, which transmits to us in a highly abstract fashion information about our external environment. Again, both Hayek and Popper share the sceptical Kantian view that the order we find in the world is given to it by the creative activity of our own minds: as Hayek himself puts it uncompromisingly in *The Sensory Order*, 'The fact that the world which we know seems wholly an orderly world may thus be merely a result of the method by which we perceive it.'[15] In his most recent, and as yet unpublished writings, Hayek has acknowledged important affinities between Popper's postulate of a 'third' world of abstract or virtual entities or intelligibles and his own conception of tradition as the bearer of knowledge and values.[16]

Later in this study, I will try to illuminate some important contrasts between Hayek and Popper in both theory of knowledge and social philosophy. Specifically, I shall argue that, some of Hayek's own statements notwithstanding, he has never accepted without massive qualifications Popper's insistence that the falsificationist methodology is appropriate in all the sciences, natural as well as social. For Hayek, the search for simple universal laws is in the social studies vain or even harmful, and there are good reasons (rooted in their different subject-matters) to support something like a dualism in methods as between natural and social sciences. In social philosophy, Hayek's outlook has an entirely different spirit and orientation from that of Popper. The distinction between 'facts' and 'decisions', which Popper elevates to the status of a fundamental tenet of liberalism, Hayek is committed to repudiate as a shadow cast by the misconceived dichotomy of nature and convention we inherit from the Greek Sophists. More generally, there are many deep contrasts between Hayek's view of a free society as one in which distinctive traditions engage in peaceful competition under the rule of law and Popper's conception of the free society as embodying openness to criticism in the ways elaborated by J. S. Mill in *On Liberty*. One of the greater achievements of Hayek's social theory is, I shall submit, its successful synthesis of insights of conservative philosophy which are fatal to the visions of Mill and Popper with the classical liberal concerns which animated Kant and Hume.

A third influence on Hayek's thought which gives his view of knowledge and the mind a very distinctive character is that of his relative, Ludwig Wittgenstein (1889–1951).[17] This influence runs deep, and is seen not only in the style and presentation of *The Sensory Order*, which parallels in an obvious way that of Wittgenstein's *Tractatus*, but in many areas of Hayek's system of ideas. It is shown, for example, in Hayek's recurrent interest in the way in which the language in which we speak shapes our thoughts and forms our picture of the world. In fact, Hayek's interest in language, and in a critique of language, predates Wittgenstein's work, inasmuch as he had an early preoccupation with the work of Fritz Mauthner, the now almost forgotten philosopher of radical nominalism whom Wittgenstein mentions (somewhat dismissively) in *Tractatus*.[18] There are, however, many evidences that Wittgenstein's work reinforced Hayek's conviction that the study of language is a necessary precondition of the study of human thought, and an indispensable prophylactic to the principal disorders of the intellect. Examples which may be adduced are Hayek's studies of the confusion of language in political thought and, most obviously, perhaps, of his emphasis on the role of social rules in the transmission of practical knowledge.

It is on this last point that one of the most distinctive features of Hayek's Kantianism, its pragmatist aspect, is clearest.[19] Of course there is a recognition in Kant himself that knowledge requires judgement, a special faculty, the *Urteilskraft*, which cannot be given any complete or adequate specification in propositional terms, and whose exercise is necessary for the application of any rule. In the sense that we must exercise this faculty of judgement even before we can apply a rule, it is action which is at the root of our very knowledge itself. Hayek's concern is not with this ultimate dependency of rule following upon judgement — which the later Wittgenstein, perhaps following Kant, emphasizes — but rather with the way that knowledge of all sorts, but especially social knowledge, is embodied in rules. Our perceptual processes, indeed all our processes of thought, are governed by rules with we do not normally articulate, which in some cases are necessarily beyond articulation by us, but which we rely upon for the efficacy of all our action in the world. Indeed, it is not too much to say that, for Hayek (notwithstanding his stress on the abstract or conceptual character of our sensory knowledge) all our knowledge is at the bottom practical or tacit knowledge: it consists, not in propositions or theories, but in skills and dispositions to act in a rule-governed fashion. There is here an interesting parallel with Popper's view, which sees even our sense organs as being themselves embodied theories.[20]

There is much in Hayek's writings to suggest that he takes what Gilbert Ryle calls 'knowing how',[21] what Michael Polanyi calls tacit knowing,[22] what Michael Oakeshott[23] calls traditional knowledge, to be the wellspring of all our knowledge. It is in this sense — in holding the stuff of knowledge to be at bottom practical — that Hayek may be said to subscribe to a thesis of the primacy of practice in the constitution of human knowledge. It is not indeed that Hayek disparages the enterprise of theory-building, but he sees the theoretical reconstruction of our practical knowledge as necessarily incomplete in its achievements. In the next section of this chapter I will discuss Hayek's view that theoretical knowledge is always and only knowledge of abstract orders or patterns and often (in the social sciences, for example) only knowledge of a principle in terms of which such patterns may be understood. Here I wish to identify another limitation of theoretical knowledge in Hayek's view: theory is for him only the visible tip of the vast submerged fund of tacit knowledge, much of which is entirely beyond our powers of articulation. Neglect of this dependency of our necessarily abstract theories on a vast range of inarticulate background knowledge has led social science astray in many fields.

The third source of influence on Hayek's sceptical Kantianism, which I have ascribed primarily to the work of his relative Wittgenstein, plainly comprehends other influences as well. Hayek cites Ryle in support of his observation that '"know how" consists in the capacity to act according to rules which we may be able to discover but which we need not be able to state in order to obey them,' and glosses the point with reference to Michael Polanyi.[24] Here the insight is that all articulated or propositional knowledge arises out of tacit or practical knowledge, the knowledge of how to do things, which must be taken as fundamental. In Polanyi's work, there is here, in fact, the fourth and final major influence on Hayek, which in conjunction with the other three further modifies his Kantianism and makes of it something that Kant himself could not have recognized. The Polanyian element which enters into Hayek's work from at least the fifties consists, first of all, in the refinement of his view of knowledge as *au fond* practical and in his exploitation of Polanyi's insight that, since much of the knowledge we use is inarticulate, we always know more than we can ever say. In *The Constitution of Liberty* and elsewhere, this insight gives a wholly new twist to the argument for liberty from human ignorance. It is not just the fact that our knowledge is extremely limited that supports a regime of liberty in which experiments in living may be tried. Rather, a regime of liberty permits knowledge to be used which we never knew (and could never have known) we had: any centralized regime which relied only on our explicit knowledge would necessarily exploit only a small part of the stock of knowledge — that small part which is expressible in statements or propositions. Only a regime of liberty can fully use that greater part of our knowledge which is not so statable. One implication of this insight of Polanyi's for social theory, recognition of which by Hayek draws his social theory away from Popper's, is that rational criticism of social life is bound to come to a stop when it reaches the tacit dimension of our practices. This is a point to which I shall recur when in a later chapter I contrast Popper's philosophy with Hayek's in a more extended and systematic way.

HAYEK'S RELATIONS WITH THE AUSTRIAN SCHOOL OF ECONOMICS AND HIS ACCOUNT OF THE METHODOLOGY OF SOCIAL SCIENCE

Hayek's debts to the Austrian School of Economics founded by Menger (1840—1921) and carried on by Hayek's teacher, F. von Wieser (1851—1926) and his colleague, L. von Mises (1881—1973), are so many and so obvious that they tend to conceal those elements of his thought which are original and which in many cases cannot be accommodated within the orthodoxy of the Austrian School. In its most general contentions, however, Hayek has followed and developed the Austrian School. He has deepened and refined the Austrian subjective theory of value — the theory that value is conferred on resources by the subjective preferences of agents and cannot be explained as an inherent property of any asset or resource. It was this profound insight which spelt the end of that tradition of classical economic theory, encompassing Ricardo, J. S. Mill and Marx, in which value was analysed in objective terms as deriving from the labour content of the asset or resource under consideration. This subjectivism regarding value in economic theory, strongly emphasized in all of von Mises's writings, is always defended by Hayek. He goes much further in the direction of subjectivism, however, by noting that the data of the social studies are themselves subjective phenomena. Such social objects as money, capital and tools can never be given an analysis in objective or physicalist terms, since they are actually constituted by human beliefs and notions. These social objects are in no sense private — their existence is always bound up with that of forms of ✔ life among communities of human beings — but their dependency on human beliefs and conceptions means that any understanding of them in mechanistic fashion is bound to be abortive.

Hayek's extension of Austrian subjectivism about value to the whole realm of social objects in no way represents a deviation from the positions of his mentors, Menger and von Mises. His earliest extensive statement on the methodology of social science, *The Counter-Revolution of Science: Studies on the Abuse of Reason* (1952) bears in many aspects the imprint of the Austrian School's doctrines, particularly in its firm assertion that the methods of social science are crucially different from those of the natural sciences. In one fundamental area, however, Hayek always differed from the Austrian School, especially as that was embodied in the person of von Mises. It was indefatigably maintained by von Mises that economic laws were deductions from a few axioms about human action. Indeed, according to von Mises, all of economic science can be derived from a proper specification of the nature of human action. Economic laws are thus apodictic truths, no less certain than the axioms which yield them as thorems, and the role of empirical evidence is secondary to identifying these necessary implications of human action in economic theory.

Hayek never accepted this apodictic–deductive or (as von Mises called it) *praxeological* conception of economic theory. His seminal paper of 1937, 'Economics and Knowledge', marks an attempt to convert von Mises to a more empirical conception of the role of theory in economics rather than any change of view on Hayek's part. In this paper Hayek seeks to distinguish those elements of economic theory which are indeed *a priori*, inasmuch as they deal with 'the pure logic of choice' as it applies to single agents, from the greater part of economics which is empirical in that it aims to account for coordinating tendencies which bring about to varying degrees integration between the activities of many people. Hayek's distinction generates problems in his economic theory, especially problems about the nature of equilibrium and the possibilites of large-scale endogenous discoordination which I shall canvass in a later chapter, but its importance here is simply to underline that Hayek always regarded the greater part of economic doctrine as testable and corrigible and having no apodictic status.

What is noteworthy about Hayek's account of the methods of the social sciences is the continuity of its development. Specifically — contrary to T. W. Hutchinson, who periodizes Hayek's work into an Austrian praxeological and a post-Austrian Popperian period, and also contrary to Norman P. Barry, who sees both trends running right through Hayek's writings — Hayek never accepted the Misesian conception of a praxeological science of human action which would take as its point of departure a few axioms about the distinctive features of purposeful behaviour over time. True, in the Introduction to *Collectivist Economic Planning* and else-where in his early writings, Hayek had (as Hutchinson notes) insisted that economics yields '"general laws", that is, "inherent necessities determined by the permanent nature of the constituent elements"'.[25] As Hutchinson himself acknowledges in passing, however, such laws or necessities function in Hayek's writings as *postulates* (rather than as axioms), and they continue to do so even in his later writings, in which (as I have already noted) a suspicion of the nomothetic paradigm of social science is expressed. It is clear from the context of the quotations cited by Hutchinson that, in speaking of the general laws or inherent necessities of social and economic life, Hayek meant to controvert the excessive voluntarism of historicism, which insinuates that social life contains no unalterable necessities of any sort, rather than to embrace the view that there can be an *a priori* science of society or human action. To this extent Barry is right in his observation that 'there is a basic continuity in Hayek's writings on methodology.'[26] Certainly, there seems little substance in a periodization of Hayek's methodological writings by reference to the supposedly Popperian paper of 1937 on 'Economics and Knowledge'.

At the same time, there seems little warrant for Barry's claim that throughout his work Hayek tries 'to combine two rather different philosophies of social science; the Austrian praxeological school with its subjectivism and rejection of testability in favour of axiomatic reasoning, and the hypothetico-decductive approach of contemporary science with its emphasis on falsifiability and empirical content'.[27] There is no evidence, so far as I know, that Hayek ever endorsed the Misesian conception of an axiomatic or *a priori* science of human action grounded in apodictic certainties. Again, as we have seen, Hayek's view that the social sciences are throughout deductive in form antedates Popper's influence and is evidenced in the Introduction to *Collectivist Economic Planning*.

Hayek's real debts to Popper are, I think, different from those attributed to him by Hutchinson and Barry. It is not that Hayek under Popper's influence abandoned an apodictic − deductive method that was endorsed (in different versions, Kantian and Aristotelian) by von Mises and Menger, but rather that he came to adopt Popper's proposal that falsifiability be treated as demarcation criterion of science from non-science.[28] Again, Hayek follows Popper in qualifying his earlier Austrian conviction that there is a radical dualism of method as between natural and social science: this conviction, he tells us, depended on an erroneous conception of method in the natural sciences: as a result of what Popper has taught him, Hayek says, 'the differences between the two groups of disciplines has thereby been greatly narrowed.'[29] Hayek's debts to Popper are, then, in his seeing that it is the falsifiability of an hypothesis rather than its verifiability which makes it testable and empirical, and, secondly, in his acknowledging a unity of method in all the sciences, natural and social, where this method is seen clearly to be hypothetico-deductive.

Even in these Popperian influences, it is to be noted, there are differences of emphasis from Popper himself. Hayek anticipates Lakatos in perceiving that the theoretical sciences may contain a 'hard core' of hypotheses, well-confirmed and valuable in promoting understanding of the phenomena under investigation, which are highly resistant to testing and refutation.[30] And Hayek explicitly states that in some fields Popper's ideas of maximum empirical content and falsifiability may be inappropriate:

It is undoubtedly a drawback to have to work with theories which can be refuted only by statements of a high degree of complexity, because anything below that degree of complexity is on that ground alone permitted by our theory. Yet it is still possible that in some fields the more generic theories are the more useful ones...Where only the most general patterns can be observed in a considerable number of instances, the endeavour to become more 'scientific' by further narrowing down our formulae may well be a waste of effort...[31]

In general, then, it seems fair to hold that Hayek acknowledges that the proper method in social and economic studies, as elsewhere, is the hypothetico-deductive method of conjectures and refutations as set out by Popper. On the other hand, he continues to recognize that in respect of complex phenomena such as are found in the social studies, testability may be a somewhat high-level and protracted process, and the ideal of high empirical content captured in a nomothetic framework a demanding and sometimes unattainable idea.

Hayek's account of the methods of the social sciences, whereas it always stressed the subjective character of the 'data' of the social studies (social objects themselves), conceived the task of social theory as that of identifying the principles governing the formation of patterns in social life rather than of working out the implications of any definition of human action. Again, Hayek shares with Popper the view that the methods of the social sciences are properly always hypothetico-deductive and conjectural, but he identifies limitations on this method in the social sciences which there is no clear evidence that Popper himself has perceived or accepted.

HAYEK ON KNOWLEDGE AND THE MIND: IMPLICATIONS FOR SOCIAL THEORY

I began by noting the striking Kantian attributes of Hayek's epistemology and philosophy of mind — aspects which Hayek himself does not stress, perhaps because he conceives the formative influence of Kantian philosophy on his thought to be self-evident. As he puts it himself in a footnote to his discussion in a recent volume of the government of conscious intellectual life by superconscious abstract rules: 'I did not mention...the obvious relation of all this to Kant's conception of the categories that govern our thinking — which I took rather for granted.'[32]

Hayek's Kantianism is seen, first in his repudiation of the empiricist view that knowledge may be constructed from a basis of raw sensory data and, second, in his uncompromising assertion of the view that the order we find in the world is a product of the creative activity of the human mind (rather than a recognition of natural necessity). His Kantian view is distinctive in that it anticipates Popper in affirming that the mental frameworks by which we categorize the world are neither universal nor invariant, but alterable in an evolutionary fashion; his Kantian view also follows Wittgenstein in grasping the role of social rules in the transmission of practical knowledge. There are, at the same time, some entirely original features of Hayek's view of the mind, which it would be hard for either Kant or Wittgenstein to accept, but which constitute one of Hayek's most intriguing contributions to philosophical speculation. Hayek suggests that, not only human social life, but the life of the mind itself is governed by rules, some of which cannot be specified at all. Note that Hayek does not contend merely that we cannot in fact specify all the rules which govern both social and intellectual life: he argues that there must of necessity be an insuperable limit beyond which we are unable to specify the rules by which our lives are governed. As he puts it:

> So far our argument has rested solely on the uncontestable assumption that we are not in fact able to specify all the rules which govern our perceptions and actions. We still have to consider the question whether it is conceivable that we should ever be in a position discursively to describe all (or at least any one we like) of these rules, or whether mental activity must always be guided by some rules which we are in principle not able to specify.
>
> If it should turn out that it is basically impossible to state or communicate all the rules which govern our actions, including our communications and explicit statements, this would imply an inherent limitation of our possible explicit knowledge and, in particular, the impossibility of ever fully explaining a mind of the complexity of our own.

Hayek goes on to observe of the inability of the human mind reflexively to grasp the most basic rules which govern its operations that 'this would follow from what I understand to Georg Cantor's theorem in the theory of sets according to which in any system of classification there are always more classes than things to be classified, which presumably implies that no system of classes can contain itself.' Again, he remarks that 'it would thus appear that Gödel's theorem is but a special case of a more general principle applying to all conscious and particularly all rational processes, namely the principle that among their determinants there must always be some rules which cannot be stated or even be conscious.' Hayek concludes this development of themes first explored in his *Sensory Order* with the fascinating suggestion that conscious thought must be presumed to be governed by 'rules which cannot in turn be conscious — by a 'supraconscious mechanism' — or, as Hayek prefers sometimes to call it, a 'meta-conscious mechanism' — 'which operates on the contents of consciousness but which cannot itself be conscious'.[33]

Hayek's argument here seems to be that there is in both action and perception a hierarchy of rules, with the most fundamental rules at any time being meta-conscious rules beyond our capacities of identification and articulation. Thus the rules of action and perception by which both intellectual and social life are governed are stratified or ranked in a hierarchy, with the most basic rules (which shape the categories of our understanding) always eluding conscious articulation. It is not that there is a set of such meta-conscious rules, co-existent with the human mind, such that we must suppose ourselves to be governed by invariant principles which we can never state and whose content must remain forever unknown to us. Rather, all the rules by which social and intellectual life is governed are conceived by Hayek to be products of a process of evolutionary selection and modification. As we acquire new, consciously articulate rules of action and perception, we will come to be governed by new meta-conscious rules, which may in turn generate further meta-conscious rules as they themselves are articulated or perhaps simply altered out of recognition.

I will return to this most fascinating idea of a meta-conscious rule in the next chapter, when I shall consider its place in Hayek's conception of a spontaneous social order. Here I wish to bring out how this idea shows Hayek's differences with Kant and Wittgenstein. For all his discussion of the antinomies of the human understanding, I do not think Kant could have accepted so drastic a limitation on the possibilities of human self-understanding as that suggested by Hayek's claim that intellectual life is always governed by inarticulable laws or principles. In this respect, Hayek's rationalism is even more self-critical than Kant's. Again, Wittgenstein's general conception of the mind would forbid any such notion of rule-following as that presupposed in Hayek's conception. For Wittgenstein, rule-following seems always to involve intentional knowledge, and, at least in the *Philosophical*

Investigations, Wittgenstein is concerned to stress the freedom of judgement we possess in applying even the most basic rules, such as those of arithmetic. Hayek's conception is here far removed from Wittgenstein's, and has closest affinities with the evolutionary epistemology developed by Popper and his disciples.

How do these considerations bear on Hayek's view of society? Hayek himself is emphatic that these insights in the theories of mind and knowledge have the largest consequences for social theory. The inaccessability to reflexive inquiry of the rules that govern conscious thought entails the bankruptcy of the Cartesian rationalist project and implies that the human mind can never fully understand itself, still less can it ever be governed by any process of conscious thought. The considerations adduced earlier, then, establish *the autonomy of the mind*, without ever endorsing any mentalistic thesis of mind's independence of the material order. Where Hayek deviates from Descartes's conception of mind, however, is not primarily in his denying ontological independence to mind, but in his demonstration that complete intellectual self-understanding is an impossibility.

Hayek's conception of mind is a view, then, whose implications for social theory are even more radical than are those of Hayek's Kantianism. It is the chief burden of the latter, let us recall, that no external or transcendental standpoint on human thought is achievable, in terms of which it may be supported or reformed. In social theory, this Kantian perspective implies the impossibility of any Archimedian point from which a synoptic view can be gained of society as a whole and in terms of which social life may be understood and, it may be, redesigned. As Hayek puts it trenchantly: 'Particular aspects of a culture can be critically examined only within the context of that culture. We can never reduce a system of rules or all values as a whole to a purposive construction, but must always stop with our criticism of something that has no better grounds for existence than that it is the accepted basis of the particular tradition.'[34] This is a useful statement, since it brings out the Kantian implication for social theory: that all criticism of social life must be immanent criticism, just as in all philosophy, inquiry can only be reflexive and never transcendential.

Hayek goes beyond Kantianism, however, in his recognition that, just as in the theory of mind we must break off when we come to the region of unknowable ultimate rules, so in social theory we come to a stop with the basic constitutive traditions of social life. These latter, like Wittgenstein's forms of life, cannot be the objects of further criticism, since they are at the terminus of criticism and justification: they are simply given to us, and must be accepted by us. But this is not to say that these traditions are unchanging, nor that we cannot understand how it is that they do change.

In social theory, Hayek's devastating critique of Cartesian rationalism entails that, whatever else it might be, social order cannot be the product of a directing intelligence. It is not just that too many concrete details of social life would always escape such an intelligence, which could never, therefore, know enough. Nor (though we are nearer the nub of the matter here) is it that society is not a static object of knowledge which could survive unchanged the investigations of such an intelligence. No, the impossibility of total social planning does not rest for Hayek on such Popperian considerations,[35] or, at any rate, not primarily on them.

Such an impossibility of central social planning rests, firstly, on the primordially practical character of most of the knowledge on which social life depends. Such knowledge cannot be concentrated in a single brain, natural or mechanical, not because it is very complicated, but rather because it is embodied in habits and dispositions and governs our conduct via rules which are often inarticulate. But, secondly, the impossibilty of total social planning arises from the fact that, since we are all of us governed by rules of which we have no knowledge, even the directing intelligence itself would be subject to such government. It is naïve and almost incoherent to suppose that a society could lift itself up by its bootstraps and reconstruct itself, in part at least because the idea that any individual mind — or any collectivity of selected minds — could do that, is no less absurd. The order we find in social life cannot, for these reasons, be the product of any rational design, and it can never become so. Social order is and must always be a spontaneous formation. /

The idea of a spontaneous social order

SPONTANEOUS ORDER VERSUS THE CONSTRUCTIVIST FALLACY

If the order we discover in society is in no important respect the product of a directing intelligence, and if the human mind itself is a product of cultural evolution, then it follows that social order cannot be the product of anything resembling conscious control or rational design. As Hayek puts it:

The errors of constructivist rationalism are closely connected with Cartesian dualism, that is, with the conception of an independently existing mind substance which stands outside the cosmos of nature and which enabled man, endowed with such a mind from the beginning, to design the institutions of society and culture among which he lives... The conception of an already fully developed mind designing the institutions which made life possible is contrary to all we know about the evolution of man.[1]

The master error of Cartesian rationalism[2] lies in its anthropomorphic transposition of mentalist categories to social processes. But a Cartesian rationalist view of mind cannot explain even the order of mind itself. Hayek himself makes this point when he remarks on 'the difference between an order which is brought about by the direction of a central organ such as the brain, and the formation of an order determined by the regularity of the actions towards each other of the elements of a structure'. He goes on:

Michael Polanyi has usefully described this distinction as that between a monocentric and a polycentric order. The first point which it is in this connection important to note is that the brain of an organism which acts as the directing centre for the organism is in turn a polycentric order, that is, that its actions are determined by the relation and mutual adjustment to each other of the elements of which it consists.[3]

Hayek states his conception of social theory, and of the central importance in it of undesigned or spontaneous orders, prorammatically and with unsurpassable lucidity:

It is evident that this interplay of the rules of conduct and of the individuals with the actions of other individuals and the external circumstances in producing an overall order may be a highly complex affair. The whole task of social theory consists in little else but an effort to reconstruct the overall orders which are thus formed...It will also be clear that such a distinct theory of social structures can provide only an explanation of certain general and highly abstract features of the different types of structures...Of theories of this type economic theory, the theory of the market order of free human societies, is so far the only one which has been developed over a long period...[4]

Because it is undesigned and not the product of conscious reflection, the spontaneous order that emerges of itself in social life can cope with the radical ignorance we all share of the countless facts on knowledge of which society depends. That is to say, to begin with, that a spontaneous social order can utilize *fragmented knowledge*, knowledge dispersed among millions of people, in a way a holistically planned order (if such there could be) cannot. 'This structure of human activities' as Hayek puts it 'consistently adapts itself, and functions through adapting itself, to millions of facts which in their entirety are not known to everybody. The significance of this process is most obvious and was at first stressed in the economic field.'[5] It is to say, also, that a spontaneous social order can use the practical knowledge preserved in men's habits and dispositions and that society always depends on such practical knowledge and cannot do without it.

Examples abound in Hayek's writings of spontaneous orders apart from the market order. The thesis of spontaneous order is stated at its broadest when Hayek says of Bernard Mandeville (1670—1733) that 'for the first time [he] developed all the classical paradigmata of the spontaneous growth of orderly social structures: of law and morals, of language, the market and money, and also the growth of technological knowledge.'[6] Note that whereas Hayek acknowledges that spontaneous order emerges in natural processes — it may be observed, he tells us, not only in the population biology of animal species, but in the formation of crystals and even galaxies[7] — it is the rôle of spontaneous order in human society that Hayek is most concerned to stress. For applying what Hayek illuminatingly terms 'the twin ideas of evolution and of the spontaneous formation of an order'[8] to the study of human society enables us to transcend the view, inherited from Greek, and, above all, from Sophist philosophy, that all social phenomena can be comprehended within the crude dichotomy of the natural (*physis*) and the conventional (*nomos*). Hayek wishes to focus attention on the third domain of social phenomena and objects, neither instinctual in origin nor yet the result of conscious contrivance or purposive construction, the domain of evolved and self-regulating structures in society via the natural selection of rules of action and perception that is systematically neglected in much current sociology (though not, it may be noted, in the writings of Herbert Spencer,[9] one of sociology's founding fathers). It is because he thinks that the sociobiologists view social order as being a mixture of instinctive behaviour and conscious control, and so neglect the cultural selection of systems and rules, that Hayek has subjected this recent strain of speculation to a sharp criticism.[10] It may be noted, finally, that Hayek's repudiation of the Sophistic nature—convention dichotomy sets him in some opposition to Popper and his talk of the critical dualism of facts and decisions and brings him close to the Wittgensteinian philosopher, Peter Winch, for whom the distinction is essentially misconceived.[11]

At the same time, Hayek's constant insistence on the competitive selection of rival rules and practices gives his conception of social life a naturalistic and evolutionary dimension which is alien to Wittgensteinian thought.

Constructivism is the error that the order we discover — in nature, in our minds and in society — has been put there by some designing mind. Hayek's conception of spontaneous order, in contesting the constructivist view, embodies an insight which goes very much against the grain of the dominant Platonist and Christian traditions in Western culture. For these traditions, order is imposed upon the world or injected into it by the exercise of reason or is found there as the reflection of a suprasensible domain of Ideas. The task of reason may be the apprehension of the eternal Forms of which all things that we can know in this world are but shadowy copies, or else the office of reason may be conceived as that of identifying a set of clear ideas whose mutual relations constitute an unchanging order. For Hayek, this cannot be the rôle of reason: the mind is as much a spontaneous order as is the human body or the human brain, and our ideas are merely the visible exfoliation of spontaneous forces. For Hayek, then, as against Plato and Descartes, the order of our ideas is supervenient upon the spontaneous order of the mind, which it can never reconstruct entirely or hope to supplant. Our conscious selves can never be governors of our mental lives, for they are at every moment utterly dependent upon the unseen (and, in large measure, uncomprehended) workings of spontaneous order in the cosmos of nature and society. In neglecting the dependency of reason itself on spontaneous order in the life of the mind, the constructivist error inverts the true relations of tacit with explicit knowledge and accords reason a prescriptive rôle it is wholly unfitted to perform in mind or society.

THE CENTRAL CONCEPTION OF SPONTANEOUS
ORDER AND ITS APPLICATIONS TO PHYSICAL AND
SOCIAL PHENOMENA

The most explicit and systematic development of the insight that order in society is a spontaneous formation is given by the economic theory of market exchanges, where the thesis that unhampered markets display a tendency to equilibrium is its most obvious application. (In a world of constantly changing beliefs and preferences, of course, equilibrium is never achieved, but is to be viewed as a constantly changing asymptote. This should warn us against construing spontaneous order as a static condition rather than a process displaying certain orderly features). At the same time, Hayek has made clear that the spontaneous-order conception has application to physical systems — to crystals, galaxies, and perhaps even, somewhat paradoxically, to certain artificial devices[12] — and it has many exemplifications in human social life apart from those in the economic realm. We find the spontaneous formation of self-regulating structures in the growth of language, the development of law and in the emergence of moral norms. (We find in David Hume, for example, a brilliant exposition of the spontaneous emergence of moral conventions, which is explicitly directed against Hobbes's constructivist rationalism).[13] In all these domains, the key idea of the spontaneous order thesis is that self-organizing and self-replicating structures arise without design or even the possibility of design, such that knowledge of some of the elements of these structures allows the formation of correct expectations about the structure of the whole.

Whereas I do not aim here to assess Hayek's conception in any definitive fashion, a number of questions are worth raising at this point. Hayek has asserted that the emergence and persistence of spontaneous orders is to be accounted for by something akin to the generalization of Darwinian evolution as it is understood in the context of the development of species. Selective evolution is the source of all order, he tells us, not only of the order we find in living things and which we recognize in the classification of species. At the same time, Hayek never maintains that the mechanism of Darwinian evolution — natural selection of genetic accidents via their reproductive fitness — must be replicated exactly in all areas where selective evolution generates spontaneous order. In the case of the capitalist market economy, there is a real analogy with Darwinian selection in that the profit-and-loss system provides a mechanism for the elimination of 'unfit' enterprises. It is less clear what it is that accounts for the emergence and persistence of orderly structures in language and law. Again, though we may indeed sensibly speak of evolution at the molecular and galactic levels, there will be nothing analogous with the mechanism of Darwinian evolution at these levels, since there appears there to be no possibility of self-replication. An evolutionary account may be given of the emergence of self-organizing systems, which invokes mechanisms of selection other than that specified in the Darwinian theory. One question that arises, then, is just what these other mechanisms may be in the areas where the Darwinian one does not apply.

In the context of social and cultural evolution, Hayek has in recent years accorded increasing prominence to the Darwinian mechanism itself. Social institutions and structures — such as religions and modes of production — come to prevail insofar as they enhance the reproductive fitness of the groups which practise them. Religions which emphasize the importance of private or several property and which support the institution of the family will enhance the life prospects of their practitioners by creating conditions of high productivity in which there will be relatively more numerous infant survivals. Modes of production which allow and encourage the identification of malinvestments and which provide incentives for their liquidation will spread, if only because they permit larger populations to be sustained than do modes of production without these features making for productivity. As Hayek sees it in his latest writings,[14] social or cultural evolution is directly continuous with evolution at the classical Darwinian level and embodies the same fundamental principle of natural selection. Hayek's conception differs from that of nineteenth century Social Darwinism, however, whether in its Spencerian—Lamarckian form or in that expounded by W. G. Sumner, inasmuch as the natural selection it speaks about is not of individuals, but of groups or populations, and it occurs via the impact of the practices and institutions, the rules of action and perception, of groups on the life chances of their members.

A further question now suggests itself — a question as to the means of identifying the rules of which Hayek speaks. He is explicit that he refers always both to rules of action and to rules of perception.[15] To take the example he mentions and which Polanyi often uses, both sorts of rule would be involved in the process of recognizing someone's face and greeting him. Perhaps, for Hayek, the differences between the two sorts of rule are less than radical, but in respect of rules of action the problem is that observed regularities of behaviour are usually compatible with a range of imputed rules. If the imputation of such rules is to *explain* the order of a group, we need some method of selection among the range of possible rules which might equally well account for the same regularities in individual behaviour. This problem may be easier with rules of perception in that techniques are available for isolating *Gestalten*, but it is still a real problem in these cases too.

Again, although I have stated it in simple, unitary fashion, the idea of a spontaneous order in society has at least three distinct aspects or elements. First, there is the thesis that social institutions arise as a result of human action but not from human design. Let us, following Robert Nozick and others[16] call this *the invisible-hand thesis* about social institutions. Intimations of this thesis are found in Mandeville and Hume, but a systematic version of it in respect of the institution of money is given by Carl Menger, founder of the

Austrian School of Economics.[17] Secondly, there is the thesis of *the primacy of tacit or practical knowledge*, which asserts that our knowledge of the world, and especially of the social world, is embodied first of all in practices and skills, and only secondarily in theories, and which speculates that at least part of this practical knowledge is always inarticulable. Thirdly, there is the thesis of *the natural selection of competitive traditions*. Here 'traditions' are understood to refer to whole complexes of practices and rules of action and perception and the claim is that there is a continuous evolutionary filtering of these traditions. This last thesis — let us call it *the thesis of cultural evolution by the natural selection of traditions* — completes the complex idea of spontaneous social order as it is expounded by Hayek.

THE APPLICATION OF SPONTANEOUS ORDER IN ECONOMIC LIFE: THE CATALLAXY

The central claim of Hayek's philosophy, as we have expounded it so far, is that knowledge is, at its base, at once practical and abstract. It is abstract inasmuch as even sensory perception gives us a model of our environment which is highly selective and picks out only certain classes of events, and it is practical inasmuch as most knowledge is irretrievably stored or embodied in rules of action and perception. These rules, in turn, are in Hayek's conception the subject of continuing natural selection in cultural competition. The mechanism of this selection, best described in Hayek's fascinating 'Notes on the Evolution of Systems of Rules of Conduct',[18] is in the emulation by others of rules which secure successful behaviour. It is by a mimetic contagion that rules conferring success — where success means, in the last resort, the growth of human numbers[19] — come to supplant those rules which are maladapted to the environment. Finally, the convergence of many rule-following creatures on a single system of rules creates those social objects — language,

money, markets, the law — which are the paradigms of
spontaneous social order.

It is a general implication of this conception that, since
social order is not a purposive construction, it will not in
general serve any specific purpose. Social order facilitates the
achievement of human purposes: taken in itself, it must be
seen as having no purpose. Just as human actions acquire
their meaning by occurring in a framework that can itself
have no meaning,[20] so social order will allow for the achievement of human purposes only to the extent that it is itself
purposeless. Nowhere has this general implication of Hayek's
conception been so neglected as in economic life. In the
history and theory of science, to be sure, where the idea of
spontaneous order was (as Hayek acknowledges)[21] put to
work by Michael Polanyi, false conceptions were spawned by
the erroneous notion that scientific progress could be planned,
whereas, on the contrary, any limitation of scientific inquiry
to the contents of explicit or theoretical knowledge would
inevitably stifle further progress.[22] In economics, however,
the canard that order is the result of conscious control had
more fateful consequences. It supported the illusion that the
whole realm of human exchange was to be understood after
the fashion of a household or an hierarchical organization,
with limited and commensurable purposes ranked in order of
agreed importance.

This confusion of a genuine hierarchical *'economy'* — such
as that of an army, a school or a business corporation — with
the whole realm of social exchange, the *catallaxy*, informs
many aspects of welfare economics and motivates its interventionist projects via the fiction of a total social product.
This confusion between 'catallaxy' and 'economy' is, at
bottom, the result of an inability to acknowledge that the
order which is the product of conscious direction — the order
of a management hierarchy in a business corporation, for
example — itself always depends upon a larger spontaneous
order. The demand that the domain of human exchange
taken as a whole should be subject to purposive planning is,

therefore, the demand that social life be reconstructed in the character of a factory, an army, or a business corporation — in the character, in other words, of an authoritarian organization. Apart from the fateful consequences for individual liberty that implementing such a demand inexorably entails, it springs in great measure from an inability or unwillingness to grasp how in the market process itself there is a constant tendency to self-regulation by spontaneous order. When it is unhampered, the process of exchange between competitive firms itself yields a coordination of men's activities more intricate and balanced than any that could be enforced (or even conceived) by a central planner.

The relevance of these considerations to Hayek's contributions to the question of the allocation of resources in a socialist economic order is central, but often neglected. It is, of course, widely recognized[23] that one of Hayek's principal contributions in economic theory is the refinement of the thesis of his colleague, Ludwig von Mises, that the attempt to supplant market relations by public planning cannot avoid yielding calculational chaos. Hayek's account of the mechanism whereby this occurs has, however, some entirely distinctive and original features. For Hayek is at great pains to point out that the dispersed knowledge which brings about a tendency to equilibrium in economic life and so facilitates an integration of different plans of life, is precisely not theoretical or technical knowledge, but practical knowledge of concrete situations — 'knowledge of people, of local conditons, and of special circumstances'. As Hayek puts it: 'The skipper who earns his living from using otherwise empty or half-filled journeys of tramp-steamers, or the estate agent whose whole knowledge is almost exclusively one of temporary opportunities, or the arbitrageur who gains from local differences of commodity prices — are all performing eminently useful functions based on special knowledge of circumstances of the fleeting moment not known to others.' Hayek goes on to comment: 'It is a curious fact that this sort of knowledge should today be regarded with a kind of contempt and that anyone who by such knowledge gains an advantage over somebody better equipped with theoretical or technical knowledge is thought to have acted almost disreputably.'[24] The 'problem of the division of knowledge', which Hayek describes as 'the really central problem of economics as a social science',[25] is therefore not just a problem of specific data, articulable in explicit terms, being dispersed in millions of heads: it is the far more fundamental problem of the practical knowledge on which economic life depends being embodied in skills and habits, which change as society changes and which are rarely expressible in theoretical or technical terms.

One way of putting Hayek's point, a way we owe to Israel Kirzner rather than to Hayek himself but which is wholly compatible with all that Hayek has said on these questions, is to remark as follows: if men's economic activities really do show a tendency to coordinate with one another, this is due in large part to the activity of *entrepreneurship*. The neglect of the entrepreneur in much standard economic theorizing, the inability to grasp his functions in the market process, may be accounted for in part by reference to Hayek's description above of the sort of knowledge used by the entrepreneur. As Kirzner puts it, 'Ultimately, then, the kind of "knowledge" required for entrepreneurship is "knowing" where to look for "knowledge" rather than knowledge of substantive market information.'[26] It is hard to avoid the impression that the entrepreneurial knowledge of which Kirzner speaks here is precisely that practical or dispositional knowledge which Hayek describes. Kirzner's account brings out a feature of entrepreneurship, crucially relevant to spontaneous order in the economic realm, which Hayek recognizes but has not developed systematically. This is that the entrepreneurial insight or perception on which the tendency to equilibrium depends, because it cannot be planned or brought about at will, but is always a matter of serendipity and flair, is itself a spontaneous phenomenon. Different institutional frameworks may encourage it in differing degrees, but it is in its nature as much beyond our powers of conscious control as are the meta-conscious rules of Hayek's theory of mind. I do not mean to suggest that entrepreneurial perception is rule-governed — though its affinities with *Gestalt*-perception would repay research — but only to stress its uncontrollability by conscious thought. One major flaw in all proposals for economic planning is that they are bound to attempt to transform entrepreneurial perception of opportunities into mechanical procedures for resource-utilization and to incur vast losses of efficiency in so attempting.

It is the neglect of how all economic life depends on this practical knowledge which allowed the brilliant but, in this respect, fatally misguided Joseph Schumpeter (1883—1950) to put a whole generation of economists on the wrong track, when he stated in his *Capitalism, Socialism and Democracy* (1942) that the problem of calculation under socialism was essentially solved.[27] It is the neglect of the same truth that Hayek expounded which explains the inevitable failure in Soviet-style economies of attempts to simulate market processes in computer modeling. All such efforts are bound to fail, if only because the practical knowledge of which Hayek speaks cannot be programmed into a mechanical device. They are bound to fail, also, because they neglect the knowledge-gathering rôle of market pricing. Here we must recall that, according to Hayek, knowledge is dispersed throughout society and, further, it is embodied in habits and dispositions of countless men and women. The knowledge yielded by market pricing is knowledge which all men can use, but which none of them would possess in the absence of the market process; in a sense, the knowledge embodied or expressed in the market price is *systemic or holisitc knowledge*, knowledge unknown and unknowable to any of the elements of the market system, but given to them all by the operation of the system itself. No sort of market simulation or shadow pricing can rival the operation of the market order itself in producing this knowledge, because only the actual operation of the market itself can draw on the fund of practical knowledge which market participants exploit in their activities. The knowledge exhibited in market prices is not only the practical knowledge possessed by millions of dispersed market actors; it is also knowledge possessed by none of them as individuals, even tacitly. It is thus systemic or holistic knowledge, knowledge generated by the market process itself and belonging (as does all traditional knowledge) to the entire society rather than to any of its separate members. It is this systemic knowledge which is destroyed or wasted when attempts are made to correct or plan market processes.

Three further points may be worth noting in respect of Hayek's refinements of the Misesian calculation debate. First, when Hayek speaks of economic calculation under socialism as a practical impossibility, he is not identifying specific obstacles in the way of the socialist enterprise which might someday be removed. Socialist planning could supplant market processes only if practical knowledge could be replaced by theoretical or technical knowledge at the level of society as a whole — and that is a supposition which is barely conceivable. The kind of omniscience demanded of a socialist planner could be possessed only by a single mind, entirely self-aware, existing in an unchanging environment — a supposition so bizarre that we realize we have moved from any imaginable social world to a metaphysical fantasy in which men and women have disappeared altogether, and all that remain are Leibnitzian monads, featureless and unhistorical ciphers.

Fortunately, such a transformation is possible, if at all, only as a thought-experiment. In practice, all supposedly socialist economies depend upon precisely that practical knowledge of which Hayek speaks, and which, though dispersed through society, is transmitted via the price mechanism. It is widely acknowledged that socialist economies depend crucially in their planning policies on price data gleaned from historic and world markets. Less often recognized, and dealt with in detail only, so far as I know, in Paul Craig Robert's important *Alienation in the Soviet Economy*,[28] is that planning policies in socialist economies are only shadows cast by market processes distorted by episodes of authoritarian intervention. The consequence of the Hayekian and Polanyian critiques of socialist planning is not inefficiency in such planning but rather its impossibility: we cannot analyze the 'socialist' economies of the world properly, unless we penetrate the ideological veil they secrete themselves behind, and examine the mixture of market processes with command structures which is all that can ever exist in such a complex society.

The third and final implication of Hayek's contribution to the calculation question is his clear statement of the truth that the impossibility of socialism is an *epistemological* impossibility. It is not a question of motivation or volition, of the egoism or limited sympathies of men and women, but of the inability of any social order in which the market is suppressed or distorted to utilize effectively the practical knowledge possessed by its citizens. Calculational chaos would ensue, and a barbarization of social life result, from the attempt to socialize production, even if men possessed only altruistic and conformist motives. For, in the absence of the signals transmitted via the price mechanism, they would be at a loss how to direct their activities for the social good, and the common stock of practical knowledge would begin to decay. Only the inventiveness of human beings as expressed in the emergence of black and gray markets could then prevent a speedy regression to the subsistence economy. The impossibilty of socialism, then, derives from its neglect of the *epistemological functions* of market institutions and processes. Hayek's argument here is the most important application of his fundamental insight into the epistemological rôle of social institutions — an insight I will need to take up again in the context of certain similarities between Hayek's conception of liberty under law and Robert Nozick's meta-utopian framework.

CULTURAL EVOLUTION AND THE NATURAL
SELECTION OF TRADITIONS

In my account of his contributions to the Misesian argument against the possibilty of rational resource-allocation under socialism, I have identified as Hayek's main contention the claim that socialist theories neglect the epistemological functions of the market process. A different way of stating the same insight, and one which Hayek himself often adopts, is to say that socialists fail to grasp the character of *the market as a discovery procedure* — as an institutionalized process for the generation and use of knowledge, tacit as well as explicit, including knowledge of men's preferences. Now, whereas the market is a paradigm case of a social institution having an epistemological rôle, it is Hayek's view that all the most important social institutions and practices have knowledge-bearing or information-carrying functions. Hayek's conception of social institutions as vehicles for the generation and dissemination of knowledge in fact represents one of the most important paradigm shifts his work brings about in social theory — a shift from the crticism and evaluation of social institutions by reference to preferred principles of morality to an assessment of them in terms of their capacity to generate, transmit and use knowledge (including tacit knowledge). One aspect of this shift is Hayek's assertion that the evolution of culture may itself be fruitfully investigated in terms of the competition between different traditions or practices, with a natural selection among them occurring which is at least partly to be explained by their relative efficiency as bearers or embodiments of knowledge. This conception of social evolution as being powered by natural selection among different knowledge-bearing institutions, practices or traditions is indeed the third element in what I earlier termed Hayek's complex idea of spontaneous social order.

Hayek's view of social rules as bearers of embodied tacit

knowledge has a number of implications for moral and social philosohpy which may be worth exploring at this point. Unlike Bentham and his disciples in the constructivist tradition of utilitarianism which for a century and a half swamped the insights of Hume, Hayek never regards social rules in an instrumental light. They are not the means to antecedently chosen goals; rather, their functional usefulness depends upon social rules being observed as it were uncritically. We cannot easily subject social rules to critical assessment, since the knowledge they embody or express is itself usually inaccessible to critical statement. The proper attitude to our inheritance of social rules is, for these reasons, one of Burkean reverence and not of reformist hubris. Such criticism of our inheritance of moral traditions as is possible and desirable is always, in Hayek's view, immanent criticism: it is a criticism in which one aspect of the whole corpus of practices we have inherited is invoked to illuminate and correct the rest. No Archimedean point of critical leverage is available for the assessment of entire moral codes, so criticism always in the end consists in the detection and removal of incoherences. At the same time, we must not fall into the intellectualist error that revision of inherited codes of conduct typically takes place as a result of the exercise of critical reason. Most often, such revision occurs as a result of innumerable small variations upon and deviations from established rules and practices, undertaken by countless anonymous individuals in unconnected but similar circumstances. So long as this process of piecemeal practical revision is allowed to proceed smoothly, unhindered either by hubristic attempts to implement synoptic reforms of the entire system or by a Romantic cult of individuality, the evolution of the code of conduct will result in social stability (though never, fortunately, in fixity).

Two points of clarification, and in part of refinement, of Hayek's conception may be inserted here. First, Hayek recognizes practical conflict or pragmatic inconsistency as one of the chief motives for revision of the inherited code

of conduct. In changing circumstances, a code of conduct
may often yield contradictory injunctions, which are incompatible at the level of practice. A point of development for
Hayek's theory exists in this aspect of his exposition, which
so far as I know is yet little explored, and which is suggested
by his recognition that the most important social rules (rules
of perception as well as of action) are efficacious not only so
far as they have been internalized and have come to govern
the personality itself. Human personality may, indeed, be
profitably regarded as a system of rules mapped into a matrix
of biological individuality. It is not that the individual personality subscribes to social rules instrumentally, in order
the better to attain his goals. Such detachment from social
rules is ubiquitous and pervasive in minor degree, but when it
is deep-seated in a personality or widespread in a culture it
spells anomie and dissolution. In most circumstances, at any
rate, we must regard the human personality as constituted by
social rules and as itself an artifact of culture. Indeed, even in
the case of anomic personality, Hayek's analysis suggests that
there will be no recognizable regularities of behaviour or
stable cognitive process unless some at least of the prevailing
social rules have been successfully internalized.

Hayek's conception suggests a line of empirical research
in social psychology and in cultural anthropology when we
come to see the psychological conflict of internalized social
rules as one of the chief sources of cultural development.
Such inner conflicts may be less likely, and in fact rare, in
simple societies which contain only a meagre range of social
rules. (I do not mean to imply that so-called primitive cultures are, necessarily or typically, simple societies of this
type. The opposite may be the case, but this is not an issue
into which I can enter here). If the conflict of internalized
social rules leads to increasing complexity in the society —
as by the exfoliation of sub-cultures, the growth of moral
pluralism or the hiving off of specific areas of social life into
enclaves having their own internal rules and practices — then
this complexity will tend to be, not merely self-replicating,

but also self-reinforcing. This thesis that cultural development may have one of its most powerful sources in the conflict of internalized norms clearly has many implications. We need some procedure for identifying norms and for detecting the frequency and severity of their practical inconsistencies. Also conflicts of internalized norms, rules or rôles will not always yield dynamic growth or increased complexity. Such psychiatric investigations of mental illness as have been conducted by Bateson and Laing suggest that, where conflicting internalized injunctions yield double-bind dilemmas, paralysis of the personality may result.[29] At the social level, too, one may easily envisage a sort of cultural stalemate resulting from such double-bind situations. What is it that determines whether internalized normative conflict engenders dynamic growth rather than paralysed fixity?

A second line of inquiry is suggested by Hayek's conception of the natural selection of competing social rules. Hayek's references to the wisdom of inherited moral convention may suggest that he sees this as massive and monolithic and recommends uncritical immersion in its practices. This cannot be so, if only because he recognizes the propensity of evolving codes to throw up contradictions of the sort we have already discussed. Hayek's Mandevillean perspective suggests another qualification for moral conservatism here, and intimates a fascinating line of empirical research. All societies contain scapegoat occupations and forbidden practices — prostitution in Western societies and witchcraft and magic in recently Christianized societies being immediate examples — which may contribute to social stability even as they are condemned by established norms. In some areas, recognition of the vital functions of these scapegoat occupations and practices may prompt demands for the revision of law and of customary morality so as to accord them a greater measure of legitimacy and social approval. It is in this spirit that Mandeville himself wrote, and in which Hayek endorsed a recent Mandevillean work by the economist Walter Block, *Defending the Undefendable*,[30] in which the social functions of such figures as the pimp, the scab and the crooked cop are vigorously expounded. Recognizing that society always contains such forbidden occupations and practices, having their own traditional codes of conduct and sometimes conferring considerable benefit on the society as a whole, may thus prompt a policy of moral reform and legal recognition in respect of them.

We may wish to push the inquiry further, however, and ask about the social functions of crime itself. Following Durkheim, we may be able to see in deviant behaviour a systemic stabilizer of the code of conduct as a whole. Without deviation, there can be no punishment and no expression of disapproval. Again, deviant behaviour (even where it confers no direct benefit on society) may be symptomatic of dysfunction in the inherited code itself. The possibility may even be entertained that a crime-free society could only be stagnant, exhibiting a degree of moral homogeneity which meant the end of further progress. Research is needed into the systemic stabilizing functions of crime which relates the type and incidence of criminal behaviours to developments of the accepted code of conduct in other areas of society.

The practical and conceptual difficulties of such research are manifest. Functional explanations in social theory face problems which are almost overly familiar. How are functional explanations to be tested (and falsified)? What is the unit of functional stability, and how is it to be identified? And is not the view of a social order as a self-regulating system at best an analogy with mechanical devices, misleading if taken too literally? Perhaps the most obscure area in functionalist sociology is, however, an unclarity as to the *mechanism* of functional adaptation. By what process does society tend towards equilibrium (however identified)? Here we reach a crux in Hayek's social theory. His thesis of the natural selection of competing practices has a rival in the economic approach to social explanation pioneered by such writers as Gary Becker. The search for the mechanism of functional adaptation in social systems generates the question:

How far is Hayek's natural selection thesis compatible with the economic approach? And, where the two methods genuinely conflict rather than complement each other, which are we to prefer? Let us see.

As a first approximation, we may characterize the economic approach to social behaviour as one which conceives human conduct to be, primarily or even as a matter of definition, purposeful and goal-orientated. Aside from reflex behaviour and states of delirium and cognitive disorganization, it is held that human action is undertaken with ends or outcomes in view. In addition, this approach often attributes a maximizing or an economizing strategy to human conduct: it is supposed that human beings are programmed, so to speak, to make the most from the resources and opportunities they have to satisfy best their wants. Even when it does not impute a process of conscious reflection, the economic approach attributes a sort of means—end, calculational rationality to agents. Indeed, in the praxeological method of L. von Mises,[31] it becomes an *a priori* truth that human conduct is rational in the sense of purposeful and goal-orientated and always involving a weighing of foregone opportunities.

It seems hard to reconcile this economic or rational-choice approach with Hayek's conception of man as rule-following animal. In the first place, some at least of the rules we follow will always be meta-conscious rules, constraining the goals we may formulate or adopt, and inaccessible to critical scrutiny. Even in the case of social rules of conduct which do not belong to the meta-conscious category, we do not adopt or subscribe to them *in order to* attain our goals. Essential as social rules are to an orderly environment in which we may achieve our purposes, they are imbibed or endorsed unreflectively, in the course of socialization. If they help us in the attainment of our ends (which they go far to shape), it is because of the natural selection process Hayek has sketched, which filters out grossly maladaptive rules. One may almost say that, if our knowledge is as restricted as Hayek supposes, with so much of it being in tacit and inarticulate form, then consciously reflective, goal-seeking behaviour cannot be the dominant paradigm of rationality in individual conduct. Rather, such calculational or consequential behaviour always presupposes a vast background of social adaptations, achieved through the mediation of internalized rules. For the most part, rationality must then consist for any individual in subscription to rules which, so far as he is concerned, are purposeless. Such purposeless rule-following is, for that reason, a mark of rationality in human beings, rather than a blemish in it.

On the other hand, such an assertion of flat incompatibility between the rule-following conception and the economic approach may be premature. Whereas the social inheritance of rules informs and governs the goals men seek, these rules will themselves be altered or abandoned if they thwart, or fail satisfactorily to promote, the goals they have themselves shaped. Systems of social rules may even have a self-defeating effect, in that the goals they suggest may destroy the overall order of the rules. Far short of a collapse of the system of rules, particular rules may be adapted, abandoned, or altered for 'economic' reasons, that is to say, so as to facilitate the achievement of already-formed goals. Consider here both the phenomenon of materialistically motivated religious conversion, and the modification of religious precepts in the course of practical life. It is plain that not only are the interstices in the system of social rules filled by calculational behaviour, but the system as a whole is stressed and reshaped by the goal-seeking and purposeful endeavours of its practitioners. In the fundamental case of the competition of religions — which Hayek has addressed profoundly in his as yet unpublished writings — there seems no necessary clash, then, between the economic approach and the Hayekian rule-following conception. We may test this result, however, more thoroughly, by way of an examination of the views of the most distinguished exponent of the economic approach, Gary Becker.

Becker has himself characterized the economic approach in a way that could not be bettered: 'The combined assumptions of maximizing behaviour, market equilibrium and stable preferences, used relentlessly and unflinchingly, form the heart of the economic approach as I see it.'[32] Qualifying this approach, Becker goes on to affirm that 'The assumption that information is often seriously incomplete because it is costly to acquire is used in the economic approach to explain the same kind of behaviour that is explained by irrational and volatile behaviour, or traditional behaviour, or "nonrational" behaviour in other discussions.'[33] The implications of this approach for social explanation by reference to traditional rules are brought out unequivocally in Henri Le Page's exposition of Becker's approach: 'Customs and traditions exist because they are valuable to most individuals; an individual chooses to adhere to them as part of his rational calculation. In other words', concludes Le Page 'customs and traditions survive because they are not detrimental to most people; they offer more benefits than costs.'[34]

Becker's argument has important affinities with Hayek's in two respects. First, Becker grasps firmly the rôle of traditions and customs in diminishing information costs. Reliance on tradition, in Becker's view, is not irrational or even non-rational, but rather eminently defensible in rational terms: if men were to calculate carefully, they would realize the insupportable costs of always calculating, and for that reason would often forego calculation by subscribing to traditional rules. Of course, when men subscribe to traditions, they are supposed in Becker's approach to be acting *as if* they had calculated information costs: Becker does not imagine that men have so calculated, any more than he is committed to regarding all behaviour as *au fond* rational. We are to explain men's proposensity for such as-if calculating behaviour, in Becker's terms, just as we explain their as-if altruistic behaviour. As Becker makes clear in his seminal paper on 'Altruism, Egoism and Genetic Fitness', both 'altruistic' and 'egoistic' behaviours can be accounted for in natural-selection terms as expressing survival-enhancing traits. Becker puts the point programmatically: 'The preferences taken as given by economists and vaguely attributed to "human nature" or something similar, the emphasis on self-interest, altruism toward kin, social distinction, and other enduring aspects of preferences — may be largely explained by the selection over time of traits having greater survival value.'[35] For Becker, as I understand him, then, the rational-choice approach and natural-selection theory are not only compatible, they are complementary and mutually supportive explanatory frameworks for social behaviour. If the economic approach explains social institutions in terms of their costs and benefits in maximizing the satisfaction of individual wants, sociobiological theory accounts for stable preferences in terms of their value in promoting survival.

In Becker's careful formulation of it, a thesis of the compatibility of natural-selection theory with the economic approach to social behaviour would seem to avoid the devastating criticism Hayek has made of those variants of sociobiology which are infected with constructivistic fallacies. Hayek's objection to at any rate the cruder and more popular versions of sociobiology is that, often enough, they treat instinct and conscious calculation as the only sources of social structures. For Hayek, indeed, one may justly say that such crudely constructivistic sociobiological theories fail to apply the natural—selection model faithfully to social institutions, inasmuch as they involve treating as primordial aspects of social life — instincts and the propensity to calculate costs and benefits — phenomena which, like important social institutions, must themselves be further explained in terms of their survival values. This vital omission in many sociobiological theories, which Hayek has identified, is remedied in Becker's account.

At the same time, this does not entail that Hayekian conception conflicts at no important point with the economic approach. Hayek's account of human action is not one which, taking wants and preferences as given or moulded by traditions and institutions, then explains behaviour as maximizing the satisfaction of these preferences. Indeed, very much in the fashion of his cousin Wittgenstein but developed entirely independently, Hayek envisages men's deliberative capacities as thoroughly shaped by their inherited traditions. In his recent writings, he has often commented on the ways in which inherited moral traditions — traditions expressing deep instinctual needs, for example, such as the moralities of tribalism — may lead individuals and societies to disaster. When this happens, we confront a 'cultural lag', in which evolved instinctual tendencies and inherited traditional sentiments both act to thwart adaptation to the beneficient order of the Great Society. On the other hand, Hayek sees also that calculational behaviour unconstrained by moral tradition may itself threaten social stability and the bases of liberty. Anticipating the findings of recent critics of act-utilitarianism such as Hodgson,[36] Hayek contends that a society of sheer calculators would fall into chaos, however 'rational' the individuals who composed it.

It is in this all-important insight into the limitations of rational choice as a source of social order that a principal contrast between the Hayekian conception and even Becker's statement of the economic approach may be found. Perfecting the argument of a long and distinguished line of liberal thinkers, such as Ferguson, Smith and Acton, Hayek has always maintained that a measure of 'uncritical' submission to social convention is an indispensable condition of stability as much as of liberty. The application of this insight to the question of the stability of market capitalist societies was made by Joseph Schumpeter, when in his *Capitalism, Socialism and Democracy*[37] he argued that the spread of the market economy tends to engender a calculational mentality which erodes the very moral traditions on which the market order depends. Similar arguments have been developed by neo-conservative writers such as Irving Kristol and Daniel Bell. In his most recent writings, Hayek has addressed this issue directly, contending (surely rightly) that the emergence and persistence of moral norms favouring market freedoms has depended crucially on widespread acceptance of religious

beliefs which embody 'symbolic truths' about the necessities
of social order. In all this, Hayek seems to be attributing a
rôle to uncritical rule-following more fundamental than the
function of diminishing information costs acknowledged in
Becker's work. His claim is that the social rules must be
regarded as vehicles of inarticulate knowledge of a kind
that is indispensable to social order. Once society comes to
be pervaded by the attitude that rules are no more than
means to known ends, much of the common stock of tacit
knowledge is inevitably lost and a measure of social chaos
must ensue.

The example of the self-destrcution of free societies
by the spread of the calculational mentality allows us to
generalize some plausible contrasts between Becker's economic approach and Hayek's conception. First, Hayek recognizes
explicitly, as Becker does not, that the inheritance of social
rules (including here rules of perception as well as of action)
shapes and moulds individual goals and structures agents'
deliberative capacities. Subscription by individuals to social
rules cannot, then, be conceived after the fashion of game
theory as a strategem designed to facilitate the achievement of consciously articulated ends. Secondly, and as a
consequence, calculation by individuals will be successful
only if it presupposes and invokes the tacit knowledge that is
embedded in the inheritance of social rules that has been
internalized in the individual personality. An attitude to
tradition of the constructivistically calculational sort described by Schumpeter as pervasive in capitalist societies
will only impoverish such societies, not just materially, but
epistemologically.

It would be thoroughly misguided to make too much of
these contrasts, however, and to overlook the deep affinities
between the Hayekian approach and that of Becker. After
all, Becker too sees character traits and social rules as survival-
enhancing adaptive devices whose emergence is to be
accounted for by natural-selection theory. No more than
Hayek does he suppose that rational calculation can be

autonomous or comprehensive, and there is nothing in his writings to support the idea that he himself *favours* a society of rational calculators. Rather, his thesis is that social institutions and many other aspects of social life may fruitfully be analysed in terms of the framework given by rational-choice theory. The crucial difference between Becker and Hayek appears to be in the area of what sort of explanation of social life is to be treated as *fundamental.* For Hayek a fundamental social explanation cannot be couched in terms of rational choice, since the latter always presupposes rules of thought, action and perception which shape individual ends and govern his deliberations. As I understand it, for Hayek rational calculation is inherently interstitial or supervenient — it fills gaps in a code of rules, resolves episodes of cognitive dissonance and aids judgement in applying norms. Whereas Hayek does not deny that the system of social rules may be altered if it does not promote the attainment of the goals it has inculcated in its practitioners, he cannot accept as fundamental an explanation of the rules themselves which is framed in terms of their contribution to the attainment of the goals of their subscribers. The fundamental explanation of the rules must rather be a natural-selection explanation of the sort given in Darwinian theory.

The upshot of the foregoing discussion of contrasts and affinities between Hayek's approach and that of Becker is that the natural selection of rival rules of action and perception is the mechanism of cultural evolution. Rational choice supervenes upon, and does not explain, this natural-selection process. A question which arises at once is whether this account of social or cultural evolution is consistent with methodological individualism. There can be no doubt that, when Hayek speaks of cultural evolution occurring by the selection of competing groups via their rival rules and practices, he sees this group selection as having a methodologically individualist character. This is to say that the group is treated as an heuristic device, and not as the fundamental unit in the theory. The fundamental unit can only be the gene or the genetic lineage. At the same time, it is at least not altogether obvious that this application of natural-selection theory to social explanation is entirely consistent with methodological individualism. On one of its formulations, at any rate, methodological individualism is an explanatory programme in which (via the resolutive—compositive method) social explanations terminate in the acts, decisions and intentions of individual agents. Such methodological individualism is surely well grounded in resisting the spurious claims to explanatory power made by reference to occult social collectivities. The problem with the natural-selection approach is that in accounting for individual character traits, dispositions, and so on by reference to their survival values, it deprives individual choices and purposes of their place at the terminal level of social explanation. The terminal level in the natural-selection theory is occupied by genetic replication. We have here an analogy with utilitarianism in moral theory, which fails to be morally individualist, not only or primarily in virtue of its collectivist policy implications, but decisively because it dissolves or disaggregates individuals into collections or series of episodes of pleasures and pains. The natural-selection theory would seem analogously to displace agents' choices from explanatory centrality by making them a dependent variable of survival chances.

A second question which arises is whether the natural-selection approach to social life is in any objectionable sense reductionist. Such a charge would certainly be made by a Wittgensteinian philosopher such as Peter Winch,[38] and by Michael Oakeshott, who both regard the assimilation of social changes to natural processes as evidencing a basic category mistake. It seems to me, though, that this *a priori* condemnation of Hayek's (and Becker's) approach is far too cavalier. Categories of thought are not given to us as Platonistic objects, immune from change, but rather emerge in the course of inquiry. The dualism of event and action which is at the back of Winch's methodological dichotomy of natural and social science cannot be taken as a fixed point in our thought, but must yield if investigation reveals the primary rôle of 'natural' processes in shaping social events. We ought to abandon, or at least drastically to modify, the act—event dichotomy, if sociobiological and natural-selection theories succeed (as they promise) in illuminating the sources of cultural change.

The question of reductionism has another aspect, however, which is connected with the issue of methodological individualism. I refer to the question of the reducibility of the order spontaneously produced by a number of rule-following individuals to the properties of the individuals concerned. In a context of inquiry closely akin to that of Hayek's, Robert Nozick has argued that invisible-hand explanations cannot be methodologically individualist.[39] Without rehearsing his arguments in detail, we may say that Nozick points to the difficulty of giving an account in individualist terms of an order which is produced by the actions of several individuals but without their intending it or even, as a rule, being able to conceive of it. In human contexts, the Menger—Mises account of the origins of money in invisible-hand terms would be almost a paradigm use of this difficulty. The question of reductionism I have in mind follows closely on consideration of such cases: are the properties possessed by the order yielded by the rule-governed actions of several individuals emergent properties wholly reducible to the elements in the order? Or is it the case that even a complete knowledge of the elements would not enable us to predict the emergence of the properties of the order they generate?

We come here, I think, to the crux of Hayek's entire conception, and to the most fascinating and profound insight in it. We have characterized Hayek's view as asserting that cultural evolution proceeds by the natural selection of rival rules of action and perception (as mediated through the practices and institutions of competing groups). Further, the evolution of rules of which he speaks encompasses the emergence of systems or structures, spontaneous orders, whose properties as wholes are not derivable from knowledge of any of their component elements. This point seems to identify a limit to reductionism wherever spontaneous orders exist.

The third element in Hayek's idea of spontaneous social order — the natural selection of traditions — thus takes him away from the Austrian commitment to the resolutive-compositive approach of methodological individualism. It does so by displacing fundamental explanation in social life from individual choices to genetic fitness on the one hand and spontaneous orders on the other hand. This displacement, in turn, sharpens the contrast between Hayek's method and that of the rational-choice theorists of the economic approach. In the last chapter of this study, I will try to assess the problems and possibilities opened up by Hayek's idea of spontaneous social order when this is viewed in all its internal complexity. Thus far, we have seen that it has important implications in the philosophy of social science. Its implications for legal and political philosophy, and its uses in the argument for individual liberty, are perhaps even more important and worthy of investigation.

The law of liberty

THE ORIGINS AND NATURE OF LAW

Hayek's understanding of law is inseparable from the account he gives of the nature of morality, and few aspects of his work are so often misunderstood as the conception he develops of morality. He has been characterized as a moral relativist, an exponent of evolutionary ethics and, less implausibly but nontheless incorrectly, as a rule-utilitarian. Let us see if we can dissipate the confusion.

In the first place, moral life for Hayek is itself a manifestation of spontaneous order. Like language and law, morality emerged undesigned from the life of men with one another: it is so much bound up with human life, indeed, as to be partly constitutive of it. The maxims of morality in no way presuppose an authority, human or divine, from which they emanate, and they antedate the institutions of the state. But, secondly, the detailed content of the moral conventions which spring up unplanned in society is not immutable or invariant. Moral conventions change, often slowly and almost imperceptibly, in accordance with the needs and circumstances of the men who subscribe to them. Moral conventions must (on Hayek's account of them) be seen as part of the evolving social order itself.

Now at this point it is likely that a charge of ethical relativism or evolutionism will at once be levelled against Hayek, but there is little substance to such criticisms. He has gone out of his way to distinguish his standpoint from any sort of evolutionary ethics. As he put it in his *Constitution of Liberty*:

It is a fact which we must recognize that even what we regard as good or beautiful is changeable — if not in any recognizable manner that would entitle us to take a relativistic position, then in the sense that in many respects we do not know what will appear as good or beautiful to another generation ... It is not only in his knowledge, but also in his aims and values, that man is the creature of his civilization; in the last resort, it is the relevance of these individual wishes to the perpetuation of the group or the species that will determine whether they persist or change. It is, of course, a mistake to believe that we can draw conclusions about what our values ought to be simply because we realize that they are a product of evolution. But we cannot reasonably doubt that these values are created and altered by the same evolutionary forces that have produced our intelligence.[1]

Hayek's argument here, then, is manifestly not that we can invoke the trend of social evolution as a standard for the resolution of moral dilemmas, but rather that we are bound to recognize in our current moral conventions the outcome of a long evolutionary process. Admittedly, inasmuch as nothing in the detailed content of our moral conventions is unchanging or unalterable, this means that we are compelled to abandon the idea that they have about them any character of universality or fixity, but this is a long way from any doctrine of moral relativism. As Hayek observes in his remarks on the ambiguity of relativism:

... our present values exist only as the elements of a particular cultural tradition and are significant only for some more or less long phase of evolution — whether this phase includes some of our pre-human ancestors or is confined to certain periods of human civilization. We have no more ground to ascribe to them eternal existence than to human race itself. There is thus one possible sense in which we may legitimately regard human values as relative and speak of the probability of their further evolution.

But it is a far cry from this general insight to the claims of the ethical, cultural or historical relativists or of evolutionary ethics. To put it crudely, while we know that all these values are relative to something, we do not know to what they are relative. We may be able to indicate the general class of circumstances which have made them what they are, but we do not know the particular conditions to which the values we hold are due, or what our values would be if those circumstances had been different. Most of the illegitimate conclusions are the result of erroneous interpretation of the theory of evolution as the empirical establishment of a trend. Once we recognize that it gives us no more than a scheme of explanation which might be sufficient to explain particular phenomena *if* we knew all the facts which have operated in the course of history, it becomes evident that the claims of the various kinds of relativists (and of evolutionary ethics) are unfounded.[2]

Hayek does not, then subscribe to any sort of ethical relativism or evolutionism, but it is not altogether clear from these statements if he thinks humanity's changing moral conventions have in fact any invariant core or constant content. In order to consider this last question, and to attain a better general understanding of Hayek's conception of morality, we need to look at his debts to David Hume, whose influence upon Hayek's moral and political philosophy is ubiquitous and profound.

Hayek follows Hume in supposing that, in virtue of certain general facts about the human predicament, the moral conventions which spring up spontaneously among men all have certain features in common or (in other words) exhibit some shared principles. Among the general facts that Hume mentions in his *Treatise*, and which Hayek cites in 'The Legal and Political Philosophy of David Hume', are men's limited generosity and intellectual imperfection and the unalterable scarcity of the means of satisfying human needs. As Hayek puts it succinctly: 'It is thus the nature of the(se) circumstances, what Hume calls "the necessity of human society", that gives rise to the "three fundamental laws of nature": those of "the stability of possessions, of its transference by consent, and of the performance of promises" And Hayek glosses this passage with a fuller citation from Hume's

Treatise: 'though the rules of justice be _artificial_, they are not _arbitrary_. Nor is the expression improper to call them *Laws of Nature*; if by natural we understand what is common to any species, or even if we confine it to mean what is inseparable from the species.'[3]

Hume's three rules of justice or laws of nature, then, give a constant content to Hayek's conception of an evolving morality. They frame what the distinguished Oxford jurist, H. L. A. Hart, was illuminatingly to call 'the minimum content of natural law'.[4] The justification of these fundamental rules of justice, and of the detailed and changing content of the less permanent elements of morality, is (in Hayek's view as in Hume's) that they form indispensable conditions for the promotion of human welfare. There is in Hayek as in Hume, accordingly, a fundamental utilitarian commitment in their theories of morality. It is a very indirect utilitarianism that they espouse, however, more akin to that of the late nineteenth-century Cambridge moralist Henry Sidgwick[5] (1838—1900) than it is to Jeremy Bentham or John Stuart Mill. The utilitarian component of Hayek's conception of morality is indirect in that it is never supposed by him that we ought or could invoke a utilitarian principle in order to settle practical questions: for, given the great partiality and fallibility of our understanding, we are in general better advised to follow the code of behaviour accepted in our own society. That code can, in turn, Hayek believes, never properly be the subject of a rationalist reconstruction in Benthamite fashion, but only reformed piecemeal and slowly. In repudiating the claims that utilitarian principles can govern specific actions and that utility may yield new social rules, Hayek makes clear that the utilitarian aspect of his moral theory is *indirect or system utilitarian*, inasmuch as the proper rôle of utility is not prescriptive or practical but rather that of a standard of evaluation for the assessment of whole systems of rules or practices. I refer here to the utilitarian aspect of Hayek's moral theory in order to stress that, for Hayek, it is not any Principle of Utility that is foundational, but rather a Kantian test of universalizability. There is no doubt that Hayek has always been an ethical Kantian for whom both the demands of justice and the claim of general welfare are derivable from Kant's idea of practical reason as involving assent to maxims of conduct in all relevantly similar cases. What is distinctive in Hayek's Kantian ethics is his insight that the demands of justice need not be competitive with the claims of general welfare: rather, a framework of justice is an indispensable condition of the successful achievement of general welfare. This insight of Hayek's was indeed nourished by his study of Hume, who always saw clearly that the utility of the rules of justice depended on their not being liable to abridgement for the sake of an apparent gain in welfare.

Again, the utilitarian aspect of Hayek's outlook is distinctive in that he explicitly repudiates any hedonistic conception of the content of utility itself.[6] How, then, does he understand utilitarian welfare? Just how are we to assess different systems of rules in regard to their welfare-promoting effects? Here Hayek comes close to modern preference-utilitarianism, but gives that view an original formulation, in arguing that the test of any system of rules is whether it maximizes an anonymous individual's chance of achieving his unknown purposes.[7] In Hayek's conception, we are not bound to accept the historical body of social rules just as we find it; it may be reformed in order to improve the chances of the unknown Man's achieving his goals. It will be seen that this is a maximizing conception, but not one that represents utility as a sort of neutral stuff, a container of intrinsic value whose magnitude may vary. Indeed, in taking as the point of comparison an hypothesized unknown individual, Hayek's conception (as he recognizes)[8] parallels John Rawls's model of rational choice behind a veil of ignorance as presented in Rawls's *Theory of Justice*.

Mention of Rawls's contractarian derivation of principles of justice at once raises the question of how Hayek's indirect or system-utilitarian argument is supposed to ground the rules of justice he defends, and, in particular, how Hayek's defence of the priority of liberty squares with his utilitarian outlook.

Several observations are apposite here. First, Hayek undoubtedly follows Hume in believing that, because they constitute an indispensable condition for the promotion of general welfare, the rules of justice are bound to take priority over any specific claim to welfare. Again, it is to be noted that Hume's second rule of justice, the transference of property by consent, itself frames a protected domain and so promotes individual liberty. Finally, Hayek argues forcefully that, if individuals are to be free to use their own knowledge and resources to best advantage, they must do so in a context of known and predictable rules governed by law. It is in a framework of liberty under the rule of law, Hayek contends, that justice and general welfare are both served. Indeed, under the rule of law, justice and the general welfare are convergent and not conflicting goals or values.

INDIVIDUAL LIBERTY UNDER THE RULE OF LAW

In Hayek's conception of it, individual liberty is a creature of the law and does not exist outside any civil society. He goes further than this, and proceeds to advance one of the most severely criticized claims of his philosophy, when he argues that the rule of law, properly understood and consistently applied, is bound to protect individual liberty. Many of Hayek's critics have urged that there is no reason why the rule of law, even as Hayek himself conceives it, should not permit highly oppressive policies and legislation. Some of Hayek's critics have linked this objection with another which they see as the most fundamental one, namely, that Hayek's political philosophy does not contain at a foundational level any commitment to inviolable human rights. The upshot of these two related critiques is that Hayek's rule of law will protect individual liberty only if it already incorporates strong moral rights to freedoms of various sorts: the Kantian test of universalizability, taken by itself, is almost without substance, in that highly oppressive laws will survive it, so long as legislators are ingenious enough to avoid mentioning particular groups or named individuals in the framing of the law itself. The core of this criticism, then, is that Hayek is constrained to demand more of the purely formal test of universalizability than it can reasonably deliver, and so comes to conflate the ideal of the rule of law with other, distinct political goods and virtues.

This fundamental criticism of Hayek, stated powerfully by Hamowy[9] and Raz[10] and endorsed in earlier writings of my own,[11] now seems to me to express an impoverished and mistaken view of the nature and rôle of Kantian universalizability in Hayek's philosophical jurisprudence. It embodies the error that, in Hayek or indeed in Kant, universalizability is a wholly formal test. Further, it fails to grasp the originality and power of Hayek's conception of justice, which is not rights-based but procedural, but which nonetheless confers a protected domain of freedom of action on individuals. Let us try to uncover the errors in this common criticism of Hayek by looking first at how the Kantian test actually functions in his philosophy.

In his 'Principles of a Liberal Social Order', Hayek tells us: The test of the justice of a rule is usually (since Kant) described as that of its "universalizability", i.e. of the possibility of willing that rules should be applied to all instances that correspond to the conditions stated in it (the "categorical imperative").[12] As an historical gloss, Hayek observes that:

It is somtimes suggested that Kant developed his theory of the *Rechtsstaat* by applying to public affairs his conception of the categorical imperative. It was probably the other way round, and Kant developed his theory of the categorical imperative by applying to morals the concept of the rule of law which he found ready made (in the writings of Hume).[13]

Hayek's own argument, that applying Kantian universalizability to the maxims that make up the legal order yields liberal principles of justice which confer maximum equal freedom upon all, has been found wanting by nearly all his critics and interpreters. Thus Raz quotes Hayek as follows:

'The conception of freedom under the law that is the chief concern of this book rests on the contention that when we obey laws, in the sense of general abstract rules laid down irrespective of their application to us, we are not subject to another man's will and are therefore free. It is because the judge who applies them has no choice in drawing the conclusions that follow from the existing body of rules and the particular facts of the case, that it can be said that laws and not men rule ... As a true law should not name any particulars, so it should especially not single out any specific persons or group of persons.'

Raz comments on this passage: 'Then, aware of the absurdity to which this passage leads, he modifies his line, still trying to present the rule of law as the supreme guarantee of freedom ...'[14]

Similarly, discussing Hayek's criteria that laws should not mention proper names and that the distinctions which the laws makes be supported both within and without the group which is the subject of legislation, Hamowy comments:

That no proper name be mentioned in a law does not protect against particular persons or groups being either harassed by laws which discriminate against them or granted privileges denied the rest of the population. A prohibition of this sort on the form laws may take is a specious guarantee of legal equality, since it is always possible to contrive a set of descriptive terms which will apply exclusively to a person or group without recourse to proper names ...[15]

How are these standard objections to be rebutted?

We must first of all note that, even in Kant and in Kantian writers other than Hayek, such as R. M. Hare and John Rawls, the test of universalizability does far more than rule out reference to particular persons or special groups. The test of universalizability does indeed, in the first instance, impose a demand of *consistency* as between similar cases, and in that sense imposes a merely formal requirement of non-discrimination. This is the first stage or element of universalization, the irrelevance of numerical differences. But the next stage of universalization is that of asking whether one can assent to the maxim being assessed coming to govern the conduct of others towards oneself: this is the demand of *impartiality* between agents, the demand that one put oneself in the other man's place. And this element or implication of universalizability leads on to a third, that we be impartial as between the preferences of others, regardless of our own tastes or ideals of life — a requirement of *moral neutrality*. I do not need to ask here exactly how these elements of universalizability are related to one another, to ask (most obviously) if the second is entailed by the first in any logically inexorable way, or similarly the third by the second. It is enough to note that this is a conception to which Hayek himself has always subscribed.[16]

Applying the full test of universalizability to the maxims that go towards making a legal order, we find that, not only are references to particulars ruled out, but the maxims must be impartial in respect of the interests of all concerned, and they must be neutral in respect of their tastes or ideals of life. If it be once allowed that the test of universalizability may be fleshed out in this fashion, it will be seen as a more full-bodied standard of criticism than is ordinarily allowed, and Hayek's heavy reliance on it will seem less misplaced. For, when construed in this fashion, the universalizability test will rule out (for example) most if not all policies of economic intervention as prejudicial to the interests of some and will fell all policies of legal moralism. Two large classes of liberal policy, supposedly allowable under an Hayekian rule of law, thus turn out to be prohibited by it.

Hayek himself is explicit that the test of universalizability means more than the sheerly formal absence of reference to particulars. As he puts it:

The test of the justice of a rule is usually (since Kant) described as that
of its 'universalizability', i.e. of the possibility of willing that the rules
should be applied to all instances that correspond to the conditions
stated in it (the 'categorical imperative'). What this amounts to is that
in applying it to any concrete circumstances it will not conflict with
any other accepted rules. The test is thus in the last resort one of the
compatibility or non-contradictoriness of the whole system of rules,
not merely in a logical sense but in the sense that the system of actions
which the rules permit will not lead to conflict.[17]

The maxims tested by the principle of universalizability,
then, must be integrated into a system of non-conflictable or
(in Leibnitz's terminology) compossible rules, before any of
them can be said to have survived the test.

Again, the compatibility between the several rules is not
one that holds in any possible world, but rather that which
obtains in the world in which we live. It is here that Hayek
draws heavily on Hume's account of the fundamental laws of
justice, which he thinks to be, not merely compatible with,
but in a large measure the inspiration for Kant's political
philosophy.[18] As I have already observed, the practical
content of the basic rules of justice is given in Hume by
anthropological claims, by claims of general fact about the
human circumstance. It is by interpreting the demands of
universalizability in the framework of the permanent
necessities of human social life that we derive Hume's three
laws of natural justice.

Note again that, in Hume, as in Hayek, the laws of justice
are commended as being the indispensable condition for the
promotion of general welfare, i.e. their ultimate justification
has a utilitarian component. But in order to achieve this
result, neither Hayek nor Hume need offer any argument in
favour of our adopting a Principle of Utility. Rather, very
much in the spirit of R. M. Hare's Kantian reconstruction
of utilitarian ethics,[19] Hayek's claim is that an impartial
concern for the general welfare is itself one of the demands
of universalizability. A utilitarian concern for general welfare
is yielded by the Kantian method itself and is not superadded

to it afterwards. Hayek's thesis, like Hume's, is that a clear view of the circumstances of human life shows justice to be the primary condition needed to promote general welfare. But, like Hare and Kant, he thinks concern for both justice and the general welfare to be dictated by universalizability itself.

Hayek's argument, then, is that the maxims of liberal justice are yielded by applying the Kantian universalizability test to the principles of the legal order. As he puts it:

It will be noticed that only purpose-independent 'formal' rules pass this (Kantian) test because, as rules which have originally been developed in small purpose-connected groups ('organizations') are progressively extended to larger and larger groups and finally universalized to apply to the relations between any members of an Open Society who have no concrete purposes in common and merely submit to the same abstract rules, they will in the proces⸱ have to shed all reference to particular purposes.[20]

Again, in listing the essential points of his conception of justice Hayek asserts:

... a) that justice can be meaningfully attributed only to human actions and not to any state of affairs as such without reference to the question whether it has been, or could have been, deliberately brought about by somebody; b) that the rules of justice have essentially the nature of prohibitions, or, in other words, that injustice is really the primary concept and the aim of rules if just conduct is to prevent unjust action; c) that the injustice to be prevented is the infringement of the protected domain of one's fellow men, a domain which is to be ascertained by means of these rules of justice; and d) that these rules of just conduct which are in themselves negative can be developed by consistently applying to whatever such rules a society has inherited the equally negative test of universal applicability — a test which, in the last resort, is nothing less than the self-consistency of the actions which these rules allow if applied to the circumstances of the real world.[21]

There seem to be several elements, then, in Hayek's contention that applying the Kantian test to the legal framework yields a liberal order. First, though he does not explicitly distinguish the three stages or phases of universalization I mentioned earlier, he is clear that the universalizability test is not only formal, and that it comprehends the requirement that the scheme of activities it permits in the real world should be conflict-free. Second, at any rate in a society whose members have few if any common purposes, law must have a largely formal character, stipulating terms under which men pursue their self-chosen activities rather than enjoining any specific activities on them; in the term Hayek adopts from Oakeshott,[22] the form of legal rule appropriate to such an abstract or open society is 'nomocratic' rather than 'teleocratic', purpose-neutral rather than purpose-dependent. Third, in a society whose members lack common purposes or common concrete knowledge, only abstract rules conferring a protected domain on each can qualify as rules facilitating a conflict-free pattern of activities. This means that the conditions of our abstract or open society will themselves compel adoption of a rule conferring just claims to liberty and private property — which Hayek rightly sees as indissolubly linked — once these conditions are treated as the appropriate background for the Kantian test.

This pattern of argument is an important and striking one, worth examining in detail on its merits, and not capable of being dismissed as prima facie unworkable. One important point may be worth canvassing, however. Hayek argues that once the legal framework has been reformed in Kantian fashion, it must of necessity be one that maximizes liberty. Hamowy goes so far as to assert that Hayek *defines* liberty as conformity with the rule of law.[23] Now, whereas not every aspect of Hayek's treatment of freedom and coercion is clear or defensible,[24] it seems a misinterpretation to say that he ever *defines* freedom as consisting solely in conformity with the rule of law. Rather, he takes such conformity to be a necessary condition of a free order. His thesis is that applying the Kantian test to the legal order will of itself yield a maxim according equal freedom to all men.[25] So it is not that the rule of law contains freedom as part of its definition, but rather that a freedom-maximizing rule is unavoidably yielded by it. In other terms, we may say that, whereas moral rights do not come into Hayek's theory as primordial moral facts, the right to a protected domain is yielded by his conception as a theorem of it.

Two points are worth making at this stage about Hayek's conception of justice in its relations with his account of law. First, Hayek's use of the test of universalizability in all its dimensions shows that the demands of law are for him as much a matter of rational discovery as they are of the spontaneous growth of a legal tradition. As against positivists, who treat law as created by legislators or judges, and who see it as having the character of commands or decisions, Hayek has always affirmed the objectivity of law. Judicial adjudication is for him a fully cognitive process (even where there are hard cases to be resolved). In this respect, he comes close to the natural lawyers for whom law occupies a pre-existing domain of objectivity, fully autonomous and independent of human decisions. On the other hand, Hayek's evolutionary perspective induces him to insist upon a much greater measure of variability and development in law than most natural lawyers can allow. In particular, Hayek thinks of the protected domain of individual liberty as having a greater degree of variability than any natural rights theorist could accept. In this, however, Hayek is surely in the right; no fixed list of rights or immunities can be drawn up which is adequate to the changing circumstances of human society. The detailed rules of property, and laws regarding privacy, for example, will need to be reworked when new technologies appear which enable unperceived invasions or privacy to be made and which generate new disputes about property rights (in air waves, for example). Adjudicating such disputes is an activity which relies on the one hand on the deliverances of legal tradition as it has evolved over the centuries and on the other upon the rational discovery process afforded by the Kantian test of universalizability.

The two-sidedness of judicial adjudication in Hayek's thought brings me to my second point about Hayek's account of law. There is throughout his writings a fascinating tension between the rational-discovery and the traditionalist models of judicial adjudication which is paralleled in his changing assessment of the place of legislation in a state governed by the rule of law. In some of his earlier writings, Hayek seemed committed to a pure form of the Kantian *Rechtsstaat*, in which the authority of the state is defined by an explicit legal constitution. Later, however, and perhaps under the influence of one of his most profound and original critics, Bruno Leoni, Hayek came increasingly to see the importance of common law as a guarantor of individual liberty. Leoni had argued penetratingly that the modern centralization of law in legislation confronted in the legal context many of the impossibilities faced by a centralized control of the economy.[26] Just as central allocation of economic resources produces chaotic waste and a degree of coordination of activities far less exact than that yielded by the market process, so centralized legislation cannot match the subtlety of common law in responding to complex and changing circumstances. In addition, common law is likely to be far more successful in giving citizens a stable framework for their activities than legislation, which is vulnerable to the whims of every transient majority. As it has evolved, Hayek's thought seems to me to have resolved his earlier ambiguity about the places of legislation and common law in the liberal state. His current view, as expounded in the last volume of his trilogy, *Law, Legislation and Liberty*, is that the liberal state has the form of a common-law *Rechtsstaat*. (He has not to my knowledge used this expression himself, but it captures his current view well.) Whereas legislation cannot be abolished altogether from the life of any modern state, it must be subject to review by a judicial process. In Hayek's latest proposals,[27] this process of judicial review is embodied in the upper chamber of a bicameral legislature, which is charged with the activity of defining law and of controlling by law the activities of the lower, legislative chamber.

Hayek's proposal that there be instituted an upper chamber authorized to pursue the demands of law, and to discover what justice requires in changing circumstances, reflects his perception that the spontaneous development of law may sometimes result in dead ends or practical deadlocks from which it has to be extricated. To some extent, this proposal accommodates some of the criticisms levelled against his work by one of Hayek's most perceptive admirers, James Buchanan. In an important paper, Buchanan observes that in Hayek's later writings we find:

the extension of the principle of spontaneous order, in its *normative* function, to the emergence of institutional structure itself. As applied to the market economy, that which emerges is defined by its very emergence to be that which is efficient. And this result implies, in its turn, a policy of nonintervention, properly so. There is no need, indeed there is no possibility, of evaluating the efficiency of observed outcomes independently of the process; there exists no external criterion that allows efficiency to be defined in objectively measurable dimensions. If this logic is extended to the structure of institutions (including law) that have emerged in some historical evolutionary process, the implication seems clear that that set which we observe necessarily embodies institutional or structural 'efficiency'. From this it follows, as before, that a policy of nonintervention in the process of emergence is dictated. There is no room left for the political economist, or for anyone else, who seeks to reform social structures, to *change* laws and rules, with an aim of security instead of efficiency in the large ... Any 'constructively rational' interferences with the 'rational' processes of history are, therefore, to be avoided.[28]

Buchanan's criticism, then, is that Hayek's apparent extension of spontaneous order or evolutionary arguments from the market processes to institutional structures is bound to disable the tasks of criticism and reform. We are left with no leverage in Hayek's account which might be used against the outcomes of the historical process. Instead, it seems, we are bound to entrust ourselves to all the vagaries of mankind's random walk in historical space.

In an earlier critique,[29] Buchanan noted perceptively the phenomenon of 'spontaneous disorder' — the emergence of patterns of activity that thwart the purposes and damage the interests of all who participate in them. Such 'spontaneous disorder' is, after all, the core of the idea of the Prisoner's Dilemma, which has been explored imaginatively in Buchanan's writing in its political and constitutional applications. In his most recent jurisprudential writings, Hayek has developed his view that one of the central tasks of the upper chamber would be to correct the evolution of the common law, and so to forestall or resolve such Prisoner's Dilemmas. We see here a very clear example of Hayek's attempt to combine respect for spontaneous traditional growths in law with the possibility of their rational assessment and critical evolution.

THE RULE OF LAW AND THE MYTH OF SOCIAL JUSTICE

Let us now recapitulate, and in some areas refine, the statement of Hayek's theory of justice which we have thus far developed. Like morality, law for Hayek is part of the natural history of mankind; it emerges directly from men's dealings with each other, it is coeval with society and so antedates the emergence of the state. For these reasons it is not the creation of any governmental authority and it is certainly not the command of any sovereign (as Hobbes surmised it to be). The principles of law are immanent aspects of social life, and their statement Hayek has called *nomos*, the law of liberty. Modern legislation he called *thesis*, and though this would have a proper place in any modern state, it has usurped many of the functions of true law, or *nomos*. Majoritarian democracy, in conjunction with legal positivism, has confused these distinctions utterly and has encouraged an identification of law with the wishes of the sovereign majority of the moment. As against these trends, Hayek has made the proposal for bicameralism mentioned in the last section, which he regards as bringing democracy back to its authentic roots in the context of a limited government (and which he calls *demarchy* to distinguish it from contemporary perversions of the democratic ideal). In making these proposals, Hayek is most concerned to lay emphasis on unencumbered judicial process as the best guarantor of individual freedom. The state, like any private citizen, is to be governed by *nomos*, the true law which defines justice and prescribes the limits of individual liberty and of governmental authority.

The most powerful threat to law thus conceived has come in recent years not so much from legal positivism or majoritarian democracy, but from contemporary ideas of distributive or social justice, and against these Hayek has directed some of his most powerful and astringent criticisms of modern thought. What are the chief features of this conception of social justice, and why does Hayek attack it so strongly? As Hayek sees it, the modern conception of social justice attributes the character of justice or injustice to the whole pattern of social life, with all its component rewards and losses, rather than to the conduct of its component individuals, and in doing this it inverts the original and authentic sense of liberty, in which it is properly attributed only to individual actions. It cannot apply to the unknown patterns which these actions form, but only to the framework within which they occur. For this reason, if for no other, Hayek argues that there cannot be the 'patterned' conceptions of justice which Robert Nozick has brilliantly criticized in his *Anarchy, State and Utopia*.[30]

Not only is the attribution of justice or injustice to social outcomes an inversion of its proper use, such a conception of justice renders it incompatible with the rule of law. As early as *The Road to Serfdom*, Hayek advanced the argument, which he refined in *The Constitution of Liberty* and completed in the second volume of *Law, Legislation and Liberty*, that the rule of law must in treating citizens anonymously and equally be indifferent to the inequalities in men's initial endowments and material fortunes. Aiming to equalize these latter would in fact involve treating men differently and unequally and could not avoid producing many serious inequities. It would also entail according to governmental authorities a span of discretionary power over the lives of citizens which could be intolerable even if it were not likely to be abused in the service of private interests. Why is this?

Contemporary distributivist conceptions, where they are not straightforwardly egalitarian, typically involve conceptions of need or merit as criteria for just distribution in society. Hayek's first observation is that not all needs or merits are commensurable with each other. A medical need involving relief of pain is not easily ranked against one involving the preservation of life and, where such needs are in practical competition for scarce resources, there is no rational principle available to settle the conflict. Such conflicts are endemic because, contrary to much social democratic wishful thinking, some basic needs, needs connected with staving off senescence for example,[31] are not satiable. Bureaucratic authorities charged with distributing medical care according to need will inevitably act unpredictably, and arbitrarily from the standpoint of their patients, for want or any overarching standard governing choice between such incommensurable needs. These dilemmas will occur elsewhere, in housing policies where these too become subject to large-scale state provision, infecting the lives of citizens with uncertainty and dependency on unforeseeable bureaucratic interventions. The situation will be the same when the occasion arises for weighing merits against each other — a process so obviously subjective as to demand no further comment. The idea that social distribution could ever be governed by these subjective and inherently disputable notions reflects the unrealism of much contemporary thought.

Even if this objection could be circumvented, and notions of need and merit given greater determinacy and commensurability, there exists a devastating criticism of distribution according to such standards, namely that it breaks the matching of reward with services rendered which is the only guarantor of economic efficiency. After all, an incompetent physician may be more needy and more meritorious than a highly competent one, but we still think that each should be rewarded according to the value of their services to their patients. The principle of rewarding people according to the value of their services to others where there is free entry to all the relevant occupations, shows clearly[32] that the only principle of justice application to distribution in a free society is that of commutative justice. Attempts to impose any other principle on the free exchanges of free men involve imposing upon them a hierarchy of ends and goals, a ranking of values and a code of judgements regarding the weightiness of competing needs and merits, about which no consensus exists in our society and which there is no reason to suppose can be achieved. Because these distributive conceptions therefore involve overriding the patterns thrown up by men's free choices, Hayek correctly observes that modern ideas of social justice threaten the transformation of the free order into a totalitarian organization.

In these powerful criticisms of contemporary redistributional aspirations, Hayek shows the incompatibility with liberty of patterned conceptions of just distribution in a manner akin to that attempted by Robert Nozick.[33] Unlike Nozick, however, Hayek relies on a theory of procedural justice instead of an assertion of fundamental rights. His criticism has in common with Nozick's that it rejects the twentieth century distinction — forged, as I shall later show, by J. S. Mill in the mid-nineteenth century — between production and distribution. For Hayek, as for Marx, economic systems are to be taken as wholes; we cannot graft a socialist distributional system on the stem of free market production. Free market production requires that negative feedback within the economy, as reflected in falling incomes and failing enterprises, be absorbed and not resisted or thwarted by governmental efforts at correcting market distribution. But it is precisely such resistance of the negative feedback essential to a dynamic economy which is sanctioned by modern distributivism. Ironically enough, the conservative implications of resisting negative feedback in the economy — which, if it could be achieved, would freeze asset distribution and the pattern of incomes and preclude all but Pareto-optimal changes which harm no one — are rarely perceived by radical exponents of social justice.

Hayek's final, and perhaps most compelling argument against social justice is an epistemological and conceptual one. Even if clear principles could be determined for correcting market distributions, no governmental authority could know enough reliably to implement and enforce them. This is a fatal blow even to Rawls's apparently attractive Difference Principle[34] enjoining that only those inequalities be permitted which benefit the worst-off group in society. All such efforts at correcting market distribution entail, not only continuous interference with men's free choices, but unsuccessful interferences at that. Hayek's argument has a conceptual side as well as this epistemological aspect in that he denies that social justice has any clear sense at all. In part this is because it inverts the original, authentic sense of justice, in which it applied to individual actions; but the greater part of Hayek's claim is that the component parts of the current conception of social justice — moral notions of desert, need and merit and so on — stand in no coherent or rational relations with each other. Failure to perceive this allows the true believers in social justice to work together in promoting an ideal which lacks any agreed content. Hayek's conclusion, then, is that whereas they could not be implemented even if they had a clear content, current distributionist views are in truth devoid of any substantial principles and so fail to provide a guide to practice. At the same time, in asserting that the primary domain of the predicate of justice is individual conduct, Hayek does not deny that just conduct occurs within a protected domain created by a legal framework, and the question naturally arises as to how this framework is to be designed or reformed.

THE JURIDICAL FRAMEWORK OF SPONTANEOUS
SOCIAL ORDER

The essential elements of Hayek's construction of juridical framework of liberty are given by his adaptation of Hume's principles of justice, to which I have already alluded. It is to be noted here that, for Hayek as for Hume, the institution of private or several property is part and parcel of justice itself. Aside from the many instrumental benefits of the institution — all of which revolve around the fact that private property allows resource allocation to occur via the decentralized decision making of very many individuals and organizations, each able to act upon its own knowledge and in pursuit of its own goals — it is indispensable in framing the protected domain for each individual. This is to say that individual liberty and private property are inseparable elements within the full conception of liberal justice. It is not to say, however, that all property in a free society may take the form of what Honoré has called full liberal ownership;[35] the property rights of a free society will in fact always be highly pluralistic, reflecting the complex mixtures of liberties and claims which free men voluntarily enter into with one another. There is room in a free society for all manner of property rights, provided always they reflect men's uncoerced choices and are not imposed on them by governmental authority.

In some respects, Hayek's view of the juridical framework of the free society is Humean and conservative, since it accepts the existing pattern of entitlements as historically given and does not seek to overturn them in the interests of any principle of rectificatory justice such as that advanced by Robert Nozick in Lockean spirit.[36] It is less conservative than Hume's account, in that Hayek sees the detailed content of property rights as open to continuous judicial revision and even (where radically new circumstances prevail) to legislative amendment. Hayek's view of the framework of a free society is thoroughly unconservative, and akin to Nozick's vision of a *meta-utopian framework*,[37] in that it allows the fullest scope to experiments in living. Using their resources, individuals and communities may in Hayek's conception initiate innovative styles of social life, just as others will pursue their long-established traditions. Indeed, one of the virtues of the institution of several property that sustains the free society is that it permits the peaceful competition of different traditions and ways of life. In facilitating this competition, private property proves essential to the cultural evolution of human society.

In Hayek's as in Nozick's account, a specific mechanism is described whereby in this peaceful competition a filtering out of maladaptive practices is achieved. The mechanism is that of *migration*: individuals will desert the practices of failing groups and so reinforce the strength of more successful ones. Hayek even introduces this mechanism to constrain some of the authorities of government: local governments, he suggests,[38] may peacefully compete in the provision of tax-supported services, since the costs of migration between them are usually not great. In this way, the process of emulation, which I earlier identified as one of the chief means whereby the natural selection of traditions occurs, achieves an institutional embodiment in the idea of competing local governments, which are constrained to adopt imitatively each other's most successful features for fear of losing their tax base by migration.

It should be stressed that, in Hayek as in Nozick, the evolutionary filter process achieves its greatest efficacy in social life to the extent that all the major social institutions (aside from those bound up with sustaining the framework itself) are privatized. Thus there will be competing types of education, of welfare provision and medical care, of family life and religion. When these aspects of social life are in the private domain, contained within institutions defined as possessing each of them its own property, the competition of groups leading to the natural selection of traditions is enhanced and we have strongest assurance that cultural evolution will proceed in the best direction. Here, as elsewhere, private property allows for diversity, and this diversity proves to be highly beneficial in terms of general welfare. The rôle of the juridical framework is, indeed, precisely to define the terms within which the continuous evolution of complex social formations may spontaneously occur.

—4—

Economic theory and public policy

SOCIAL SCIENCE AND PUBLIC POLICY

Hayek's account of human knowledge, in which a thesis of
the primacy of practice supports the claim that theoretical
knowledge is always of a highly abstract and necessarily
incomplete order, has important implications for the proper
method for the practice of social science. To begin with,
Hayek's affirmation of 'the primacy of the abstract' in all
human knowledge means that social science is always a
theory-laden activity and can never aspire to an exhaustive
description of concrete social facts. More, the predictive
aspirations of social science must be qualified: not even the
most developed of the social sciences, economics, can ever
do more than predict the occurrence of general classes of
events. Indeed, in his strong emphasis on the primacy of the
abstract, Hayek goes so far as to question the adequacy of
the nomothetic or nomological model of science (i.e. exact
prediction through 'laws'), including social science. At least
in respect of complex phenomena, all science can aim at is an
'explanation of the principle', or the recognition of a pattern
— 'the explanation not of the individual events but merely of
the appearance of certain patterns or orders. Whether we call
these merely explanations of the principle or mere pattern
predictions or higher level theories does not matter.'[1] Such
recognitions of orders or pattern predictions are, Hayek
observes, fully theoretical claims, testable and falsifiable:

but they correspond badly with the usual cause—effect structure of nomothetic or law-governed explanation.

In his most important later statement on these questions, 'The Theory of Complex Phenomena', Hayek tells us that, because social life is made up of complex phenomena, 'economic theory is confined to describing the kinds of patterns which will appear if certain general conditions are satisfied, but can rarely if ever derive from this knowledge any predictions of specific phenomena.'[2] If we ask why it is that social phenomena are complex phenomena, part of the reason at any rate lies in what Hayek earlier characterized[3] as the subjectivity of the data of the social sciences: social objects are not like natural objects whose properties are highly invariant relatively to our beliefs and perceptions; rather, social objects are in large measure actually constituted by our beliefs and judgements. Social phenomena are non-physical, and Hayek has stated that 'Non-physical phenomena are more complex because we call physical phenomena what can be described by relatively simple formulae.'[4] And, because of the subjectivity of its data, social life always eludes such simple formulae.

Hayek's view that we can at best attain abstract models of social processes, whereas the concrete details of social life will always largely elude theoretical formulation, has large and radical implications in the field of public policy. In brief, it entails that the object of public policy should be confined to the design or reform of institutions within which unknown individuals make and execute their own, largely unpredictable plans of life. In a free society, in fact, whereas there may be a legal policy in respect of economic institutions, there cannot be such a thing as economic policy as it is presently understood, for adherence to the rule of law precludes anything resembling macroeconomic management. Here I do not wish to take up this point, which I will consider later, but rather to spell out the connection between Hayek's methodological views and his belief that most, if not all economic policy as practised in the post-war world has had a self-defeating effect.

We have seen that, for Hayek, the most we can hope for in understanding social life is that we will recognize recurring patterns. Hayek goes on to observe:

Predictions of a pattern are ... both testable and valuable. Since the theory tells us under which general conditions a pattern of this sort will form itself, it will enable us to create such conditions and to observe whether a pattern of the kind predicted will appear. And since the theory tells us that this pattern assures a maximisation of output in a certain sense, it also enables us to create the general conditions which will assure such a maximisation, though we are ignorant of many of the particular circumstances which will determine the pattern that will appear.[5]

Hayek's view stands in sharp opposition to any idea of a policy science or a political technology aimed at producing specific desired effects. Such a policy science demands the impossible of its practitioners, a detailed knowledge of a changing and complex order in society. Even Popper's conception of 'piecemeal social engineering', Hayek tells us, 'suggests to me too much a technological problem of reconstruction on the basis of the total knowledge of the physical facts, while the essential point about the practical improvement is an experimental attempt to improve the functioning of some part without a full comprehension of the structure of the whole.'[6] Indeed Hayek's central point is that understanding the primacy of the abstract in human knowledge means that we must altogether renounce the modern ideal of consciously controlling social life: a better ideal is that of *cultivating* the general conditions in which beneficial results may be expected to emerge.

Hayek's critique of the constructivistic or engineering approach to social life parallels in an intriguing way that of Michael Oakeshott and of the Wittgensteinian philosopher Rush Rhees. Consider Oakeshott's statement: 'The assimilation of politics to engineering is, indeed, what may be called the myth of rationalist politics.'[7] Or Rhees's observation (made in criticism of Popper): 'There is nothing about human societies which makes it reasonable to speak of the application of engineering to them. Even the most important "problems of production" are not problems in engineering.'[8] The conception of social life which talk of social engineering expresses is at fault not only because it presupposes an agreement on goals or ends which nowhere exists but also because it promotes the illusion that political life may become subject to a sort of technical or theoretical control.

The idea of a policy science, which Hayek sees as embodying the constructivistic approach to social life, tends in the economic area systematically to neglect the tendencies to self-regulation which the market process displays. For Hayek, the catallaxy is but one instance of spontaneous order, it is the sort of spontaneous order whose control mechanism is the profit-and-loss system of market competition. Rival enterprises, using the tacit as well as the theoretical knowledge of their managers and entrepreneurs, discover the wants of their customers and bring about an unplanned integration of the activities and preferences of the various market participants. Note here that, though Hayek often stresses the production and efficiency of the market process, and contrasts this with the chaos and waste of socialist and interventionist systems, he is emphasizing the harmony and self-regulating properties of the market process when he characterizes it as a spontaneous order. In laying down as the central problem of economic theory the mechanisms whereby dispersed knowledge is put to social use, Hayek is breaking with the conception of economics endorsed by all the classical economists. With the partial exception of Adam Smith, the classical economists altogether failed to grasp the epistemological foundations of market institutions and they all tended to conceive of economics as the science of wealth creation − a science of *plutology* − or else as the general study of economizing or maximizing behaviour. As my analysis of Hayek's relations with such advocates of the economic approach to social life as Gary Becker has shown,

however, Hayek's view of society does not fit easily or well
with any of these rational-choice models. In its applications
to economics, in particular, Hayek has, at least since the
crucial year of 1936, in which he wrote his important paper
on 'Economics and Knowledge', seen the central economic
problem as having to do, not with the efficient utilization of
scarce resources, but rather with the generation and utilization of dispersed knowledge. Many errors in economic theory
are made when it invokes the unreal postulate of perfect
information in describing the behaviour of market participants.
This postulate of omniscience becomes positively pernicious
when it is invoked as a standard of criticism of real-world
market processes and used thereby as a support for interventionism. Neglect of the market's informational functions
almost inevitably issues in demands for economic planning in
which the ineradicable ignorance of governmental authorities
of the complex data in which economic order rests is dis-
regarded. More fundamentally, the assumption of perfect
information gives a distorted bias to economic theory as
a whole.

NEOCLASSICAL EQUILIBRIUM, THE THEORY OF CAPITAL AND THE CHARACTER OF THE BUSINESS CYCLE

Hayek's insight that it is the division of knowledge in society
that gives economic theory its main problem yields one
of its most important results in his criticisms of the idea of
equilibrium in classical and neoclassical economics. The
assumption of omniscience which is made in classical
accounts of perfect competition destroys their usefulness
as models for any real market process. In addition, however,
such a conception of equilibrium fails to make a crucial
distinction between what Hayek calls *the pure logic of choice*
— the body of principles which explain the rational choices
of individuals — and the market processes which tend to

produce coordination in the economy. The difference here is between the equlibrium position achieved by a single rational chooser, given his preference function and his opportunities and constraints and the equilibrium which may emerge through the interaction of several agents. The former equilibrium is one that may be attributed to any individual, while the latter designates a degree of coordination among many individuals. The importance of this distinction is that, whereas the pure logic of choice may be given an axiomatic formulation, the theory of coordination in the real economy is part of empirical economic science. In criticizing the classical conception of equlibrium for conflating individual choice at one time with market processes over time, Hayek also distinguished his own view from that of von Mises, for whom propositions about market equilibrium had themselves an axiomatic character. It is not that von Mises ever subscribed to the unreal neoclassical view of equilibrium, but rather that he insisted that the account he gave of equilibrium was, like the rest of economics, deducible from axioms about human action. Hayek had never accepted this view of economics, and his distinction between the pure logic of choice and the empirical parts of economic theory was in fact an attempt at a fundamental criticism of the Misesian view.

Equilibrium, then, is for Hayek a matter of market actors behaving in ways which allow their activities to mesh or integrate. Whether they succeed in coordinating will depend on how accurate their beliefs and expectations about each other's behaviour turn out to be. The question now arises as to how this very general account of equilibrium illuminates or applies to historical episodes of depression and large-scale discoordination, and here we come to Hayek's version of the Austrian theory of the trade cycle. As it had been developed by Hayek's colleague, von Mises, the Austrian theory explains the boom—bust cycle of modern capitalist economics by invoking the credit policies of the banking system. At its simplest, the Austrian view is that the contemporary banking system tends to lower the market rate of interest below the

natural rate — where the natural rate is understood to be the
interest rate that would match the investment level with
the level of voluntary savings — and so communicates to
businessmen misleading and incorrect signals regarding
the condition of the economy. In acting on these false
signals, businessmen take the economy further away from
coordination and reinforce existing distortions in relative
price structures. Bankruptcies and unemployment are bound
to follow the period of malinvestment induced by unsound
credit expansion and are in fact signs of the market process
attempting to move back to coordination.

Two points of theoretical interest may be made about this
very brief sketch of Austrian trade cycle theory. First of all,
it embodies a strong insistance on the *non-neutrality of
money*. Changes in the quantity of money (as this is produced by governmental and banking institutions) do not act
at once to alter the general price level. Rather, they enter the
economy at specific points and act to alter the *relative* price
structure. They do this — and here is the second point — by
altering the time structure of the production process. Austrian
theory is distinctive in its characterization of production as a
process having several stages or phases, consumption goods
being at the nearest stage and investment or capital goods at
the furthest stage. Each phase of the production process
requires a combination of complementary goods, many of
which are specific to that phase of production and so cannot
easily be switched to other stages of the process. The effect
of credit expansion induced governmentally or via unsound
banking practices is to 'lenghten' the production structure
artificially so that resources are drawn into long-term investment at the furthest end of the process. Since, however,
people's real preferences have not altered, the malinvestment
in capital goods can be sustained only by further credit
expansion. When this is not forthcoming the discoordination
of the economy is disclosed in rising unemployment and
business failures. In a nutshell, the credit laxity which the
modern banking system tends to display distorts the allocation

of resources from its natural, if constantly changing home where it reflects the actual preferences (including the time-preferences) of all market actors (consumers as well as producers). It does so, more specifically, by inducing over-investment at the furthest end of the production process. Depressions represent a spontaneous process in which market factors attempt to restore the lost meshing between demand and supply at all stages of the production process.

Hayek's version of this Austrian account, developed in book form first in his 1931 study, *Prices and Production*, is distinctive by emphasizing strongly the theme that realistic economics is microeconomics, dealing with the subtle and complex world of relative price structures which change over time. Drawing on von Mises and in some measure upon Knut Wicksell, Hayek attempted to link up the central claims of his monetary theory – which, as we have seen, emphasizes the non-neutrality of money in the real world – with capital theory and price theory. In both the area of capital forma-tion and that of price determination Hayek was concerned to correct the schematic account given in neoclassical theory of the impact of monetary changes and to argue that the effect of such changes was in both areas to be conceived in qualitative and microeconomic terms. The aggregative type of theorizing favoured by econometric approaches using statistical data, useful though it is for some purposes, risks postulating entities and causal relationships that do not in fact exist in the real world. As Hayek put the point in programmatic form:

The best known instance [of this aggregative method], and the most relevant case in point, is the resuscitation by Irving Fisher some twenty years ago of the more mechanistic forms of the quantity theory of the value of money in his well-known 'equation of exchange'. That this theory, with its apparatus of mathematical formulae constructed to admit of statistical verification, is a typical instance of 'quantitative' economics, and that it indeed probably contributed a good deal to influence the methodology of the present representatives of this school, are propositions which are not likely to be denied. I do not propose to quarrel with the positive content of this theory: I am even ready to concede that so far as it goes it is true, and that, from a practical point of view, it would be one of the worst things which would befall us if the general public should ever again cease to believe in the elementary propositions of the quantity theory. What I complain of is not only that this theory in its various forms has unduly usurped the central place in monetary theory, but that the point of view from which it springs is a positive hindrance to further progress. Not the least harmful effect of this particular theory is the present isolation of the theory of money from the main body of general economic theory.

For so long as we use different methods for the explanation of values as they are supposed to exist irrespective of any influence of money, and for the explanation of that influence of money on prices, it can never be otherwise. Yet we are doing nothing less than this if we try to establish *direct* causal connections between the *total* quantity of money, the *general level* of all prices and, perhaps, also the *total* amount of production. For none of these magnitudes *as such* ever exerts an influence on the decisions of individuals; yet it is on the assumption of a knowledge of the decisions of individuals that the main propositions of non-monetary economic theory are based. It is to this 'individualistic' method that we owe whatever understanding of economic phenomena we possess; that the modern 'subjective' theory has advanced beyond the classical school in its consistent use is probably its main advantage over their teaching.

If, therefore, monetary theory still attempts to establish causal relations between aggregates or general averages, this means that monetary theory lags behind the development of economics in general. In fact, neither aggregates nor averages do act upon one another, and it will never be possible to establish necessary connections of cause and effect between them as between individual phenomena, individual prices, etc. I would even go so far as to assert that, from the very nature of economic theory, averages can never form a link in its reasoning ...[9]

As Hayek understands it, then, correct methodology in economic theory always involves reducing aggregative statements to their micoreconomic foundations. It is their departure from this individualist and subjectivist stance in methodology which does much to explain the errors in policy and theory not only of the Keynesians, but also of many contemporary monetarists.

HAYEK VERSUS KEYNES AND FRIEDMAN
ON THE RÔLE OF MONEY IN THE REAL ECONOMY

These general views illuminate much of the rationale of Hayek's opposition not only to Keynesian policies of macroeconomic demand management but also to Friedmanite monetarism. Of course, in the great debates of the thirties, Hayek had argued forcefully that Keynes in no way provided a general theory of economic discoordination. Again, Hayek always argued that the policies Keynes suggested, depending as they did for their success upon institutional and psychological irrationalities which their very operation would undermine, were bound over the longer run to be self-defeating. In particular, Hayek maintained that Keynesian policies of deficit financing depended for their success upon a widespread money illusion which the policies themselves could not help but erode. Hayek's further objection to Keynesian policies is that, in part because they depend on a defective understanding of the business cycle (which is seen as expressing itself in aggregate variations in total economic activity rather than a discoordination of relative price structures brought about by a governmental distortion of the structure of interest rates) Keynesian policy-makers find it hard to avoid committing a sort of fallacy of conceptual realism: statistical artefacts or logical fictions are allowed to blot out the qualitative relationships which make up the real economy. Quite apart from its technical details, however, it is clear that Hayek's critique of Keynesian policies is of a piece with his emphasis on the primacy of the abstract and with his insight into the indispensability of conventions for the orderly conduct of social life. Policies of macroeconomic demand management ask more in the way of concrete knowledge of the real relationships which govern the economy than any adminstrator could conceivably acquire, and their operation is in the longer run self-defeating. More generally, Hayek's challenge to Keynesian theory is a demand that Keynesians specify in detail the mechanisms whereby an unhampered market could be expected to develop severe discoordination. Only if such mechanisms could be clearly described and (crucially) given a plausible historical application, would a serious challenge to Hayek's own Austrian view — in which it is governmental intervention in the economy which is principally responsible for discoordination — enter the realm of critical debate.

Contrary to popular opinion, Hayek has always disassociated himself from orthodox monetarism on grounds closely akin to his objections to Keynesianism. It is important here, however, to note that both 'Keynesianism' and 'monetarism' refer to complex patterns of ideas, whose contents have changed much over time. Thus Hayek actually endorsed Keynes's first departures from orthodox quantity theory of money[10] and, on the other hand, he has repeatedly asserted that it was a disaster when the crude view of the quantity theory was dropped from public doctrine. These are not all inconsistent statements, since Hayek's positions in the theory and policy of money have always differed from those developed by Keynes (and, especially, by Keynes's disciples) and from those espoused by such modern monetarists as Milton Friedman. In theory, both the Keynesians and the monetarists adopt the aggregative approach which Hayek as an Austrian economist in the tradition of von Wiser and von Mises regards as methodologically unsound. In the area of public policy, the quantity theorists made the error of suggesting that a successful stabilization of the general price level would of itself coordinate economic authority. Keynes himself, throughout many changes of view, seems to have held that the coordination of economic activity could be *restored* by an increase in aggregate purchasing power. In both cases, the error is committed of supposing that qualitative and structural economic discoordinations may be overcome by policies which act upon statistical aggregates and averages. Both Keynesian and monetarist analyses mislead public policy, which ought rather simply to allow the spontaneous cleansing process of recession to take its course. We see here that nice questions in the methodology of economic theory may have massive repercussions in public policy.

It is beyond the compass of the present study, which aims to exhibit Hayek's positions in economic theory and public policy as implications of his fundamental philosophical outlook, to assess the technical aspects of his contributions to the theory and policy of money in modern economies. A few observations on the general outlines of his monetary economics may be in order nonetheless. An initial point to grasp is that since, for Hayek, money is an evolved social institution and not the creation of government, it is unlikely that government will achieve anything resembling full control of it. More specifically, in respect to Friedman's proposals for monetary regulation by a fixed rule, Hayek has argued that in a modern democracy no governmental or quasi-governmental agency can preserve the independence of action essential if such a monetary rule is to be operated consistently. Most fundamentally, such a policy of adopting a fixed rule in the supply of money is opposed by Hayek on methodological grounds. Such a policy calls for an exactitude in modeling and measuring economic life, and an unambiguity in the definition of money, which it is beyond our powers to attain. Hayek's own objection to Friedman's monetarist proposals is, then, most substantially that money is not the sort of social object that we can define precisely or control comprehensively; Hayek has even suggested that, in recognition of the elusiveness of the monetary phenomenon, we should treat 'money' as an adjectival expression.[11] applicable to indefinitely many distinct and disparate instruments. Monetary policy, strictly speaking, is neither desirable nor possible in a modern economy which contains many money-creating institutions aside from government. Under the gold standard or its surrogate, a regime of fixed exchange rules, something like monetary policy could be pursued since the definition of money was then controlled by impersonal convention. Since the collapse of the gold standard and of the fixed exchange system, we have experienced a monetary chaos, in which rival governments engage in a sort of competitive monetary nationalism. Hayek's proposal has[12] now become the radical and even revolutionary one that we transform this monetary chaos into *a monetary catallaxy* by depriving government of its monopoly powers over the creation of money. Currency competition by private suppliers would, he argues, not only act as an effective constraint upon government inflation, but also (by bringing money into the market process) remove the main cause of economic recession and of the trade muscle, namely, the existence of money as a 'loose joint in the economic system', outside the market process and subject to constant political control. Subjecting money to market forces would not of course remove all of the endogenous sources of market disturbance, but it would eliminate its single greatest exogenous source in governmental monetary manipulation.

Hayek's most original and radical proposal in the area of public policy, the opening up of money creation to market processes by abolishing legal tender laws and allowing private issuance of money, is one that follows directly from his deepest philosophical and methodological commitments. When money was controlled by an unchallenged convention (as in the days of the gold standard) or by an impersonal and international fixed rule (as during the period of fixed exchange rates), he saw no pressing need for introducing market competition into the monetary area. (Even then,[13] however, he argued in favour of allowing monetary freedom as an aspect of individual liberty.) In his later writing, in which he despairs of controlling governmental monetary activity by any fixed rule, he sees the only way to stable money values as being one which exploits spontaneous market forces. In this he sees further than even the classical laissez-faire liberals and in my judgement takes the consistent and necessary step of recognizing that even the stability of the real market economy depends upon its monetary instruments becoming part and parcel of the market process itself.

SHACKLE'S CRITIQUE OF HAYEK

There is a fundamental criticism of Hayek's economic thought which is suggested at once by the arguments we have just been exploring. Much in Hayek's account of the business cycle, as in his general view of spontaneous social order, seems to suggest that he believes economic discoordination results always from institutional factors, so that at any rate large-scale disequilibrium would be impossible in a catallaxy of wholly unhampered markets. Against this view, Hayek's brilliant and somewhat neglected pupil, G. L. S. Shackle, has argued that the subjectivity of expectations must infect the market process with an ineradicable tendency to disequilibrium.[14] It must be allowed that, if we accept Hayek's view of equilibrium as a process in which men's plans are coordinated by trial and error over time, there can be nothing apodictically certain about this process: conceivably, under some conditions of uncertainty in which hitherto reliable expectations are repeatedly confounded, large scale discoordination could occur in the market process. Shackle's argument here depends on extending Hayek's subjectivism regarding valuation to the process of forming expectations about the economy. In Shackle's subjectivist and indeterminist view, forming expectations is a highly creative process, not significantly governable by any algorithm or mechanical rule. Follwing Keynes on this point,[15] Shackle sees business confidence as an almost irrational datum, a matter of animal spirits or creative imagination rather than of rational assessment. If Shackle is right, a large-scale economic collapse of the Keynesian sort could occur in the absence of any governmental intervention. It could happen in the ways Keynes described, even if Keynes was wrong about the causes of the boom—bust cycle of the twenties and thirties. This is a powerful objection to Hayek's position, and one which poses a severe problem for all who support unregulated market processes, since it tends to restore credibility to Keynes-type macroeconomic management policies in at least some imaginable circumstances. Four counter-observations are in order, however. First, nothing in Shackle's argument tells against the point, defensible both on theoretical grounds and as an historical interpretation, that in practice by far the most destabilizing factor in the market process is provided by governmental intervention. The sort of endogenous instability of which he speaks may remain a theoretical possibility, but it fails to explain the historical phenomena which are the classical subject matter of the theory of market disequilibrium. Secondly, and relatedly, it is unclear that the kind of disequilibrium of which Shackle speaks — disequilibrium generated by divergency in subjective expectations — could amount to anything resembling the classical business cycle, which is more plausibly accounted for in Austrian and Hayekian terms as a consequence of governmental intervention in the interest rate structure.

Thirdly, it is unclear that Shackle's argument shows the presence in the market process of any *tendency to disequilibrium*. What we have in the market process is admittedly a 'kaleidic' world, in which expectations, tastes, and beliefs constantly and unpredictably mutate. Yet, providing market adaptation is unhampered, what we can expect from the market process is an uninterrupted series of momentary equilibrium tendencies, each of them asymptotic — never quite reaching equilibrium — and each of them soon overtaken by its successor. In this kaleidic world there may well be no apodictic certainty that we shall never face large-scale, endogenous discoordination, but we are nevertheless on safe ground in preferring that the self-regulating tendencies of the process be accorded unhampered freedom and that governmental intervention be recognized as the major disruptive factor in the market process. We are on strong ground, then, in discerning in the tendency to equilibrium in the market process the formation of spontaneous order in the economic realm.

Fourth and last, we are on safest ground in trusting to the self-regulating tendencies of the catallaxy, when money itself forms an integral part of the market process in the fashion envisaged by Hayek's proposal for the denationalization of money. Hayek's proposal addresses one of the most common objections to his policy prescription for letting recession run its course, namely that a sudden and drastic restriction of governmental money supply might initiate a secondary deflation[16] and thus deepen the recession. Even if it had some force in the thirties, this objection is countered by Hayek's new proposal. For, in a circumstance where governmental restriction of its own money supply went too far, private issuers would have an incentive to step in and fill the unmet need for money. Hayek is surely right in arguing that a 'big bang' monetary contraction, in shattering inflationary expectations decisively, is likely to be the quickest way to restore confidence to a depressed economy. The relative failure of the phased anti-inflation strategies of the governments of Thatcher and Reagan in the United Kingdom and the United States, which have achieved a moderate reduction in inflation at severe cost in employment, only reinforces the strength of Hayek's case. If there remain real dangers in Hayek's prescription for a drastic contraction of government money, these are accommodated by his complementary proposal of freeing private issuance of money. Hayek in no way claims to be able to predict the forms in which private money creation will develop — and his proposal is, for this and many other reasons, and contrary to his critics,[17] entirely in the spirit of his critique of constructivist rationalism. The evidences of spontaneous order in every other field of human activity support his conviction that even in this area, where it is largely untried, its result will surpass anything that conscious contrivance of social life can achieve.

Some contrasts and comparisons

J. S. MILL

Throughout his intellectual life Hayek has always displayed a pronounced interest in John Stuart Mill's work in epistemology, social philosophy and economic theory, and a fascination with his personality. He has had a substantial, if in some ways indirect impact on Mill scholarship through his book on Mill's relationship with Harriet Taylor and, before that, his rediscovery of and republication of Mill's positivistic tract, *The Spirit of the Age*.[1] Notwithstanding his life-long preoccupation with Mill's work, Hayek has never endorsed the central tenets of Mill's liberalism. Indeed, he sees Mill as in many ways a watershed figure whose ambiguities and innovations mark the historical moment in which the development of classical liberalism was halted in England. In Mill, according to Hayek, a number of elements alien to the genuine liberal tradition as it was developed by the writers of the Scottish Enlightenment came to occupy a central place and thereby to deflect and distort the main current of liberal thought. Among these, Mill's disastrous disseveration of laws of production from laws of distribution and his invention of the contemporary conception of social justice, his concessions to nationalism and socialism and his absorption of a Romantic conception of individuality are identified by Hayek as decisive in Mill's breach with classical liberalism. These infuences, he believes, were received by Mill from

Continental sources, specifically from French Positivism and German Romanticism, and have persisted in English liberalism ever since. In Acton and the classical liberals of the Gladstonian circle, to be sure, the old tradition survived, but it was intellectually moribund and decreasingly influential in public affairs. For Hayek, then, John Stuart Mill is a decisive figure, whose ambiguities have greatly contributed to the degeneration and near extinction of classical liberalism.

How far is this Hayekian critique of Mill's liberalism — a critique nowhere developed in a systematic or extended fashion in Hayek's writings, but explicit in many of his detailed discussions of questions of philosophy and policy — one that we are bound to accept? Before we try to pronounce on this, it may be worth underlining some clear areas of parallelism and of agreement as between Hayek and Mill. There is, first of all, some real affinity between Hayek's use of an indirect utalitarian pattern of moral argument and Mill's elaboration of a version of indirect utilitarianism in *A System of Logic* and his applications of it in *Utilitarianism* and *On Liberty*. In Mill, indirect utilitarianism means above all that the test of utility — the promotion of greatest happiness — is to be applied, not to specific practical questions, but to whole systems of rules or codes of conduct. The Principle of Utility is a standard of evaluation for social systems or networks of practices and will be self-defeating if attempts are made to turn it into a maxim for practical life. In practical life, we are generally best advised to rely upon maxims much more specific than the Principle of Utility. Further, as Mill suggests in many of his writings — his review of Tocqueville's *Democracy in America*, for example[2] — there is a strong presumption that the inherited moral code embodies wisdom not otherwise available to any one generation of men. There is in all this a powerful affinity between Mill's Coleridgean variant of indirect utilitarianism and Hayek's synthesis of Humean indirect utilitarian argumentation with a Kantian test of universalizability.

Even in moral philosophy, however, these affinities between Hayek and Mill should not be taken too far. In Mill, the Principle of Utility is the supreme maxim of practical reasoning and ultimately governs all domains of practical life. For Hayek, practical reasoning is governed by the Kantian test of universalizability which, once certain Humean constraints on viable morality have been identified, yields the liberal conception of justice. Hayek's Kantian approach seems to have several advantages over Mill's effort at a post-Benthamite indirect utilitarianism. In the first place, Mill never shows what claim the Principle of Utility itself has on reason: it is left dangling in mid-air despite all his efforts to adduce 'considerations … capable of determining the intellect to give or withhold its assent'.[3] In Hayek, as in R. M. Hare,[4] the claims of general welfare are themselves yielded by our assent to the more formal Kantian principle. Indeed Hayek is on strong ground when he denies that he is a utilitarian of any sort, since his use of indirect utilitarian arguments — arguments showing that acceptance of constraints on the promotion of general welfare are themselves necessary for the promotion of general welfare — may be seen as an application of his ethical Kantianism to the problem of designing a framework within which human purposes are best likely to be achieved. In this connexion it is crucial to note that, like Hume, Hayek does not regard the maintenance of a framework of rules of justice and the promotion of general welfare as competitive aims. Rather, he sees the existence of a stable framework of justice-preserving rules as an indispensable condition of the attainment of general welfare. As we have seen, he conceives the latter, however, not as some hierarchy of values, nor yet as an agreed body of ends, but rather in terms of maximizing the chances of any unknown person of achieving his ends. As a test of the utility of different systems of rules, this seems to have important advantages over any proposed by Mill.

Hayek's Kantian standpoint in fundamental ethics illuminates another difference with Mill — a difference as to the principles of liberty which they defend. Mill's Principle of Liberty is one instance of the harm principle, which states that harm to others is a necessary condition of justified invasion of individual liberty. Hayek sees, as Mill did not consistently see, that the notion of harm itself invokes a sphere of protected liberty, and cannot be detached from that moral content. Rules of justice generated by the Kantian apparatus give the notion of harm all the purchase it has in discussions of justified limitation of liberty. Even if Mill's conception of harm could be given a determinate content independent of prior rules of justice — as I myself argued it could in my book on Mill[5] — it would do far too much. There are so many cases in which we may rightfully harm one another that it is implausible to regard it as even a necessary condition of the restriction of liberty. Rather, Hayek prefers to defend the Kantian (and Spencerian) principle of equal freedom, which confers on us all liberty of action which may justly be used in harmful ways. Hayek does not deny that infliction of some harms may be a sufficient condition of the restriction of liberty, but where this is the case, it is the principle of equal liberty which is being qualified and not Mill's harm principle that is being invoked. In shifting discussion away from intractable arguments about rival criteria of harm to the delimitation of the protected sphere, Hayek initiated a move in liberal theory away from the Millian paradigm which others have followed (Rawls, Dworkin and Ackerman) and which promises much for social philosophy.

Hayek's conception of the task of a principle of liberty has more in common with Mill's than does their view of the content of such a principle. I mean here that both writers distinguish sharply between a principle laying down the limits of coercion and a maxim specifying the proper functions of the state. Neither Hayek nor Mill is a minimum-statist who restricts the state to preventing force and fraud: each of them accepts a distinction between the state's 'authoritative' and 'non-authoritative' (in Mill's terms), coercive and non-coercive activities, such that the state is prohibited from no non-coercive, service activity. Again, both Hayek and Mill accept a presumption in favour of laisser-faire, or state non-interference, but they are clear that this is defensible by expediency, provided the state exercises no coercion in addition to that involved in enforcing the principle of liberty (as it is differently understood by the two writers) and in raising revenue through the tax mechanism. No doubt (as Hayek is quick to insist) state spending may be indirectly jeopardize liberty even when it is non-coercive; but in this area, at least, there is no principled disagreement between the two liberal writers.

Hayek's approach to the character of a free society differs in several important respects from Mill's. In regard to its dominant principle — the principle of equal liberty — Hayek's conception is, as I have already noted, more favourable to liberty than is Mill's. Again, Hayek has explicitly dissociated himself from Mill's paternalistic and culturally chauvinistic assertion that liberty is to be granted to men only when a certain level of economic and cultural development — roughly, that of England in Mill's time — has been securely attained. This restriction is rightly abhorrent to Hayek for, aside from underrating the contribution of individual liberty to the raising of economic and cultural standards, it unduly limits the scope of the Kantian argument for liberty as a condition of human autonomy. In a different area, however, Hayek's conception may appear more restrictive of liberty than Mill's. I refer to Hayek's denial that the sanctions of convention, to which Mill refers as a form of moral coercion, constitute an abridgement of individual autonomy. Hayek has two crucial objections to this view of Mill's. First, strong conventions about acceptable behaviour form part of the stable social environment which we all need for the exercise of our liberty. We cannot act effectively if we are unable to form sound expectations about the reactions of others, and this can occur only if social relations are in major part governed by conventions which constrain the expression of individuality. Such conventions will in turn be effective in governing conduct only if they are allowed to provide, by way of social censure and disapprobation, negative feedback on the conduct of others. As Thomas Sowell has justly put this Hayekian point in criticism of Mill:

> ... the demands of unbounded individualism need to be weighed in the light of inherent social constraints which can only change their form but cannot be eliminated without eliminating civilization. Moreover, the claim for individual toleration cannot extend to cancelling other people's right to judge as they will what a given individual does. Much of the modern demand for individualism − including John Stuart Mill's *On Liberty* − is a plea for exemption from social feedback from those negatively judging individual behaviour.[6]

There are, no doubt, important questions as to how far society may go in enforcing by censure the dominant moral conventions, but these questions are not answered, or even addressed, by Mill's repudiation of all such enforcement as a form of moral coercion. The important point is that a society without such strong moral conventions would unavoidably be chaotic. Most likely, coercion would have to fill the gaps left by the erosion of moral convention, since some means of social coordination there must be. The real alternative to a society containing strong conventions enforced by public opinion is not a Millian bohemia, but a Hobbesian state of nature. This remains the case, even when one recognizes that Hayek's free society would contain several, and not a single dominant cultural tradition. Each of these traditions would exercise upon its practitioners a constraint of opinion which Mill would absurdly condemn as moral coercion. The free society does not need to be unified by a single moral tradition; but it cannot do without the coherence given by most social interaction being regulated by convention, albeit as given by diverse traditions. In this sense, convention is a condition of liberty and not (as Mill supposed) one of its enemies.

The second Hayekian objection to Mill's vision of the free society goes deeper than the first. Not only must the expression of individuality be constrained by moral convention; individuality is itself always formed and partly constituted by moral convention. We must conceive of human individuality as a cultural achievement and not as a natural endowment. Though human individuals are always more than shadows cast by social conventions, Hayek sees (as Mill did not consistently see) that the deliberative and affective capacities that enter into the formation of personality, and that are necessary conditions of the exercise of individual judgement, presuppose a continuing background of social convention. The relations between human personality and social convention are thus not purely external relations in Hayek's conception, but partly mutually constitutive. One may go even further, and observe that an array of flourishing traditions, each with its own sanctions against deviancy, enhances the options of the choosing individual. A society in which tradition has become attenuated, or in which a diversity of traditions has been eroded, is likely to be one in which the differences between men have become trivial or idiosyncratic rather than rich and weighty.

We see in this latter point a crucial difference between Mill and Hayek in their view of the rôle of experiments in living. For Mill, these are affairs of the individual in which he asserts his inborn individuality against the pressures of social convention. Hayek rejects this conception as embodying a Romantic cult of individuality. Experiments in living are undertaken, not by assertive individuals, but by distinct traditions or ways of life which compete for practitioners. Indeed, Hayek perceives[7] that a post-traditional society of the sort Mill envisaged would (if it could ever be achieved, and lasted for more than a generation or so) seriously impoverish the options of its individual members. A society will do most for the autonomy of its members if it is rich in distinctive traditions between which migration is possible (but not necessarily easy, or common). The benefits of liberty in terms of its promotion of the growth of knowledge are in fact most likely to be achieved when society does encompass such a peaceful competition of rival traditions.

The other area of deep difference between Hayek and Mill is in their views of distribution and justice. For Hayek, as we have seen, a productive system incorporates a set of rules for distribution, and the two cannot be severed. In particular, it is folly to suppose that men will perform the same services, if the incomes accruing to them are distorted by attempts to 'correct' market distribution. Yet it is precisely this error that Mill makes in his disastrous dichotomy between production and distribution. As he famously puts it:

> The laws and conditions of the production of wealth partake of the character of physical truths. There is nothing optional, or arbitrary in them ... this is not so with the distribution of wealth. That is a matter of human institutions solely. The things once there, mankind, individually or collectively, can do with them as they like.[8]

Here we have, in the crudest imaginable form, a statement of the 'manna from heaven' presumption of contemporary distributivist theories. It may be said that what distinguishes Mill from Hayek — and, for that matter, form Marx — is Mill's lack of any clear view of production and distribution as inseparable parts of a single economic system. We may have a choice between economic systems (though it is the burden of the Mises—Hayek—Polanyi argument about resource-allocation under socialism that our freedom is far more restricted than we suppose); we do not have the freedom to mix the productive arrangements of one system with the distributive arrangements of another. This is a truth understood by all the classical economists, including Marx, which Mill's influence has helped to obscure.

I shall say less about Mill's attitudes to nationalism and socialism. Hayek is on strongest ground when he sees the classical liberal opposition to nationalism as being carried on by Acton, whose criticisms of Mill on the principle of national self-determination are still well worth reading. In regard to socialism, Mill was characteristically ambiguous, at most favouring a sort of market syndicalism, in which most enterprises would be turned into self-governing workers' cooperatives. Such a system is in all probability entirely unworkable, involving as it does the break-up of large corporations and consequent sacrifices of economies of scale and institutionalizing a wholly undesirable fusion of job-security with share-holding. But Mill's utopian fantasies of self-management are still not the Fabian centralist socialism which came to prevail in British progressive circles, and they retain a realism and sobriety about market determination of wages and the dubious advantages to the working class of trades unions which Hayek is bound to endorse. (I do not say that Hayek approves of Mill's many changes of stance on wages and unions, but only that Mill's vision of a market syndicalism is in these respects superior to anything produced in the Fabian tradition, and to that extent meets with Hayek's approval). This is only to say that, whatever confusions Mill introduced into the liberal tradition, he remained an economic liberal in that he never supposed that the central allocative functions of the market could be abolished in the context of the generation of incomes.

HERBERT SPENCER

One of the great gaps in Hayek scholarship is any detailed comparison of his views with those of his classical liberal predecessor, Herbert Spencer. This is surprising, since Hayek's philosophy has many affinities with Spencer's, including the aspiration of embedding the defence of liberty in a broad evolutionary framework, without at the same time committing the fallacies in evolutionary social theory which vitiate Spencer's synthetic philosophy. Neglect of these important affinities is perhaps best accounted for by neglect of Spencer himself — a neglect encouraged, in Spencer's case as in Mill's, by G. E. Moore's unfortunate influence on the history of ideas. The clearest of these many affinities is in moral theory, where Spencer commits none of the howlers intellectual historians (following Moore and other secondary sources) habitually attributive to him.

Spencer's moral theory, like J. S. Mill's and like Hayek's own, is a species of indirect utilitarianism. By indirect utilitarianism, it will be recalled, I intend that theory of morality and practical reasoning which evaluates all states of affairs by reference to the utility they contain but which condemns any strategy of direct utility-maximization as self-defeating.

What evidence is there that Spencer adhered to the moral theory I have imputed to him? By far the most direct avowal of his utilitarian commitment occurs in the second volume of Spencer's *Autobiography*. There Spencer recalls discovering to his surprise that he had been classed as anti-utilitarian by J. S. Mill in his *Utilitarianism*. Spencer wrote at length on the subject in a letter to Mill which (since it is not readily accessible) is worth quoting fully:

I have never regarded myself as Anti-utilitarian. My dissent from the doctrine of Utility as commonly understood concerns not the object to be reached by men, but the method of reaching it. While I admit that happiness is the ultimate end to be contemplated, I do not think it should be the proximate end. The Expediency-Philosophy having concluded that happiness is a thing to be achieved, assumes that morality has no other business than empirically to generalise the results of conduct, and to supply for the guidance of conduct nothing more than its empirical generalisations.

But the view for which I contend is, that Morality so-called — the science of right conduct — has for its object to determine *how* and *why* certain modes of conduct are detrimental, and certain others beneficial. The good and bad results cannot be accidental, but must be necessary consequences of the constitution of things: and I conceive it to be the business of moral science to deduce, from the laws of life and the conditions of existence, what kinds of action necessarily tend to produce happiness, and what kinds to produce unhappiness. Having done this, its deductions are to be recognised as laws of conduct; and are to be conformed to irrespective of a direct estimation of happiness and misery.

... corresponding to the fundamental propositions of a developed Moral Science, there have been, and still are, developing in the race, certain fundamental moral intuitions; and ... though these moral intuitions are the results of accumulated experiences of utility, gradually organised and inherited, they have come to be quite independent of conscious experience ... just as space-intuition responds to the exact demonstrations of Geometry, and has its rough conclusions interpreted and unified by them, so will moral intuitions respond to the demonstrations of Moral Science, and will have their rough conclusions interpreted and unified by them.[9]

Spencer concludes this part of his autobiography by opposing 'the contented resting in empirical utilitarianism' and observing 'that the connexions between conduct and consequences are in every case causal, and that ethical theory remains but rudimentary until the causal relations are generalised, was a truth not recognized by them (i.e. the early, "empirical" utilitarians)'.

It should be noted that the moral theory which Spencer expounds here under the name 'rational utilitarianism', and which he contrasts so sharply with the merely 'empirical' ethics of the early utilitarians, is in fact little different from the doctrine espoused by J. S. Mill, against whose misinterpretation of his doctrine Spencer protested. For it was Mill's view that the principles of morality and of justice, such as his own famous principle of liberty, were secondary maxims derivable from the principle of utility itself and based on the utility-promoting and utility-diminishing tendencies of the classes of acts they variously prescribed and prohibited. That these principles are not 'empirical' in the weak, objectionable sense which Spencer criticizes is shown clearly enough in a passage from Mill's 'Dr. Whewell on Moral Philosophy':

If the effect of a 'solitary act upon the whole scheme of human action and habit' is small, the addition which the accompanying pleasure makes to the general mass of human happiness is small likewise. So small, in the great majority of cases, are both, that we have no scales to weigh them against each other, taken singly. We must look at them multiplied, and in large masses. The portion of the tendencies of an action which belong to it individually, but as a violation of a general rule, are as certain and as incalculable as any other consequences; only they must be examined not in the individual case, but in classes of cases.[10]

Again, in one of his later letters, Mill observes that 'the right way of testing actions by their consequences, is to test them by the natural consequences of the particular action, and not by those which would follow if everyone did the same. But, for the most part, the consideration of what would happen if everyone did the same, is the only means we have of discovering the tendency of the act in the particular case.'[11]

As D. G. Brown has put it in an article in which these statements of Mill's are cited, they show Mill arguing that 'the tendency of a particular act literally is a causal tendency, statable in an empirical law.'[12] Further, we find Mill working with a conception of the place of rules in moral and political life which is neither the 'practice' conception adumbrated by Rawls,[13] nor yet the rule-of-thumb view defended by Smart.[14] For Mill, as for Spencer, moral rules such as those defining the juridical framework of a liberal order are injunctions to act or to abstain which supersede in the guidance of conduct any appeal to ultility but the content of which is derivable wholly in utilitarian terms. It seems that neither Mill nor Spencer noticed the striking family resemblance between their respective theories.

It was left to the penetrating intelligence of Henry Sidgwick, whose *Lectures on Mr. Spencer's Ethics*[15] remains by far the most acute criticism of Spencer, to note the affinity between Spencer's own doctrine and those of the utilitarians, whom Spencer largely misunderstood. Sidgwick observes of Bentham that he argues 'in a manner not unlike Mr. Spencer's, against the absurd supposition that each could make the happiness of others his *primary aim*'.[16] Spencer's advocacy of egoism, like Bentham's, is, as Sidgwick sees, strategic and not ethical. Sidgwick goes on further to remark that,[17] whereas the influence of Comte upon J. S. Mill renders Spencer's misunderstandings of J. S. Mill somewhat more intelligible than the mistakes he commits in his exposition of Benthamism, yet Spencer could not have represented Mill in the way he does had he read Mill's criticism of Comte's altruistic universalism in his *Auguste Comte and Positivism*.[18]

Despite their mutual misunderstandings, then, it is true that for Spencer and for Mill the tendencies of actions were captured in statable empirical laws. Both Spencer and Mill adhered to what Spencer called 'rational utilitarianism'.

It is extraordinary that Hayek's own moral theory — what I have called a Kantian version of indirect utilitarianism — should resemble so strikingly that endorsed by Spencer. For the nub of both theories is that endemic human ignorance justifies the self-denying ordinances of liberal justice *as efficacious means of promoting utility*.

Spencer's moral theory, like Hayek's, was connected by him with his broader philosophy. What, specifically, connects Spencer's moral theory with his larger synthetic philosophy? In value-theory, Spencer's hedonism committed him to the view that life is worthless in the absence of pleasure or happiness. His evolutionist beliefs, however, encouraged him to suppose that a balance of pleasure over pain, happiness over misery would ultimately come to prevail in human life. A number of difficulties beset this view. First, there are overwhelming obstacles in the way of giving anything like quantitative exactitude to comparative judgements about pleasure and pain. These are ancient and well-worn problems, but it remains true that the lack of any proposal in Spencer's writings for a workable *measure* of utility undermines his confident affirmation of the progressively increasing balance of pleasure over pain in human life. It may well be doubted, of course, that Spencer's belief that the course of social evolution promoted happiness was based on empirical observation. More likely, it had its source in Spencer's unyielding metaphysical and moral optimism, his faith in the evanescence of imperfection, a doctrine to which empirical beliefs are not obviously salient, but which Spencer sought scientific support for in his evolutionary speculations. Here Sidgwick's comment on Spencer seems irresistibly persuasive:

> In criticising this [Spencer's] 'evolutionary optimism', as we may call it, I ought to explain that I am not opposing optimism as a philosophical doctrine. I am not myself an optimist; but I have a great respect for the belief that, in spite of appearances to the contrary, the world now in process of evolution is ultimately destined to reveal itself as perfectly free from evil and the best possible world. What I would urge is that, in the present stage of our knowledge, this belief should be kept as a theological doctrine, or, if you like, a philosophical postulate, and that it should not be allowed to mix itself with the process of scientific inference to the future from the past.[19]

Spencer's mistaken belief that evolutionary theory might give support to moral optimism by demonstrating the necessity of moral progress has its source in a central defect of his evolutionary theory itself, namely, that it specified no plausible *mechanism* for the evolution of societies. Indeed, unless we accept Spencer's Lamarckian belief in the inheritability of acquired characteristics, we have no reason within Spencer's system for supposing that the evolution of species and the evolution of societies occurs on a single scale. While we have in Darwinian theory an intelligible mechanism of biological evolution in the natural selection of genetic accidents, Spencer identifies no analogous mechanism in society whereby from the competition of customs and practices those prevail which are on some independent (and, typically, unspecified) criterion 'the fittest'. Certainly, Spencer's references to the pressure of population growth on resources and on existing forms of social life are wholly inadequate in this context. Different societies react in different ways to the pressure imposed on them by growth of population — some by technological and social innovation, others (historically the vast majority) by curbing the growth in their numbers. There is, in any case, no automatic and invariant connection between either a society's productivity or its populousness and its chance of survival in a competition with other societies. While these are complex and disputed matters, everything suggests that Malthus and Darwin are better guides in these areas than Lamarck and Spencer.

Hayek's system is free from most, if not all of the difficulties that plague Spencer's. In the first place, Hayek is at pains to identify both the similarities and the differences between biological and cultural evolution. Whereas they have in common that, in both, selection proceeds by way of reproductive advantage, they differ in that cultural evolution works by the selection of groups via their inherited practices whereas biological evolution is of individuals via their genes or lineages. Though Hayek does not espouse Lamarckism in its biological applications, his conception of cultural evolution simulates Lamarckian selection in that it deals entirely with inheritable traits — that is, with customs, practices and traditions — with, in short, those rules of action and perception that are *not* imprinted in the gene. Like Spencer, Hayek sees population pressure as the most importent spur to cultural evolution, but he ascribes no necessity to the relations between the two and he certainly does not suppose that cultural evolution tends to produce a balance of pleasure over pain. Hayek proposes as a *measure* of utility a calculus of lives — that is, a social system is presumed to generate greater utility if it can support a greater population — but his *criterion* of utility, as we have seen, is probabilistic and preference-based and expressed in terms of the unknown man's chances of attaining his aims. In other words, Hayek is not saddled with Spencer's hedonistic value-theory, and he does not make Spencer's implausible claims about the connections between cultural evolution and the maximization of happiness. Indeed, Hayek is careful to identify cultural evolution (meaning the spontaneous formation and selection of social practices) as a *necessary* condition of the kind of progress towards the maximization of life-chances which he identifies with the utilitarian goal. Whereas there may remain in his conception of the competition of traditions many areas of obscurity, Hayek's identification of the basic mechanism at work in both biological and cultural evolution as proceeding

Darwinianly (by reproductive advantage) solves many puzzles which debilitate Spencer's account.

In one area, however, Hayek and Spencer are strikingly at one – that is, along with C. S. Pierce, in their elaboration of an evolutionary epistemology in which the Kantian categories are themselves viewed as products of natural selection. This mention of a natural-selection epistemology at once brings us back to a comparison with the most prominent and profound defender of an evolutionary theory of knowledge, and it is to him that I now turn.

KARL POPPER

Hayek is united in deep and long-standing bonds of friendship with Popper and is at pains to emphasize the affinities in their thought. A brief survey, however, soon shows there to be differences of emphasis of some importance. Let us look at the central ideas of Popper's philosophy and see how they square with Hayek's system of ideas.

The central core of Popper's epistemology is the proposal[20] that falsifiability be treated as a criterion of demarcation between empirical and non-empirical statements, propositions and theories; Popper suggests that we use the falsifiability of its theories to distinguish science from myth and metaphysics, for example, and he points out that the adoption of the proposal will enable us to characterize as pseudo-scientific such enterprises as psychoanalysis, astrology and Marxism. Contrary to innumerable accounts of his philosophy,[21] Popper's demarcation criterion was never intended as a criterion of the meaningfulness of sentences. As well as supplying a demarcation criterion between science on the one hand and metaphysics, myth and pseudo-science on the other, Popper's falsificationism enabled him to propose a solution to Hume's problem of induction. For, accepting the validity of Hume's arguments against the propriety of reasoning from instances of which we have had experience, to the truth of the corresponding laws of nature, and trading on the (purely logical) assymmetry between verification and refutation, Popper's falsificationism allowed him to characterize science as a strictly deductive enterprise in which conjectures are boldly propagated and then severely tested by attempted refutations. When science is so understood, the growth of scientific knowledge is seen to occur, not through the use of any form of 'inductive inference' by means of which theories might be verified, confirmed or probabilified, but by an error-elimination procedure in which hypotheses of ever-increasing empiirical content (or versimilitude) are corroborated by withstanding ever more stringent tests. Unlike Hume, Popper draws no irrationalist conclusions from the collapse of induction: rather, appealing to a principle of transference from validity in logic to efficacy in psychology, he rehabilitates rationality in thought and action with the conjecture that learning occurs in human beings and all other problem-solving organisms, not through any (mythical and logically invalid) piling up of inductive confirmations in support of general hypotheses, but by an error-elimination process closely analogous to evolution by natural selection.

With his account of scientific progress as a process in which theories of increasing versimilitude are developed in response to ever deeper problems, Popper links the growth of knowledge with the evolutionary passage from lower to higher forms of life, preserving a qualitative distinction between problem-solving in the lower organisms and in science by emphasizing the self-critical character of error-elimination procedures in the latter. Popper's evolutionism is further linked with his pluralist theory of a three-tiered world, comprising not only material things and states of mind (which he calls 'World 1' and 'World 2' respectively), but also a domain of intelligibles, virtual objects or objective structures (which he calls 'World 3'). It is in this third world, man-made but autonomous in that objective problems and theories await discovery within it, that man's cultural evolution mainly occurs, and it is the central thesis of Popper's

philosophy that growth in human knowledge and understanding presupposes the adoption of a method of criticism.
A critical approach to empirical science is shown in the
adoption of the method of conjectures and refutations, but
Popper has himself applied the critical method to the study
of irrefutable theories of philosophy. Popper's 'critical
approach' embodies a theory of rationality as consisting in
openess to criticism. It is in its critical theory of rationality,
together with its combination of fallibilism or dynamic
scepticism in epistemology and realism or objectivism in
ontology — a combination which he characterizes as involving
rejection of the commonsense theory of knowledge with
retention of the commonsense theory of the world — that the
chief interest of Popper's general philosophy lies.

Many of Popper's themes of openess to criticism, falsificationism and negative dialectic are strikingly anticipated in
J. S. Mill's *On Liberty*. These themes effectively distance
Popper's thought from Hayek's in which the dangers of
critical rationalism are emphasized more strongly than its
utility. Hayek's social philosophy may here fruitfully be con-
trasted with Popper's. Popper's 'critical dualism of facts and
decisions' embodies that very nature—convention dichotomy
which Hayek deplores. Further, it leads him to treat social
institutions as if they were no more than instruments for the
attainment of human purposes. This instrumentalist or
externalist approach to social institutions in turn supports
Popper's advocacy of piecemeal social engineering — a sort of
political technology in which 'social problems' are supposed
to become amenable to scientific discussion and rational
settlement. We have here an attempted assimilation of
democratic policy-making to Popper's ideal—typical scientific
community. Popper's talk of improving civilization, of solving
common problems by implementing a political technology,
endorses a view of society no less monistic than that of the
utopian social engineers he is concerned to criticize. At the
same time, in transposing to areas of social conflict the
shared standards of objectivity and impartiality which

characterize scientific communities, Popper's interventionist social engineering brings about a dualism in society between those, the rational planners, who possess political power, and the rest, who do not. Popper's social thought is permeated by a somewhat monistic interventionism, which receives support from his doctrine of the critical dualism of facts and standards.

Hayek's work intimates a very different approach. His criticisms of scientism in the social studies and his espousal of a qualified methodological dualism as between natural and social science express his conviction that there is little in common between the growth of knowledge in the physical sciences and the acquisition and use of knowledge of the social world. His defence of market competition as a discovery procedure, and of purpose-independent legal rules as the indispensable framework within which individuals may pursue their own purposes, reflects his belief that our explicit knowledge of society is unavoidably so abstract as to preclude anything like conscious planning even of specific social institutions ('piecemeal social engineering'). Further, a major part of Hayek's argument for a system of liberty is in his claim that it is precisely the presence of conflicting moral and intellectual traditions in our society that warrants the institution of a liberal order. For such an order provides a neutral framework within which peaceful competition may occur between rival forms of social life, so that those best adapted to changing circumstances may come to prevail. Hayek differs from Popper, then, in his highly conservative view of the limitations of reason and the dangers of theoretical inquiry into the social order and in his correspondingly modest account of the rôle of the state in social life.

These specific considerations aside, the most general difference between Hayek and Popper appears to lie in their attitudes to reason. It would be a mistake to exaggerate this difference: both, after all, are critical rationalists, sharing a common attitude to the constructivism of Bacon and Descartes in the theory of knowledge. Again, each endorses an

evolutionary perspective on epistemological questions. At
the same time, Hayek's sense of the limitations of reason is
greater, and his conviction of the dangers of the uncritical
use of reason correspondingly sharper than anything that
is evident in Popper (though there may be important shifts
of emphasis in Popper between the radical criticalism of
The Open Society and the more self-critical rationalism
of *Conjectures and Refutations*). The difference here may
not be one merely of optimism or pessimism in the assessment of the social prospects of the use of reason. It may go
deeper, in that Hayek has on occasion embraced a view of the
limits of reason, akin to that found in Polanyi, Wittgenstein
and Oakeshott, according to which our reasonings always
come to a stop at our most basic practices. This view — which
in a Popperian view might seem a residue of *justificationism*
in Hayek — poses a problem for Hayek, when he comes to see
large elements of contemporary practice — especially moral
practice — as standing in need of radical revision. The justificationist view that all criticisms must presuppose uncriticizable
postulates or assumptions seems to be abandoned by Hayek
in practice when he condemns large areas of current moral
sentiment and practice as inimical to liberty, social stability
and indeed to the continuance of our civilization. The
radicalism of Hayek's criticism of modern civilization seems
to belie his occasional endorsement of the justificationist
doctrine that all criticism must invoke absolute presupposi-
tions which are themselves beyond criticism and to take him
close to the theory of pan-critical rationalism developed by
some of Popper's disciples.[22] On the other hand, Hayek's
insistence that our intellectual life is always governed by
some inarticulable rules states a limit to criticism which it is
hard to see any Popperian accepting. Hayek's position in the
theory of rationality seems distinct from Popper's in its
explicit recognition of these insuperable limits to criticism.
It seems to offer, subtly but importantly, from the account
of rationality given by Oakeshott, Polanyi and (above all) by
Wittgenstein, in that the basic practices, forms of life or

meta-conscious rules at which criticism comes to a stop are none of them given unalterably by nature or society. All of them are subject to natural selection in cultural evolution and (in this sense) to the continuous criticism of practice. It is in his thesis that the processes of social life itself contain filter devices (in Robert Nozick's useful terminology)[23] for the elimination of inadequate beliefs and values that Hayek's distinctive insight is to be found. The conception of rationality which this insight yields — in which reason is embodied in the evolving practices of society — is one which has echoes in both Popper and Wittgenstein, but is developed in a fashion which neither could easily accept.[24] In this regard Hayek has staked out a position in the theory of rationality which deserves our most careful scrutiny.

—6—

Assessment and criticism

THE UNITY OF HAYEK'S SYSTEM OF IDEAS

If this study has a single unifying theme, it is that Hayek's work is to be viewed and understood as a whole. Though his work has developed over six decades and has crossed many disciplinary boundaries, it has throughout exemplified a distinctive conception of the powers of the mind and of the character of human knowledge. As I have tried to show, this conception animates and explains many of the positions Hayek has adopted even in the areas of technical controversy within economic theory. His criticisms of macroeconomics and of policies based upon macroeconomic theories express his belief that the real economy consists of microeconomic or qualitative realtionships between individual market participants. These relationships are not captured by models whose central elements are aggregates and averages of economic activity which can never exert a causal influence on real market actors. Public policies which treat these statistical fictions as if they had a reference in the real world not only commit a fallacy of conceptual realism, they also inevitably have a self-defeating affect, for, in so far as the policies themselves become part of the environment of expectations within which market participants act, their intended affect will be discounted. In respect of Keynesian policies of deficit financing, we may say that they achieve their intended results only in so far as they are not expected — only in so far as market participants have pre-Keynesian expectations and habits.[1] Friedmanite indexation policies, on the other hand, whatever rôle they may have in a disinflationary policy, may actually worsen the discoordination of relative prices and incomes, and may breed expectations which are in the long run unsustainable. All these macroeconomic policies embody the deep philosophical and methodological errors of ascribing causal or ontological status to heuristic fictions and, conversely, of ignoring the subjective character of the central objects of economic life (costs, opportunities, expectations and so on). Hayek's central theory — that most social knowledge is unavoidably practical knowledge resistant to theoretical statement, while social theories are always and only conjectural models of the general conditions under which abstract patterns of activity will form — by itself disqualifies many dominant recent positions in economic theory and in public policy.

That Hayek's thought hangs together in this way, constituting a system in which detailed positions implement fundamental philosophical insights, cannot now responsibly be denied. At the same time, it would be mistaken to suppose that the relations between the several elements of Hayek's system are always ones of strict mutual entailment. Within his theory of knowledge, for example, his sceptical Kantianism and his assertion of the primacy of tacit knowledge do not entail each other. An Aristotelean who supposes that we may have knowledge of the natural kinds of things of which the world is composed, and who conceives of explanations as always referring to the nature of the thing whose behaviour is to be explained, may consistently allow that much, if not most of our knowledge is embodied or tacit knowledge.[2] Indeed, it may not be impossible to give Hayek's version of evolutionary epistemology an Aristotelean statement in which our theories and our sense organs are bearers of fallible conjectures about the real natures of things. In this connection, as in others, Hayek's thought contains important insights which may be put to use by many who do not accept his sceptical Kantianism.

In social philosophy, Hayek's insights might be accepted, at least in part, by some who are not themselves liberals. His view of law as among the natural conventions of evolving human society might be illuminating to many conservatives and traditionalists who have only a highly qualified commitment to individual liberty. Hayek's evolutionist account of law and morality might well be invoked by traditionalist opponents of current policies of rapid modernization in developing nations. His view of law as an integral part of social life, immanent in human interaction rather than imposed upon them from without, would of itself suggest the counter-productivity of policies which seek to redesign traditional social structures and their sustaining legal traditions. The chaos and anomie of many African states, in which tribal law and convention have been laid waste by ambitious development programs, and the debacle of over-rapid modernization efforts in Iran, are phenomena not only compatible with, but even predictable with the aid of Hayek's general account of cultural evolution in its application to the development of law. If Hayek's central ideas are in this way acceptable even to some critics of liberalism, however, the question arises whether his system hangs together even in the thematic way I have suggested. Might not the theory of spontaneous social order be in competition with the commitment to individual liberty? It is to this objection to the unitary character of Hayek's system, an objection put as much by rationalist libertarians as by traditionalist conservatives, that I now turn.

THE STATUS AND CONTENT OF THE IDEA
OF SPONTANEOUS ORDER IN SOCIETY

As I analysed it in the second chapter of this study, Hayek's complex conception of spontaneous order has three elements, which I named: the invisible-hand thesis; the thesis of the

primacy of tacit or practical knowledge; and the thesis of the
natural selection of traditions. It is to the last and first of
these three elements that Hayek refers when he speaks
of 'the twin ideas of evolution and of the spontaneous
formation of an order',[3] but I think the second element
captures the indispensable epistemological component of the
conception. Once stated, the conception suggests a fundamental question. Where are the implications of spontaneous
order for social philosophy? Most particularly, how does
the idea of spontaneous order support the argument for
individual liberty? Or, to put the same question in different
words, does the idea of spontaneous order itself have a
liberal content?

An initial uncertainty which must be dispelled before we
can answer these questions, is the uncertainty whether the
notion of spontaneous order has any normative content at
all. As Hayek himself explicates it, and as I have analyzed it,
it has no such content, and figures rather as a value — free
explanatory schema for natural and social phenomena.
Hayek's own formal statement of the concept of order is
entirely value-neutral: 'By order', he tells us, 'we shall throughout describe a state of affairs in which a multiplicity of
elements of various kinds are so related to each other that
we may learn from our acquaintance with some spatial or
temporal part of the whole, to form correct expectations
concerning the rest, or at least expectations which have a
good chance of proving correct.'[4] He goes on to state: 'The
study of spontaneous orders has long been the peculiar task
of economic theory, although, of course, biology has, from
its beginning, been concerned with that special kind of
spontaneous order which we call an organism. Only recently
has there arisen within the physical sciences under the name
of cybernetics, a special discipline which is also concerned
with what are called self-organizing or self-generating systems
... It would be no exaggeration to say that social theory
begins with — and has an object only because of — the
discovery that there exist orderly structures which are

the product of the actions of many men, but are not the result of human design.'[5] These statements indicate that, for Hayek the idea of spontaneous order has its central use as an explanatory framework for the complex phenomena we find in nature and human society. If this is so, then it has, in itself, no normative content, and in particular, no liberal content. Thus we may use the invisible-hand component of the idea of spontaneous order to explain developments — such as the rise of modern statism — which a classical liberal viewpoint condemns. Throughout the world, and certainly in Britain, the emergence of the modern welfare and administrative state occurred via a long series of piecemeal and unplanned responses to specific problems. No doubt there are those, such as the Webbs, who welcomed this development, but the dynamic impulse of the modern trend to statism was only reinforced, and not initiated, by such thinkers. We best understand the growth of the interventionist state if we apply to it the analysis of the Virginia School of public choice theorists. As it has been expounded by Buchanan and Tulloch,[6] public choice theory explains and even predicts the growth of interventionism whenever the constitutional framework of the free society becomes subject to alteration by a democratic competition for votes. In this circumstance, every agent will be constrained to seek governmental privileges, if only as an act of self-defence against all other agents. The failures of interventionist policies to obtain their goals will only rarely lead to their abandonment, since they will always have the support of vociferous interest groups who are their beneficaries. Once the constitutional framework of society becomes an object of political struggle, as it is bound to do in an age of unlimited democracy, there is a momentum in the trend to statism which transcends the interests, and even the wishes of the political actors involved. When he fears that every other actor will use the power of government against him, each man will be impelled to seek to use governmental power in his own interests. We will have then, *a legal war of all against all*, a recreation in the context of civil society of Hobbes's state of nature. This is indeed the mechanism of Hayek's road to serfdom, a mechanism he identifies himself when in his famous book he shows why the worst are bound to come out on the top in a totalitarian state.[7]

If we treat it as a value free explanatory scheme, then the idea of spontaneous order can help to explain the emergence and operation of twentieth-century statism, in both its interventionist and its totalitarian forms. It does so by invoking the idea of a Prisoner's Dilemma in which agents acting severally produce a social situation which thwarts their goals and harms their interests. In an interventionist democracy, as David Friedman has observed,[8] every man is in a public-good trap in virtue of which he is constrained to act against his own interests. This is the dark or maleficent side of spontaneous order in its invisible-hand aspect, that human action can bring about a bad state of affairs without anyone intending it, and even against most people's intentions. It is in this way, as a value-free explanatory device, that I believe Hayek's idea of spontaneous order is to be understood. This interpretation forswears the device of building into spontaneous order explanations a definite moral content — given by a theory of individual rights, or a libertarian side constraint against aggression, perhaps — which would disallow an explanation of statism as a spontaneous formation. Such an interpretation is difficult to sustain in the context of Hayek's work, since a theory of rights is not foundational in it and he does not restrict the operation of spontaneous order to non-coercive situations. Thus we can see that spontaneous-order explanations may illuminate contemporary departures from liberty, just as they help us understand the development of pre-liberal societies. Indeed it may be among the most powerful uses of spontaneous-order explanation, that it illuminates both the emergence of liberal society and its waning in the twentieth century.

If spontaneous order is to be understood in this value-free way, it will have no necessary connection with individual liberty, and may be found illuminating even by some avowed enemies of individual freedom. A traditionalist conservative, for example, might favour the anti-liberal practices thrown up by cultural evolution in some societies and resist their reform or revision. Some such position was adopted by the French reactionary thinker, Josef de Maistre, when he praised Russian political culture as a spontaneous growth, and compared it favourably with that of the culture of Western Europe whose cultures had been 'scribbled over' by enlightened philosophers.[9] How then does spontaneous order enter the argument for liberty, if liberty is not an integral part of spontaneous order itself? It has been argued by some rationalist libertarians, such as James Buchanan and Murray Rothbard,[10] that spontaneous-order theses have no application to the basic framework of liberty and may confuse the argument for liberty. The charge is a weighty one since, though he regards it as a spontaneous growth, Hayek certainly does not view the free society as a necessary or inevitable terminus of cultural evolution. He is insistent that there is no law of evolution,[11] and acknowledges that the trend to liberty may always be defeated (as when free societies are swept away by expansionist tyrannies). How then does the idea of spontaneous order strenghten the case for liberty?

It does so, negatively and in the first place, by showing that constructivist planning is bound to be always limited in success and often self-defeating, in social life. The paradigm case of this self-defeating effect of constructivist planning is the case of socialism, which has everywhere reduced living standards, including those of the poorest groups, from what they would have been had a market catallaxy been allowed to operate. Precisely the same self-defeating mechanism is at work in more prosaic instances, such as rent control, which has produced a situation of scarcity and costliness of rental accommodation worse than any it was intended to remedy. More positively, the idea of spontaneous order supports the argument for liberty by showing that social order does not depend upon any kind of hierarchical structure.

As Hayek put it:

Living as members of society and dependent for the satisfaction of most of our needs on various forms of co-operation with others, we depend for the effective pursuit of our aims clearly on the correspondence of the expectations concerning the actions of others on which our plans are based with what they will really do. This matching of the intentions and expectations that determine the actions of different individuals is the form in which order manifests itself in social life; and it will be the question of how such an order does come about that will be our immediate concern. The first answer to which our anthropomorphic habits of thought almost inevitably lead us is that it must be due to the design of some thinking mind. And because order has been generally interpreted as such a deliberate *arrangement* by somebody, the concept has become unpopular among most friends of liberty and has been favoured mainly by authoritarians. According to this interpretation order in society must rest on a relation of command and obedience, or a hierarchical structure of the whole of society in which the will of superiors, and ultimately of some single supreme authority, determines what each individual must do.

This authoritarian connotation of the concept of order derives, however, entirely from the belief that order can be created only by forces outside the system (or 'exogenously'). It does not apply to an equilibrium set up from within (or 'endogenously') such as that which the general theory of the market endeavours to explain. A spontaneous order of this kind has in many respects properties different from those of a made order.[12]

In this passage Hayek gives a more definite content to the thought contained in Proudhon's dictum, 'Liberty is the mother of order.' Orderly relationships among men do not, as a general rule, presuppose command structures, and coercion is not the commonest, and certainly not the most efficacious way of integrating human activities. An entire society is not akin to any of its component organizations, and is not to be modelled on the analogy of an army or a factory. If an analogy is to be found, a whole society is more like a forest than it is like any organization. We can expect the most exact and sensitive meshing of the activities and plans of people, if they are left free to act on their own purposes and with the aid of their own knowledge, and the social processes in which their plans are rendered compatible are actually obstructed by attempts at comprehensive planning based on a pretense at synoptic knowledge of society which no one can possess.

The idea of spontaneous order supports liberty in yet a third way. We have seen that the social circumstance of men in interventionist and totalitarian regimes simulates that of men in a Hobbesian state of nature inasmuch as each is constrained by fear of the power-seeking activities of others to engage in a predatory political competition for resources which undermines production and is ruinous for all. The insight of spontaneous-order theory is that, *once a stable juridical framework of liberty under the law is established*, the Hobbesian Prisoner's Dilemma is circumvented, and social competition ceases to be mutually harmful. Spontaneous order generalizes the insight contained in the theory of peaceful trading, that voluntary exchanges are not typically zero-sum exchanges (in which what one side gains the other loses) or negative-sum exchanges in which both parties lose (as is the case in Hobbes's state of nature). Rather, once the juridical framework guarantees Adam Smith's *system of natural liberty*, in which individual freedom is maximal and equal across society, men will have the greatest possible opportunity to make voluntary exchanges that are to mutual benefit. Under the system of natural liberty, there is a harmony of interests among men in which each man has the greatest chance of achieving his purposes. The general welfare is maximized in these circumstances, not by charging any authority with the task of its promotion, but by guaranteeing the framework within which each may pursue his own purposes. Whereas the idea of spontaneous order may not of itself have a liberal content, it has a liberal implication in that it suggests that order, harmonious interests and the general welfare will flow from a system of natural liberty of the sort Smith advocated. The idea of spontaneous order does have a liberal character, in other words, once it is specified that the formation of spontaneous order is subject to the requirement that they emerge from voluntary transactions undertaken within a stable framework of law.

HAYEK'S CONSTITUTION OF LIBERTY:
SOME CRITICISMS ASSESSED

The general idea of the system of natural liberty which Hayek adopts from Adam Smith is clear enough, it is the idea that there be equal and maximal freedom of action across the whole of society. It is not so clear, however, how this system of natural liberty is to be given juridical protection.

Hayek has, in recent years, advanced proposals of his own as to how this framework of natural liberty is to be sustained. His proposal is for a bicameral constitution in which a legislative assembly or upper chamber lays down the rules under which the lower house, or governmental assembly, may act. As he recognizes,[13] Hayek's proposal has affinities with that of J. S. Mill in his *Considerations on Representative Government*, which proposes the institution of a *nomothetae* or law-making body to control the activities of day-to-day legislation. Hayek's proposal for bicameralism is intended to make secure the framework within which the operatives of spontaneous order tends to general benefit, but does it achieve its end? Two sorts of criticism have been levelled against Hayek's proposals. The first of these, which I shall contend is the less important, is the objection that the division of powers proposed in the bicameral constitution is either unworkable or, if workable, unlikely to protect liberty as strongly as Hayek hopes it might. This first criticism has been made by one of Hayek's libertarian critics, Ronald Hamowy, who focuses on the jurisdictional problems that would be faced in Hayek's bicameral constitution and argues that no additional protection to liberty is afforded by such a constitution. His argument seems to be that, since there are no inviolable limitations on the authority of government in Hayek's constitution, there is no reason to suppose that it will protect liberty any better than existing constitutional arrangements do.

As Hamowy puts it:

> The constitution itself neither solves these jurisdictional problems nor, more importantly, does it contain any substantive limitations on the powers of the legislature, regardless of which of its two houses might have jurisdiction. The constitution, we are told,
>
>> ought to consist wholly of organizational rules, and need touch on substantive law in the sense of universal rules of just conduct only by stating the general attributes such laws must possess in order to entitle government to use coercion for their enforcement.
>
> Thus, despite his elaborate and complex schema of government, in the end Hayek returns to his original restrictions on the formal qualities of rules of conduct that he first laid down in his *Constitution of Liberty* as the only protection against arbitrary government.
>
> I would suggest that this approach has been discredited and that it has been shown that no purely formal criteria of the sort Hayek has offered, that is, that all laws be general, predictable, and certain, can effectively curtail the extent of governmental intrusion, all the structural changes notwithstanding.[14]

As against this criticism, I would maintain that nothing in historical experience suggests that the jurisdictional problems to which Hamowy alludes are insoluble. No doubt, as in every other area of law, there will be hard cases in Hayek's constitution in which a dispute will arise as to which house has jurisdiction over which area of policy or governmental activity. Such disputes are perfectly familiar features of constitutional development and, as in the British case, are often resolved by the evolution of constitutional conventions. Accepting that there will be these jurisdictional hard cases in no ways concedes that they pose undecidable questions within Hayek's constitution of liberty. As to the claim that Hayek's general requirements for true law are purely formal and so incapable of protecting liberty, I have already argued in chapter 3 of this book that this criticism embodies an inaccurate and impoverished understanding of the rôle of the Kantian test in Hayek's philosophical jurisprudence. Given certain assumptions about the natural necessities of the human circumstance, the Kantian test will yield a domain of individual liberty — roughly, that which is captured by Adam Smith's system of natural liberty — which, though not invariant or inviolable, nontheless imposes strong restrictions on governmental authority. It is not a relevant criticism that Hayek's theory fails to yield individual rights that are well-defined and inviolable, since no theory of natural rights has achieved that result. Rather, recognizing that the scope of individual liberty must be the subject of continuous legal redefinition and judicial review, Hayek is seeking to frame a constitution in which the expansionist momentum of modern government is curbed. His thesis is that a constitution in which there is a clear (if not always indisputable) division of powers of the sort his bicameral proposal envisages is one less likely to tolerate the endless expansion of the scope of government activity and intervention found in all modern societies.

It is true enough — and here we come to the second, and far more substantial criticism of Hayek's constitution — that there can be no cast-iron guarantee that it will be stable or that it will consistently protect liberty. No institutional framework has been devised or is imaginable, which will infallibly protect individual liberty from all unjustified encroachment. In part, this is because there are hard cases, areas where reasonable men may reasonably differ about whether a given measure constitutes an invasion of liberty and, if so, whether it is justified. We do not possess, and are unlikely ever to have, a theory which gives completely definite answers to all substantial questions about the justified limitations of individual liberty. Even if a comprehensive theory of rights were available, its applications would remain areas of reasonable controversy as it had to be extended into novel areas created by changes in society and in technology. This underdetermination of reasoned judgements about the limits of liberty by any imaginable theory of the subject is wisely recognized by Hayek and addressed by his proposal that the upper chamber be made up of men and women of proven judgement. Hayek's intuition here is surely the sound one that, when questions about justice and liberty are not clearly decidable by any existing theory, we are likely to achieve the best results by relying on the judgements of an experienced and independent elite of persons who have been tested in the wider society. What other recourse have we, in fact?

Our best bulwark against the erosion of liberty lies in some such control of governmental legislation by a Hayekian upper chamber. That this is so is shown by the evidence of history and contemporary experience. In the English case, a century of unparalleled individual freedom was achieved (from the Napoleonic wars to the outbreak of the First World War) despite the fact that no former constitutional barriers existed against any governmental intervention. On the other hand, an elaborate apparatus of judicial review by the Supreme Court, a written constitution and a federal system has not prevented an expansion of governmental activity, and a consequent contraction of individual liberty in the United States, of equal or greater dimensions than that experienced in England. To be sure, nothing in a Hayekian constitution would render it immune to large-scale instability. Just as in the economic domain an unhampered market renders large-scale discoordination unlikely but not unthinkable, so in the constitutional area an unfixed Hayekian constitution would diminish the chances of massive crisis but never altogether eliminate them. All economies and all polities confront what may be called *the Shackle—Buchanan problem* — the problem, explored in economic theory by G. S. L. Shackle and by James Buchanan in political philosophy, of coping with chaos in society.[15] Whereas Hayek's proposals for emergency provisions within the constitution for enabling government to extricate society from such deadlocks and dilemmas may not give a complete response to the prospect of social chaos which every society must recurrently face, there is no reason to suppose that any better response exists. Detailed proposals along the lines that Buchanan has made[16] for refining the constitution of the free society could further strenghthen our protection against disorder and invasion of liberty. It is not a reasonable criticism of Buchanan's proposals, or of Hayek's that they fail to provide infallible protection in a world of ineradicable uncertainty.

CONSERVATISM AND RADICALISM
IN HAYEK'S SOCIAL PHILOSOPHY

A different range of objections to the integrity or unitary character of Hayek's system focuses upon its combination of demands for radical reform of existing attitudes and institutions with its strong affirmation of the wisdom and efficacy of the social inheritance of tradition. This kind of objection may have several variants, of which I shall select two as being especially significant. The first objection suggests that Hayek's social philosophy embodies conflicting commitments to libertarian individualism and cultural traditionalism. This is to say that Hayek seeks to combine two outlooks, that of classical liberalism in which the individual is sovereign and conceived as the bearer of weighty moral claims against society, and that of traditional conservatism, for which human individuality is itself a cultural achievement and in which individuals are subject to the claims of their society's moral practices. The two-sidedness of Hayek's thought, always decidedly radical in its attitude to received opinions at the same time that it displays a marked conservatism in its evaluation of cultural tradition, is here represented as a tension between libertarian and traditionalist commitments in political philosophy.

This is a common objection to Hayek's thought, and one

that I once endorsed myself,[17] but it betrays a lack of insight into one of the most centrally important arguments in his work. I refer to his claim that human individuality depends for its exercise and even its existence on a cultural matrix of traditional practices which shape and permeate the moral and intellectual capacities of the individual. For Hayek, as for Oakeshott,[18] human individuality is a fruit of tradition and cannot for that reason stand in opposition to tradition's claims. In making this claim, Hayek is synthesizing the insights of conservative philosophy — especially the insights that the human individual is not a natural datum but rather a social achievement, while human reason must similarly be viewed as an element in the growth of culture and never as its guide — with the central concerns of classical liberalism. He is offering us a more humble, sceptical and modest form of liberalism than that found in the French philosophers, a liberalism that has rid itself of the incubus of an hubristic rationalism — and which has most in common with the social philosophy of the thinkers of the Scottish Enlightenment, and, above all, with the outlook of David Hume. Hayek is, in effect, refining and completing this non-rationalist tradition of classical liberalism when he makes his crucial distinction between true and false individualism[19] — between the individualism which sets man apart from society and the liberalism which sees man's individuality as organic part of social life. The key element in the distinction he finds in the different rôle alloted within each individualist tradition to the use of reason. In the one, reason has an architectonic and constructive rôle, whereas in the other it is critical, exploratory and only one aspect of the process of cultural evolution. Hayek's social philosophy in fact embodies a fusion of the conservative view of reason as inherently limited in its uses with the Scottish Enlightenment's conception of man as the creature (and not creator) of social life.

There remains to be considered the second strand of criticism of Hayek's system, which focuses on a tension in his view of morality. This second criticism has itself two variants which it is important to distinguish. The first, which I shall call the *neoconservative objection*, charges that the Hayekian liberal order is dependent upon a moral capital which its workings, and even Hayek's own theories, tend to deplete. This is a criticism of market freedoms as old as classical liberalism itself (and perhaps even older, since traces of it may be detected in Aristotle's writings) and expressed by many of the founders of classical liberalism, including Adam Ferguson and Adam Smith. The key idea expressed by these classical writers, and by their modern counterparts, such neoconservatives as Irving Kristol and Daniel Bell,[20] is that a market process in which rewards are distributed regardless of deserts or moral virtues must at length destroy the moral foundation of bourgeois virtue on which the stability of the market order depends. In both Adam Smith and the neo-conservatives it is suggested that the unregulated market or commercial society tends to produce a sort of mindless hedonism which renders it defenceless against more vital tyrannies. In Kristol's argument, not only are the martial virtues lost in the commercial society, but (and here Kristol follows Joseph Schumpeter)[21] the capitalist milieu becomes an ideal breeding ground for all manner of subversive and nihilist movements.

Now it can by no means be denied that Hayek's defence of capitalism goes against the grain of some traditional as well as much contemporary moral sentiment. His recognition that in the game of catallaxy sheer luck is sometimes decisive breaks the link, preserved only in popular mythology, between market success and moral deserts. It is not clear to me, however, that the force of his breach with an element in the traditional defence of capitalism is in fact to weaken the market order. Traditional notions of desert, need and merit have been the moral inspiration of the most determined twentieth-century enemies of the capitalist order which (with many reservations) neoconservatives too wish to defend. It was popular notions of distributive justice that were (and are) invoked by communist critics of capitalism and, not so long ago, by National Socialist enemies of the free economy. As against the neoconservatives, recent history suggests that Hayek is right in his judgement that the successful defence of market capitalism requires a revision in conventional morality in which despised occupations and practices — such as those of the speculator and middleman — are morally rehabilitated. Since the anti-capitalist movements of our time have all drawn on popular morality for their inspiration, Hayek's seems an inescapable conclusion.

There is a second variant — I shall call it *the radical argument* — which attacks the same problem from an opposed angle. In his writings on Mandeville and in his recent writings, Hayek has in fact demanded rather substantial revisions of customary or traditional morality. Following Mandeville, he has argued that private vices are sometimes public goods, and he has cautioned that we have most to fear from group rivalries (and not from the egoism of individuals). Traditional morals are, he has pointed out, the morals of the small group or the tribe, and not the morals of free men in an open society. Our ingrained moral sentiments, though they may express primordial instincts or ancient moral traditions, will often embody attitudes that are inimical to the stability and good functioning of the market order in an abstract or open society. As Hayek has put it trenchantly:

The Rousseauesque nostalgia for a society guided not by learnt moral rules which can be justified only by a rational insight into the principles on which this order is based, but by the unreflected 'natural' emotions deeply grounded on millenia of life in the small hords, leads thus directly to the demand for a socialist society in which austerity ensures that visible 'social justice' is done in a manner which gratifies natural emotions.[22]

This is an important statement since it illustrates how within the critical rationalist framework of Hayek's doctrine, judgements may be made condemning large segments of inherited and contemporary moral life as incompatible with the market order to which mankind owes its present numbers. In his reflections on the contemporary moral passion for 'social justice' Hayek has gone further and has recognized that cultural evolution may throw up 'unviable moralities'[23] — forms of moral life destructive of the very societies in which they are practised. Here Hayek may be echoing the insight of his friend, Michael Polanyi, who identifies in modern times the growth of what he calls *moral inversion*,[24] a mutation of ancient moral traditions into forms of moral sentiment hostile to all established social order. Indeed Hayek is clear that much in both ancient and modern morality condemns the market order outright. As he observes:

Though they (constructivist moral philosophers) all appeal to the same emotions, their arguments take very different and in some respects almost contradictory forms. A first group proposes a return to the older rules of conduct which have prevailed in the distant past and are still dear to men's sentiments. A second wants to construct new rules which will better serve the innate desires of the individuals. Religious prophets and ethical philosophers have of course at all times been mostly reactionaries, defending the old against the new principles. Indeed, in most parts of the world the development of an open market economy has long been prevented by those very morals preached by prophets and philosophers, even before governmental measures did the same. We must admit that modern civilization has become largely possible by the disregard of those indignant moralists. As has been well said by the French historian Jean Baechler, 'the expansion of capitalism owes its origins and raison d'être to political anarchy.' That is true enough of the Middle Ages, which, however, could draw on the teachings of the ancient Greeks who — in some measure also as a result of political anarchy — had not only discovered individual liberty and private property, but also the inseparability of the two, and thereby created the first civilisation of free men.[25]

Hayek here recognizes that the modern defence of individual liberty demands a radical revision both of current and ancient morality. In pursuing the re-evaluation of values that are necessary to the stability of the market order we are guided only by our rational insight into the general conditions of its successful operation. Despite its thesis of the primacy of practice, then, Hayek's doctrine issues in judgements critical of large segments of moral practice. Hayek's example suggests that radicalism and conservatism in intellectual and moral life may not be in conflict at all. If his argument about the sort of morality essential to the stability of the market order is sound, it has the paradoxical result that a contemporary conservative who values private property and individual liberty cannot avoid being an intellectual and moral radical.

THE HAYEKIAN RESEARCH PROGRAMME
AND THE PROSPECTS OF SOCIAL PHILOSOPHY

What, in conclusion, are the central elements of Hayek's system of ideas as they bear on the present condition and future prospects of social philosophy? The first important element I have identified as *the epistemological turn* in Hayek's social theory. He breaks with the predominant model of normative social theory as a conjunction of conceptual analysis with cost-benefit deliberations in terms of preferred values and instead proposes that we assess social systems by reference to their capacity to generate and use knowledge. This proposal is in effect an implication of his evolutionary epistemology. Hayek's contribution to evolutionary epistemology is the insight that social institutions and rules of conduct may profitably be viewed as vehicles of knowledge about man and the world. More precisely, he urges us to recognize that much of our knowledge is, and will always be embodied in the skills and dispositions of human beings as practitioners of cultural traditions and participants in social institutions. Whereas Popper sees our sense-organs as embodied theories, Hayek conceives of social institutions similarly as embodied knowledge. In both Hayek and Popper the Kantian categories are subject to an evolutionary interpretation. Popper and Hayek differ in that for Popper it is the scientific community that is the centre of attention as the bearer of growing knowledge, whereas for Hayek the social process as a whole is the object of assessment as a generator and filter for practical knowledge. Hayek's strategy here is of the greatest importance for social theory in that it relinquishes the quest for a blueprint of the best social order in favour of an investigation of the sort of framework within which theoretical and practical knowledge best grows. His argument is that anyone who values the satisfaction of human purposes is bound to approve and prefer that social system which maximizes the production, dissemination and use of human knowledge. All societies contain knowledge-bearing institutions, of course, but those societies whose institutions encourage the discovery and communication of decentralized practical knowledge will best promote the achievement of human purposes. Among the social institutions which have this knowledge-enhancing effect, private property and market competition are fundamental, but the rôle of the family in transmitting a growing fund of practical knowledge across the generations is not to be neglected.

The second paradigm shift in social thought initiated by Hayek's system is closely related, and may be termed *the evolutionist turn*. Here the claim is that distinct traditions and social systems, each of them a bearer of information about man and the world, enter into a practical competition with each other in which there is a tendency for error to be filtered out and an approximation to truth to occur. Further, it is claimed that there exists a tendency in any society for traditions and practices to be sifted by a competitive process in virtue of which there is always a presumption that existing traditions are adapted to the needs and circumstances of their practitioners. In Hayek's view, then, the traditions and practices prevailing in any society are to be regarded as the residue of an evolutionary process of trial and error, in which various experiments in living are undertaken collectively and those which are maladaptive or dysfunctional discarded.

A society's dominant traditions will accordingly embody an inheritance of successful adaptations in the past, even if they do not (and cannot) embody knowledge needed to make successful adaptations in an unknown future.

In respect of each of these aspects Hayek's social philosophy, hard questions can reasonably be asked. Hayek's version of evolutionary epistemology arguably confronts the same formidable difficulty facing Popper's version — the likelihood that the human mind, as it has been shaped by evolutionary pressure, in no way mirrors accurately the actual structure of the world. All that an evolutionary account of human knowledge can tell us is that there must be some sort of fit between man's inborn categories and expectations and the regularities that exist in nature. In the absence of such a complementarity between the inborn structure and content of the human mind and the order of nature, the human species could not presumably have survived. That some sort of matching of the contents of the human mind with the natural order is required by man's evolutionary situation and record cannot support the claim that the evolution of the human mind exhibits a tendency to approach the truth. The categories and expectations that have enabled us to survive up to now might, after all, be merely lucky errors, falsehoods with a chance affinity to longstanding conditions in our part of the universe. In carving out an ecological niche for itself, the human species may well have evolved a view of the world which it cannot transcend, but which embodies only the fictions that have proved profitable to it across a long period of its history. The self-critical enterprise of scientific research might indeed overturn some of the errors contained in our natural interpretation of things, but there is no reason to suppose that it can detect and eradicate our most deep-seated errors. For all we know, the evolutionary trend of the human mind may be leading us ever further away from truth.

In his commitment to an evolutionary epistemology, then, Hayek confronts a difficulty that afflicts, and may perhaps prove fatal to evolutionary epistemology in general. The difficulty may perhaps be resolved in Hayek, though not in Popper, by the adoption of a more explicitly pragmatist account of truth. The conjectural realism of Hayek's version of evolutionary epistemology might be abandoned and the truth-content of a theory explicated entirely in terms of its contribution to efficacious action. In this revision of Hayek's view, all ideas of an evolutionary approximation to reality would be forsworn, though it might still be affirmed that the evolution of mind in nature tends to an approximation of truth insofar as beliefs and categories become more coherent and better fitted to yield efficacious practice. If, in order to circumvent the difficulties of his theory of knowledge, Hayek's system took this pragmatist turn, it would link up with the thought of C. S. Pierce, the great American pragmatist philosopher in whose writings the evolutionary epistemology is first advanced.

There is a second range of questions for Hayek's social philosophy which would remain pressing even if the very general objection to his evolutionary epistemology that I have mentioned could be met. These questions relate to his claim that, because they are at any time the result of a natural selection of rival practices over many generations, the dominant traditions in society must be presumed to be functional or adaptive in respect of the needs and circumstances of its members. Against this claim, there are familiar criticisms of functionalism in social theory, which bear on Hayek's theory even if it does not embody the common functionalist fallacies. We need to have a definite criterion of the function of social institutions, and it is not clear that Hayek's theory provides one. The population test — which assesses the functional value of an institution or practice by its capacity to increase human numbers — is indeterminate in its results, if only because the calculus of lives needs to be applied over a given time-span if it is to yield any definite result. (A primitive neolithic economy may do better on the population test than a modern industrial economy, if its stability allows it to reproduce a small population across thousands of generations, and if the industrial economy is short-lived because of its lack of control of dangerous technologies.) There is in any case an unclarity in the relation of population size as the *measure* of the utility of an institution or a social system and Hayek's proposal that the maximization of the unknown man's chances of attaining his goals be adopted as the *criterion* of social utililty.

These problems of the definition of functionalism apart, there are questions to be asked about the mechanism whereby rival traditions are subject to natural selection. The two mechanisms Hayek mentions − emulation and migration − may well contingently account for the spread of some traditions, but they cannot always be invoked to explain great historical changes. When one religion prevails over its competitors, for example, it is often because it has succeeded in capturing state power rather than because it has any direct Darwinian advantage. Hayek's evolutionist view of human social development, in imposing a naturalistic scheme of interpretation on history, may (as Michael Oakeshott has) suggested all such schemes must)[26] do violence to the sheer contingency of historical events. This is a point Hayek implicitly recognizes when he acknowledges that barbarous militarist states may win out over more pacific free societies, but it has large implications which may demand a revision of his system. It seems plain, in any case, that the competition between rival social systems need have no sort of liberal outcome when, as in the modern world, the mechanisms of migration and emulation are not allowed to operate as between collectivist and free systems.

These considerations suggest a final question about the Hayekian system. Hayek in his Polanyian reflections on the emergence of unviable moralities, on the lack of understanding of those at work in large organisations of the market process and on the tacit commitment to interventionist solutions to social problems that is now all but universal in modern populations, has recognized that unplanned social evolution may throw up results deeply subversive of the liberal order. If we recognize that cultural evolution has generated unviable moralities and a fund of tacit ignorance or error in the common people, Hayek's sytem faces a crisis, not so much in virtue of a tension between its traditionalist and its libertarian components as because of a conflict between its rationalist and its sceptical aspects. It is after all, a rational insight of his social theory that allows Hayek to identify some components of modern morality as destabilizing the market order. If the rational claims of his social theory are in this way to take precedence over important elements in the fund of tacit understanding shared by modern populations, then the evolutionist endorsement of man's random walk in historical space has been withdrawn. If this ultimate tension in Hayek's system is resolved in the rationalist fashion his social theory suggests, the resulting philosophy will come to resemble that of James Buchanan (in which a neo-Hobbesian contractarian constitutionalism in political ethics is married to a Hayekian account of social evolution)[27] more than it does Hayek's recent thought. If, on the other hand, the rational claims of Hayek's social theory are abandoned as being in conflict with his sceptical insistence on our necessary ignorance of the sources of order in society, the ambition of Hayek's social philosophy to guide practice is forsworn and (not unlike that of Michael Oakeshott) its content becomes primarily elucidatory and explanatory. In either case, whereas its systematic character is not thereby destroyed, the unity of Hayek's thought is endangered by the uncertainty at its very centre as to the relations of tacit knowledge with theoretical insight in political life.

Whereas it may not in the end cohcrc completely as a system, Hayek's thought is far more than a series of scattered insights. It is unified by the governing ideas of spontaneous social order and the competitive selection of rival practices, and it suggests a new research programme for the social studies. Many of its specific proposals may need revision, refinement or development, as when over shorter periods of history the Becker economic approach to social life may prove indispensable in filling in the gaps left by Hayek's scheme.[28] None of these revisions compromises the central insights of Hayek's research programme — that social institutions emerge as the unintended consequence of human actions, and are fruitfully to be conceived as vehicles or bearers of tacit social knowledge. In displacing social thought from a constructivist conception of social institutions, and in giving an epistemological turn to our assessments of rival social systems, Hayek has pioneered a new way in social thought.

The two paradigm shifts which Hayek's system initmates frame a new research programme for social philosophy. The dominant research programme of conceptual analysis and cost-benefit research is plainly degenerate, petering out all too easily into a no-man's land of intuitionistic ethical and linguisitc judgements, and of minute technical studies of social choice. Contemporary social philosophy has for too long lacked a promising method and even a distinctive subject matter. Hayek's conception of the undesigned formation of social institutions, and of the rôle of those institutions as bearers of practical knowledge, generates a massive research programme for social science even if his own system may in the end contain conflicting elements. In advancing this new research programme for social theory, Hayek liberates contemporary inquiry from the dead weight of the superseded intellectual tradition of constructivist rationalism. By making this advance, however, he returns thought about man and society to the great tradition of the Scottish Enlightenment, and opens up to us the abandoned road to genuine knowledge of man and of the conditions of his freedom and welfare first laid down by the thinkers of classical liberalism.

Biographical Note on Hayek

Friedrich August von Hayek was born in Vienna on 8 May 1899, into a distinguished family of scientists and academics. The family lineage goes back to Bohemia in the fifteenth century, while in modern times it has links with that of the philosopher, L. Wittgenstein. The academic interests of Hayek's family were predominantly in the natural sciences on the paternal side and in law on his mother's side.

Hayek earned two doctorates at the University of Vienna – Dr Jur. in 1921 and Dr Rer. Pol. in 1923 – and became *Privatdozent* in Political Economy in 1929. His teacher was the great economist of the Austrian tradition, F. von Wieser, but he later attended the seminar of L. von Mises (with whom he had worked as a legal consultant in the civil service from 1921–6 apart from a period in the United States in 1923–4. Hayek was appointed Tooke Professor of Economic Science and Statistics in the University of London in 1931 and in 1944 he was elected a Fellow of the British Academy. During this period (in 1938) he acquired British citizenship, which he has retained. In 1950, he was appointed Professor of Social and Moral Sciences and member of the Committee on Social Thought at the University of Chicago. After retiring from Chicago in 1962, he became Professor at the University of Freiburg and after retirement in 1967, became honorary professor at the University of Salzburg in Austria and at present occupies an emeritus professorship at the University of Freiburg. In 1974 the Swedish Academy of Sciences awarded him, together with Gunner Myrdal, the Nobel Prize in Economics.

Now in his eighty-fifth year, Hayek is currently at work revising for publication the manuscript of a new three-volume work entitled *The Fatal Conceit: The Intellectual Error of Socialism.*

Bibliography

The following bibliography of writings by and about F. A. Hayek is an expanded and revised version, made by the author in October 1983, of a bibliography compiled near the end of 1982 by John V. Cody and Nancy Ostrem, whose invaluable assistance I would like to acknowledge. In addition, I wish to acknowledge the helpful suggestions of Kurt R. Leube (Editor-in-Chief of the International Carl Menger Library, Vienna), Prof. Albert H. Zlabinger of Jacksonville University (and co-editor with Kurt Leube of Philosophia Verlag), Prof. Paul Michelson of Huntington College, Paul Varnell of Chicago, and members of the Institute for Humane Studies staff, including Leonard P. Liggio, Walter Grinder, and John Blundell. Finally, I would like to thank Professor Hayek himself who, with the help of his secretary Mrs Cubitt, brought many additional items to my attention.

While aiming to be the most comprehensive, accurate, and up-to-date listing of Hayekian scholarship yet assembled, this bibliography — owing to the prolific and dispersed nature of the materials involved — must unavoidably contain errors, incomplete citations, and omissions. Among the omissions are a great many of Hayek's voluminous letters to editors, short notes or comments, interviews (including tape recordings, video-cassettes, and films), and book reviews. Such journals as the *Schriften des Vereins für Sozialpolitik, Jahrbücher für Volkswirtschaft und Sozialpolitik* (after 1927 superseded by *Zeitschrift für National-ökonomie*), and *Economica* contain many items not listed in this edition of the bibliography. I hope that these omissions may be rectified in subsequent editions of this book.

Earlier bibliographical orientations to Hayek's writings that proved helpful in creating the present Bibliography are:

Erich Streissler, Gottfried Haberler, Friedrich A. Lutz, and Fritz Machlup (eds.) 'Bibliography of the Writings of Friedrich A. von Hayek,' in *Roads to Freedom: Essays in Honour of Friedrich A. von Hayek*. London: Routledge & Kegan Paul, 1969, pp. 309—315.

Walter Eucken Institut. 'Bibliographie der Schriften von F. A. von Hayek.' ['Bibliography of the Writings of F. A. von Hayek.'] in *Freiburger Studien. Gesammelte Aufsätze von F. A. Hayek.* Tübingen: J. C. B. Mohr/Paul Siebeck (Wirtschaftswissenschaftliche und wirtschaftsrechtliche Untersuchungen 5), 1969, pp. 279—284.

Fritz Machlup, 'Friedrich von Hayek's Contribution to Economics.' *The Swedish Journal of Economics* 76 (December 1974): 498—531.

——. 'Hayek's Contribution to Economics,' in *Essays on Hayek*. Edited by Fritz Machlup. Foreword by Milton Friedman. New York University Press, 1976, pp. 13—39. [Machlup's 1974 and his updated 1976 bibliographical essays are indispensable guides to Hayek's writings through the mid-1970s. Adhering to the fourfold classification system of Hayek's writings laid out in the Streissler 1969 *Roads to Freedom*, Hayek 'Bibliography,' Machlup devised an alphabetical numerical identification code for easy reference to Hayek's books (B—), pamphlets (P—), edited or introduced books (E—), and articles in learned journals or collections of essays (A—).]

——. *Würdigung der Werke von Friedrich August von Hayek*. Translated by Kurt R. Leube. Tübingen: Walter Eucken Institut (Vorträge und Aufsätze 62), 1977, pp. 63—75. [This 'Assessment of the Works of Friedrich August von Hayek' is the German translation of the preceding Machlup Bibliography of Hayek.]

Leube, Kurt R. 'Anhang: Bibliographie der Schriften von F. A. von Hayek,' ['Appendix: Bibliography of the Writings of F. A. von Hayek'] in F. A. von Hayek, *Geldtheorie und Konjunkturtheorie*. Reprint of the 1st edition (Vienna, 1929; see B—1). Salzburg: Philosophia Verlag, 1976. pp. 148—160. This is identical to Leube's Hayek Bibliography in Friedrich A. von Hayek, *Individualismus und wirtschaftliche Ordnung*. Reprint of the 1st German edition (Erlenbach—Zurich, 1952; see B—7). Salzburg: Philosophia Verlag, 1976, pp. 354—357.

——. 'Ausgewählte Bibliographie der Arbeiten F. A. Hayeks zu verwandten Problemkreisen' ['Selected Bibliography of the Works of F. A. Hayek to Related Problem Areas'], in the German reprint of the first edition (Vienna, 1931; see B—2) of *Preise und Produktion*. Vienna: Philosophia Verlag, 1976, pp. 13--18.

HAYEK'S WORKS

Books

B—1 *Geldtheorie und Konjunkturtheorie.* (Beiträge zur Konjunkturforschung, herausgegeben vom Österreichischen Institut für Konjunkturforschung, No. 1). Vienna and Leipzig: Hölder-Pichler-Tempsky,
1929/2, xii, 147 pp. (England 1933, Japan 1935, Spain 1936.)
Translated into English by N. Kaldor and H. M. Croome with an
'Introduction to the Series, Library of Money and Banking History'
by Lionel Robbins as *Monetary Theory and the Trade Cycle.* Lon-
don: Jonathan Cape, 1933, 244 pp. American edition, New York:
Harcourt Brace & Co., 1933. Reprinted New York: Augustus M.
Kelley, 1966. The German 1st edition of *Geldtheorie* is described as
'Contributions to Trade Cycle Research, published by The Austrian
Institute for Trade Cycle Research, No. 1.' This Institute was founded
by Ludwig von Mises, and Hayek was its Director from 1927—1931.
See also foreword and bibliography to the 2nd German edition by
Kurt R. Leube, 'Vorwort und Bibliographie zur Wiederauflage F. A.
Hayek: *Geldtheorie und Konjunkturtheorie.*' Salzburg: (W. Neuge-
bauer) Philosophia Verlag, 1976.
[Hayek's *Geldtheorie* (1929) together with its English translation
(1933) is an expanded version of the paper (A—7a) delivered at a
meeting of the Verein für Sozialpolitik, held in Zurich, in September
1928 (See A—7a with annotations). Hayek cites earlier studies as the
foundations for his *Geldtheorie*: A—2a, A—6, A—7a, A—9a, A—13.
Hayek presents, from the Austrian School perspective, a critical
assessment of rival theories on the cause of trade cycle. He argues
that the cause of all significant trade cycle fluctuations are monetary
interventions which distort relative price relationships.]

B—2 *Prices and Production.* (Studies in Economics and Political Science,
edited by the director of the London School of Economics and
Political Sciences. No. 107 in the series of Monographs by writers
connected with the London School of Economics and Political
Science.) London: Routledge & Sons, 1931/2, xv, 112 pp. 2nd
revised and enlarged edition, London: Routledge & Kegan Paul,
1935/9, also 1967 edition, xiv, 162 pp. American edition, New
York: Macmillan, 1932. German edition. *Preise und Produktion.*
Vienna, 1931/2, also 1976 edition. (Japan 1934, China (Taipei)
1966, France 1975.)

See also the selected bibliography to the 2nd German edition: Kurt
R. Leube, 'Ausgewählte Bibliographie zur Wiederauflage F. A. Hayek:
Preise und Produktion.' Philosophia Verlag, 1976.
[The 1st edition of *Prices* (1931) literally reproduced Hayek's four
lectures on industrial fluctuations presented at the University of
London (LSE) during the session 1930–1931. The 'Preface to the
Second Edition' of *Prices* (1935) states how Hayek developed
Austrian capital theory following the four lectures. These develop-
ments were contained in the 2nd edition and prepared for by A—11a,
A—12, A—13, A—14, A—21, A—22, A—23, A—24a, as well as by the
first German edition of *Preise* (1931), the English version (B—1), and
A—9a. Economist Sudha R. Shenoy, in an unpublished manuscript,
has done a detailed comparative analysis of the differences between
the 1931 and 1935 editions of *Prices.*]

B—3 *Monetary Nationalism and International Stability.* Geneva, 1937;
London: Longmans, Green (The Graduate Institute of International
Studies, Geneva, Publication Number 18), 1937, xiv, 94 pp. Reprinted New York: Augustus M. Kelley, 1964, 1971, 1974.
[Revised version of five lectures delivered at the *Institut Universi-
taire de Hautes Études Internationales* at Geneva. Hayek surveys the
consequence of alternative monetary arrangements, such as gold vs.
paper currency and flexible vs. fixed exchange rates.]

B—4 *Profits, Interest and Investment: and Other Essays on The Theory
of Industrial Fluctuations.* London: Routledge & Kegan Paul, 1939/3,
viii, 266 pp., also 1969 edition. Reprinted New York: Augustus M.
Kelley, 1969, 1970: Clifton, New Jersey: Augustus M. Kelley, 1975.
[Collection of essays, mostly reprints or revised versions of earlier
essays, which are attempts 'to improve and develop the outline of a
Theory of Industrial Fluctuations contained in' B—1 and B—2. The
first chapter, 'Profits, Interest and Investment' is new; the other
chapters are revisions of A—37a, A—27a, A—26, A—19, A—21,
A—14, A—9a. Hayek's essays defend the Austrian School's theory of
the trade cycle. He argues that monetary interventions cause far-
ranging economic distortions that bring about malinvestment and
unemployment.]

B—5 *The Pure Theory of Capital.* London: Routledge & Kegan Paul,
1941/2 (also 1950 edition); Chicago: University of Chicago Press,
1941 (also 1950, 1952 and 1975 editions); xxxi, 454 pp. (Spain
1946, Japan 1951 and 1952.)
[Growing out of Hayek's concern for the causes of the trade cycle or

industrial fluctuations, this work deals with capital, interest, and time components in the structure of production.]

B—6 *The Road to Serfdom*. London: George Routledge & Sons, 1944/ 1945/20 (also 1969 edition); Chicago: University of Chicago Press, 1944/1945/20 (also 1969 edition), 250 pp. (Sweden 1944; France 1945; German version 1945: *Der Weg zur Knechtschaft*. Zurich 1945/3 (also 1952 edition); the German translation by Eva Röpke is available in paperback from Deutscher Taschenbuch Verlag (Munich, 1976); Denmark, Portugal, and Spain 1946; Netherlands 1948; Italy 1948; Norway 1949; Japan 1954; China (Taipei) 1956/1965/1966; Iceland 1980.)

Reprinted in two different paperback versions with new Prefaces by F. A. H. Chicago: University of Chicago Press, Phoenix Books, 1956 (see B—13, chapter 15) and also 1976 paperback edition by University of Chicago Press and Routledge & Kegan Paul.

[Hayek wrote *The Road to Serfdom* in his 'spare time from 1940 to 1943' while he was engaged in pure economic theory. The central argument was first sketched in A—37b (1938) and expanded in P—2 (1939). Hayek's thesis is that social—political planning endangers both political and economic liberties of the individual.]

B—7 *Individualism and Economic Order*. London: George Routledge & Sons, 1948/5, also 1960, 1976; Chicago: University of Chicago Press, 1948/5, also 1969, 1976, vii, 272 pp. Paperback edition, Chicago: Henry Regnery Co., Gateway edition 1972 (out of print), but now available in a University of Chicago paperback edition. (German edition, Zurich, 1952, Norway (shortened version) 1953, Spain 1968, Netherlands no date.)

See also bibliographic postscript in the German reprint of the 1st edition, Erlenbach-Zurich: 1952: Kurt R. Leube, 'Bibliographisches Nachwort zur Wiederauflage F. A. Hayek: *Individualismus und wirtschaftliche Ordnung*.' Salzburg: Philosophia Verlag, 1977.

[*Individualism* reprints P—5, A—34, A—49, A—50, E—5 (chapter 1: 'The Nature of the Problem'), E—5 (chapter 5: 'The (Present) State of the Debate'), A—41, A—48, A—45, A—38; and some previously unpublished lectures: chapter 5: 'The Meaning of Competition' and chapter 6 '"Free" Enterprise and Competitive Order.' These articles and speeches sound the Hayekian warning against economic and social planning.]

B—8 *John Stuart Mill and Harriet Taylor: Their Friendship and Subsequent Marriage*. London: Routledge & Kegan Paul, 1951/1969;

Chicago: University of Chicago Press, 1951/1969, 320 pp.

[During the 1920s the Mill—Taylor correspondence became available for scholarly assessment of how much ideological influence Harriet Taylor exerted on the political, economic and social ideas of her intimate friend and eventual husband, John Stuart Mill. Hayek's volume presenting their correspondence allows the reader to judge the nature of their relationship.]

B—9 *The Counter-Revolution of Science: Studies on the Abuse of Reason.* Glencoe, Illinois: The Free Press, 1952, 255 pp; new edition New York, 1964; 2nd edition with 1959 Preface to German edition, Indianapolis, Indiana: Liberty*Press*, 1979, also available in Liberty-*Press* paperback. (Germany 1959, Frankfurt am Main edition published under the title *Missbrauch und Verfall der Vernunft* or 'The Abuse and Decline of Reason'; German reprint of Frankfurt edition, Salzburg: Philosophia Verlag, 1979; France excerpts, 1953; Italy 1967.)

[The two major sections of this volume first appeared as articles in *Economica* as A—46 (1942—1944) and A—42 (1941), respectively: the third study first appeared as A—70 (1951). Hayek analyses the intellectual origins of social planning and engineering. Topics covered include: scientism and the methodology of studying society, collectivism, historicism, non-spontaneous or rationalistic social planning, as well as the role of Saint-Simon, Comte, and Hegel in legitimizing scientistic sociology.]

B—10 *The Sensory Order: An Inquiry into the Foundations of Theoretical Psychology.* London: Routledge & Kegan Paul, 1952; Chicago: University of Chicago Press Press, 1952, xxii, 209 pp; new edition 1963/1976. Reprinted Chicago: University of Chicago Press, Phoenix Book paperback, 1963 (out of print). University of Chicago Press has reissued the paperback in a Midway Reprint, 1976, with the Heinrich Klüver Introduction.

[Though published in 1952, the 'whole principle' of *The Sensory Order* was conceived 30 years earlier by Hayek in a draft of a student paper composed around 1919—1920, while he was still uncertain whether to become a psychologist or an economist. Three decades later his concern about the logical character of social theory led him to re-examine favourably his youthful conclusions on certain topics of epistemology and theoretical psychology: concepts of mind, classification, and the ordering of our mental and sensory world. In his 1952 Preface Hayek acknowledges his indebtedness 'particularly' to Ernst Mach and his analysis of perceptual organization.]

B—11 *The Political Ideal of the Rule of Law.* Cairo: National Bank of Egypt, Fiftieth Anniversary Commemorative Lectures, 1955, 76 pp. [Publication of four lectures Hayek delivered at the invitation of the National Bank of Egypt. These essays form a historical survey of the evolution of freedom and the rule of law in Britain, France, Germany, and America.]

[Reprinted in a revised, edited, and abridged format as chapters 11 and 13—16 of Hayek's B—12: chapters 11 and 16 of the B—12 version were reprinted under the title, *The Rule of Law.* Menlo Park, California: Institute for Humane Studies (Studies in Law, No. 3), 1975.]

B—12 *The Constitution of Liberty.* London: Routledge & Kegan Paul, 1960; Chicago: University of Chicago Press, 1960/1963/5 (also 1969 edition); Toronto: The University of Toronto Press, 1960, x, 570 pp. Also available in paperback: Chicago: Henry Regnery Co. Gateway Edition, 1972.

German translation: *Die Verfassung der Freiheit.* Tübingen: Walter Eucken Institut (Wirtschaftswissenchaftliche und wirtschaftsrecht-liche Untersuchungen No. 7), [J. C. B. Mohr/P. Siebeck], 1971. (Spain 1961), Italy 1971, China (Taipei) 1975.)

[Hayek composed the Preface of *The Constitution of Liberty* on his 60th birthday (8 May, 1959). He intended this survey of the ideals of freedom in Western civilization to commemorate the centenary of John Stuart Mill's *On Liberty* (1859). In 'Acknowledgements and Notes' he describes the various preliminary drafts and versions he incorporated into this volume; also see B—11. Hayek stresses the working of the liberal, spontaneous order of society, which is too complex to be subjected to social planning and engineering.]

B—13 *Studies in Philosophy, Politics and Economics.* London: Rout-ledge & Kegan Paul, 1967/1969; Chicago: University of Chicago Press, 1967/1969; Toronto: University of Toronto Press, 1967/1969, x, 356 pp. Reprinted in paperback New York: Simon and Schuster Clarion Book, 1969.

[This volume of 25 essays contains reprints of articles and speeches by F. A. H. as well as previously unpublished writing and speeches over a 20-year period preceding 1967. Reprints (often revised) include: A—76, A—102, A—103b, A—112, A—108, A—115, A—65, A—68, A—99a, etc. Consult volume to determine other essays published for the first time. The scope of topics includes essays on epistemology, history of ideas, specialization, Hume, spontaneous order, the liberal social order, the transmission of liberal economic ideas, and a variety of other topics on philosophy, politics, and economics.]

B—14 *Freiburger Studien. Gesammelte Aufsätze.* Tübingen. Walter Eucken Institut (Wirtschaftswissenschaftliche und wirtschaftsrechtliche Untersuchungen 5) J. C. B. Mohr/P. Siebeck, 1969, 284 pp.

['Freiburg Studies. Collected Essays.' German anthology of Hayek's essays. Contains German versions of such items as P—9 and P—10.]

B—15 *Law, Legislation and Liberty: A New Statement of the Liberal Principles of Justice and Political Economy*, vol. I, *Rules and Order*. London: Routledge & Kegan Paul; Chicago: University of Chicago Press, 1973, xi, 184 pp.

A trilogy published in the following sequence:

Vol. I, *Rules and Order*, 1973

Vol. II, *The Mirage of Social Justice*, 1976

Vol. III, *The Political Order of a Free People*, 1979

These volumes are also available in paperback, Phoenix Books editions of the University of Chicago Press. A French translation, *Droit, Législation et Liberté*, is available from Presses Universitaires de France in the Collection Libre Échange, edited by Florian Aftalion and Georges Gallais-Hamonno.

[Vol. I distinguishes between liberal spontaneous order (*'cosmos'*) and planned or engineered, rationalistic social orders (*'taxis'*). Hayek also traces the changing concept of law, principles vs. expediency in politics, and the 'law of legislation'.]

B—16 *Law, Legislation and Liberty: A New Statement of the Liberal Principles of Justice and Political Economy*, vol. II, *The Mirage of Social Justice*. London: Routledge & Kegan Paul; Chicago: University of Chicago Press, 1976, xiv, 195 pp.

[Vol. II outlines the meaning of justice in the free, liberal social order, critiques the notion of 'social' or distributive justice, and contrasts it with the market order or 'catallaxy', the regime of the Open Society.]

B—17 *New Studies in Philosophy, Politics, Economics and the History of Ideas*. London: Routledge & Kegan Paul, 1978; Chicago: University of Chicago Press, 1978.

[This volume of 20 essays supplements Hayek's earlier *Studies* (B—13) by reprinting in a more accessible form some of his earlier articles and unpublished lectures not reprinted in *Studies*. Reprints include P—11a, P—9, A—121, P—10, A—127, P—9, A—131a, A—136a,

A—116, A—113. Consult *New Studies* for titles of essays not previously published. Ranging over themes from philosophy, politics, economics, and the history of ideas, Hayek analyses such topics as constructivism, the 'atavism of social justice', liberalism, the dangers of economic planning, and the ideas of Mandeville, Smith, and Keynes. Chapter 2 reprints his 1974 Nobel Prize speech, 'The Pretence of Knowledge.']

B—18 *Law, Legislation and Liberty: A New Statement of the Liberal Principles of Justice and Political Economy*, vol. III, *The Political Order of a Free People*. London: Routledge & Kegan Paul; Chicago: University of Chicago Press, 1979, xv, 244 pp.

[Vol. III concludes Hayek's trilogy. Hayek exposes the weakness inherent in most forms of democratic government and outlines his alternative constitutional, political, and legal arrangements to create a democratic order that would be consistent with the free society. The Epilogue, 'The Three Sources of Human Values,' reprints Hayek's Hobhouse Lecture delivered at the London School of Economics, 17 May 1978.]

Pamphlets

P—1 *Das Mieterschutzproblem, Nationalökonomische Betrachtungen.* Vienna: Steyrermühl-Verlag, *Bibliothek für Volkswirtschaft und Politik*, No. 2, 1929.

['The Rent Control Problem, Political Economic Considerations.' Hayek's later article (A—9b) was adapted from P—1 (the more detailed study on the effects of rent control) and both were used to form the substance of Hayek's 'The Repercussions of Rent Restrictions,' in F. A. Hayek, Milton Friedman, *et al.*, *Rent Control: A Popular Paradox. Evidence on The Effects of Rent Control*. Vancouver: The Fraser Institute, 1975, pp. 67—83; this last volume grew out of an earlier version: Arthur Seldon (ed.) *Verdict on Rent Control*. London: Institute of Economic Affairs, 1972.]

P—2 *Freedom and the Economic System*. University of Chicago Press (Public Policy Pamphlet No. 29. Harry D. Gideonse (ed.) 1939, iv, 38 pp.

[Reprinted in an enlarged form from *Contemporary Review* (April 1938).]

P—3 *The Case of the Tyrol*. London: Committee on Justice for the South Tyrol, 1944.

[F. A. H. advocates Tyrolean autonomy independent of Italian hegemony. Compare with Hayek's article A—53 (1944).]

P—4 *Report on the Changes in the Cost of Living in Gibraltar 1939— 1944 and on Wages and Salaries.* Gibraltar, no date (1945).

P—5 *Individualism: True and False.* (The Twelfth Finlay Lecture, delivered at University College, Dublin, on 17 December, 1945.) Dublin: Hodges, Figgis & Co. Ltd., 1946; and Oxford: B. H. Blackwell Ltd., 1946, 38 pp.

[Reprinted in *Individualism* (B—7), chapter 1. German edition: 'Wahrer und Falscher Individualismus.' *Ordo* 1, 1948. Spain, 1968. Also reprinted in the various translations of B—7.]

P—6 *Two Essays on Free Enterprise.* Bombay: Forum of Free Enterprise, 1962.

P—7 *Wirtschaft, Wissenschaft und Politik.* Freiburger Universitätsreden, N.F. Heft 34, Freiburg im Breisgau: H. F. Schulz, 1963, 24 pp.

[English version, 'The Economy, Science and Politics,' chapter 18 of B—13. The original (in German) was Hayek's inaugural lecture on the assumption of the professorship of Political Economy, Albert Ludwig University at Freiburg im Breisgau, 18 June 1962.]

P—8 *Was der Goldwährung geschehen ist. Ein Bericht aus dem Jahre 1932 mit zwei Ergänzungen.* Tübingen: Walter Eucken Institut (Vorträge und Aufsätze 12), 1965, 36 pp. (France 1966): *Revue d'Économie Politique* 76 (1966), for French version.

['What Has Happened to the Gold Standard. A Report Beginning with the Year 1932 with Two Supplements.']

P—9 *The Confusion of Language in Political Thought, With Some Suggestions for Remedying It.* London: Institute of Economic Affairs (Occasional Paper 20), 1968/1976, 36 pp.

[Lecture originally delivered in 1967 in German to the Walter Eucken Institut at Freiburg im Breisgau. Reprinted in English as chapter 6 of B—17, and in German as 'Die Sprachverwirrung im politischen Denken' in B—14.]

P—10 *Der Wettbewerb als Entdeckungsverfahren.* Kiel: (Kieler Vorträge, N.S. 56), 1968, 20 pp.

['Competition as a Discovery Procedure.' Originally delivered in English as a lecture to the Philadelphia Society at Chicago on 29 March 1968 and later on 5 July 1968, in German, to the Institut für Weltwirtschaft of the University of Kiel. The German version was published first, but it lacked the final section found in the English version published in chapter 12 of *New Studies* (B—17). The German version also was reprinted in F. A. H.'s German collection of essays entitled *Freiburger Studien* (B—14), 1979.]

P—11a *Die Irrtümer des Konstruktivismus und die Grundlagen legitimer Kritik gesellschaftlicher Gebilde.* Munich-Salzburg 1970/2 (also 1975 edition). Tübingen: Walter Eucken Institut (Vorträge und Aufsätze 51), 1975. (Italy, 1971).
[Reprinted with some changes as 'The Errors of Constructivism' (chapter 1) of B—17.]

P—11b *A Tiger by the Tail: The Keynesian Legacy of Inflation. A 40 Years' Running Commentary on Keynesianism by F. A. Hayek.* Compiled and introduced by Sudha R. Shenoy. London: Institute of Economic Affairs (Hobart Paperback No. 4), 1972; 2nd edition 1978, xii, 124 pp. Also reprinted, San Francisco: The Cato Institute (The Cato Papers, No. 6), 1979. See A—130.

P—11c *Die Theorie Komplexer Phänomene.* Tübingen: Walter Eucken Institut (Vorträge und Aufsätze 36), 1972.
[English version, 'The Theory of Complex Phenomena' appears in chapter 2 of B—13. This essay originally appeared in English in M. Bunge, ed. *The Critical Approach and Philosophy. Essays in Honour of K. R. Popper.* New York: The Free Press, 1964.]

P—12 *Economic Freedom and Representative Government.* Fourth Wincott Memorial Lecture delivered at the Royal Society of Arts, 21 October 1973. London: The Institute of Economic Affairs (Occasional Paper 39), 1973, 22pp.
[Appears as chapter 8 of B—17.]

P—13 *Full Employment at Any Price?* London: Institute of Economic Affairs (Occasional Paper 45), 1975/1978, (Italy 1975), 52 pp.
[Three Lectures. Lecture 1: 'Inflation, The Misdirection of Labour, and Unemployment'; Lecture 2: 'The Pretence of Knowledge' (Hayek's 1974 Nobel Prize Speech); Lecture 3: 'No Escape: Unemployment Must Follow Inflation.' A Short Note on Austrian Capital Theory is added as an Appendix. Reprinted as *Unemployment and Monetary Policy.* San Francisco: Cato Institute (Cato Paper No. 3), 1979, 53 pp.]

P—14 *Choice in Currency. A Way to Stop Inflation.* London: Institute of Economic Affairs (Occasional Paper 48), February 1976/1977, 46 pp.
[Based on an Address entitled 'International Money' delivered to the Geneva Gold and Monetary Conference on 25 September 1975 at Lausanne, Switzerland.]

P—15 *Drei Vorlesungen über Demokratie, Gerechtigkeit und Sozialismus.*
Tübingen: Walter Eucken Institut (Vorträge und Aufsätze 63
B. Mohr/P. Siebeck)). 1977.
['Three Lectures on Democracy, Justice, and Socialism.']

P—16a *Denationalisation of Money: An Analysis of the Theory and Practice of Concurrent Currencies.* London: The Institute of Economic Affairs (Hobart Special Paper 70), October 1976, 107 pp.

P—16b See, along with P—16a, the revision: *Denationalisation of Money — The Argument Refined. An Analysis of the Theory and Practice of Concurrent Currencies.* Hobart Special Paper 70, Second (Extended) edition, 1978, 141 pp.

P—17 *The Reactionary Character of the Socialist Conception, Remarks by F. A. Hayek.* Hoover Institution, Stanford University, 1978.

P—18 *Economic Progress in an Open Society.* Seoul, Korea: Korea International Economic Institute (Seminar Series No. 16), 1978.

P—19 'The Three Sources of Human Values.' The Hobhouse Lecture given at the London School of Economics, 17 May 1978. Published in the Epilogue to *Law, Legislation and Liberty*, vol. III. London: Routledge & Kegan Paul, 1979 (B—18).
[German translation: 'Die drei Quellen der menschlichen Werte.' Tübingen: Walter Eucken Institut (Vorträge und Aufsätze 70) [J. C. B. Mohr/P. Siebeck], 1979.]

P—20 *Social Injustice, Socialism and Democracy.* Sidney, Australia. 1979.

P—21 *Wissenschaft und Sozialismus.* Tübingen: Walter Eucken Institut, (Vorträge und Aufsätze 71) [J. C. B. Mohr/P. Siebeck], 1979.
['Science and Socialism.']

P—22 *Liberalismus.* Translated from English by Eva von Malchus. Tübingen: Walter Eucken Institut (Vorträge und Aufsätze 72) [J. C. B. Mohr/P. Siebeck 1979], 47 pp. ['Liberalism'] Reprint—translation into German of article in *New Studies* (B—17).

P—23 *A Conversation with Hayek.* American Enterprise Institute, Washington, D. C., 1979.

P—24 *Nineteen-eightees Unemployment and the Unions.* London: The Institute of Economic Affairs (Hobart Paper 87), 1980.

P—25 *Evolution und Spontane Ordnung.* Zurich: Bank Hoffman, July 1983.

Books edited or introduced

E—1 Hermann Heinrich Gossen. *Entwicklung der Gesetze des menschlichen Verkehrs und der daraus fliessenden Regeln für menschliches Handeln.* Introduced by Friedrich A. Hayek. 3rd edition. Berlin: Prager, 1927, xxiii, 278 pp.
['The Laws of Human Relationships and of the Rules to be Derived Therefrom for Human Action.' Cf.: A—15. Gossen's (1810—1858) fame rests on this one book, first published in 1854, in which he developed a comprehensive theory of the hedonistic calculus and postulated the principle of diminishing marginal utility. He thereby anticipated the marginal utility breakthrough in the theory of economic value in 1871 by Menger, Jevons, and Walras.]

E—2 Friedrich Freiherr von Wieser. *Gesammelte Abhandlungen.* Edited with an introduction by Friedrich A. von Hayek. Tübingen: Mohr, 1929, xxxiv, 404 pp.
[This edition includes von Wieser's Collected Writings published between 1876 and 1923. Friedrich Freiherr von Wieser (1851—1926) was Hayek's mentor at the University of Vienna and represented the 'older Austrian school' of Economics. See A—4 and A—125b.]

E—3 Richard Cantillon. *Abhandlung über die Natur des Handels im Allgemeinen.* Translated by Hella von Hayek. Introduction and annotations by F. A. von Hayek. Jena, 1931, xix, 207 pp.
[A French translation of Cantillon's 'Essay on the Nature of Trade in General' appeared as *Essai sur la Nature du Commerce en Général* in *Revue des Sciences Économiques* (Liège, April—October, 1936). Italian translation by the Italian liberal editor of *Il Politico*, Luigi Einaudi appeared in *Riforma sociale* (July 1932).]

E—4 *Beiträge zur Geldtheorie.* Edited and prefaced by Friedrich A. Hayek. Contributions by Marco Fanno. Marius W. Holtrop, Johan G. Koopmans, Gunnar Myrdal, Knut Wicksell. Vienna, 1933, ix, 511 pp.
['Contributions on Monetary Theory.']

E—5 *Collectivist Economic Planning: Critical Studies on the Possibilities of Socialism.* Edited with an Introduction and a Concluding Essay by F. A. Hayek. Contributions by N. G. Pierson, Ludwig von Mises, Georg Halm, and Enrico Barone. London: George Routledge & Sons, 1935, v, 293 pp. (France 1939, Italy 1946.)
[Reprinted New York: Augustus M. Kelley (1967), 1970 from the 1935 edition; reprinted Clifton, New Jersey: Augustus M. Kelley,

1975. Hayek's Introductory chapter 1 deals with 'The Nature and History of The Problem' of socialist calculation. Hayek's concluding chapter concerns 'The Present State of the Debate.' Mises' (1881–1973) article 'Economic Calculation in the Socialist Commonwealth' (translated from the German by S. Adler), chapter 3, had set off the debate when it appeared originally under the title 'Die Wirtschaftsrechnung im sozialistischen Gemeinwesen' in the *Archiv für Sozialwissenschaften* 47 (1920). N. G. Pierson's (1839–1909) article, 'The Problem of Value in the Socialist Community,' chapter 2, originally appeared in Dutch in *De Economist* 41 (s'Gravenhage, 1902): 423–456.]

E–6 Boris Brutzkus. *Economic Planning in Soviet Russia*. Edited and prefaced by Friedrich A. Hayek. London: George Routledge & Sons, 1935; xvii, 234 pp.

E–7 *The Collected Works of Carl Menger*. 4 volumes with an Introduction by F. A. von Hayek. London: The London School of Economics and Political Science (Series of Reprints of Scarce Tracts in Economic and Political Science No. 17–20), 1933–1936.

> Vol. 1, *Grundsätze der Volkswirtschaftslehre* (1871) 1934.
> Vol. 2, *Untersuchungen über die Methode der Sozialwissenschaften* (1883) 1933.
> Vol. 3, *Kleinere Schriften zur Methode und Geschichte der Volkswirtschaftslehre* (1884–1915) 1935.
> Vol. 4, *Schriften über Geldtheorie und Währungspolitik* (1889–1893), 1936.

[Vol. 1 contains a bibliographical introduction to Menger by Hayek. Vol. 4 contains a complete list of Menger's known writings.]

Later 2nd German edition: Carl Menger, *Gesammelte Werke*. 4 vols. Tübingen, 1968–1970.

['Collected Works.']

E–8 Henry Thornton. *An Enquiry into the Nature and Effects of the Paper Credit of Great Britain* (1802). Edited and introduced by Friedrich A. Hayek. London: Allen and Unwin, 1939, 368 pp.

E–9 *John Stuart Mill, The Spirit of the Age*. Introduced by F. A. Hayek. Chicago: University of Chicago Press, 1942, xxxiii, 93 pp.

[Hayek's Introduction is entitled, 'John Stuart Mill at the Age of Twenty-Four,' and surveys Mill's intellectual development at the time of Mill's famous essay. 'The Spirit of the Age,' which represented important deviations from Benthamite utilitarian liberalism.]

E–10 *Capitalism and the Historians*. Edited and introduced by

F. A. Hayek. London: Routledge Kegan Paul, and Chicago: University of Chicago Press, 1954, 188 pp.

[The inspiration for the several papers presented was The Mont Pélèrin Society meetings held at Beauvallon in France in September 1951 on the distortions of historians and intellectuals in describing Capitalism and The Industrial Revolution. Hayek's Introduction (pp. 3–29) is entitled 'History and Politics' and is reprinted in B–13 and (in German) as 'Wirtschaftsgeschichte und Politik' ['Economic History and Politics'] in *Ordo* 7 (1955): 3–22. T. S. Ashton's first chapter is 'The Treatment of Capitalism by Historians'; L. M. Hacker's second chapter is entitled 'The Anticapitalist Bias of American Historians'; Bertrand de Jouvenel contributed chapter 3, 'The Treatment of Capitalism by Continental Intellectuals'; T. S. Ashton's chapter 4, 'The Standard of Life of the Workers in England, 1790–1830,' originally appeared in *The Journal of Economic History*, Supplement 9, 1949; the final article by W. H. Hutt, 'The Factory System of The Early Nineteenth Century,' originally appeared in *Economica* (March 1926). Hayek's volume provoked many pro and con reviews. A sampling: Arthur Schlesinger, Jr, *The Reporter* (30 March 1954): 38–40; Oscar Handlin, *The New England Quarterly* (March 1955): 99–107; Charles Wilson. *Economic History Review* (April 1956); Asa Briggs, *The Journal of Economic History* (Summer 1954); T. W. Eastbrook, *The American Economic Review* (September 1954); Max Eastman, *The Freeman* (22 February 1954); Helmut Schoek, *U. S. A.* (14 July 1954); Eric E. Lampard, *The American Historical Review* (October 1954): and John Chamberlain, *Barron's* (4 January 1954.)]

E–11 F. Bastiat, *Selected Essays in Political Economy*. Introduction by F. A. Hayek, Princeton University Press, 1964.

E–12 Louis Rougier. *The Genius of the West*. Introduction by F. A. v. Hayek. Los Angeles: Nash Publishing (published for the Principles of Freedom Committee), 1971, pp. xv–xviii.

E–13 Gerald P. O'Driscoll, Jr. *Economics as a Coordination Problem*. The Contributions of Friedrich A. Hayek. Foreword by F. A. Hayek. Kansas City: Sheed Andrews and McMeel, Inc., 1977, pp. xi–xii.

E–14 Ludwig von Mises. *Socialism: An Economic and Sociological Analysis*. Translated by Jaques Kahane. 1981 Introduction by F. A. Hayek. Indianapolis: Liberty Classics, 1981, pp. xix–xxiv. Dated August 1978.

[Hayek's Foreword pays tribute to Mises for the anti-socialist impact that Mises' *Die Gemeinwirtschaft: Untersuchungen über den Sozialismus* (Jena: Gustav Fischer, 1922) created on many intellectuals after the First World War.]

E—15 Pascal Salin, *European Monetary Unity: For Whose Benefit?* Foreword by F. A. Hayek. Brussels: Institutum Europaeum, 1980.

E—16 Ewald Schams. *Gesammelte Aufsätze.* Prefaced by F. A. Hayek. Ready in Spring 1983. Munich: Philosophia Verlag.

Articles in journals, newspapers, or collections of essays

A—1a 'Das Stabilisierungsproblem in Goldwährungsländern.' *Zeitschrift für Volkswirtschaft und Sozialpolitik*, N. S. 4 (1924).

['The Stabilization Problem for Countries on the Gold Standard.' See note A—2a for the biographical context of Hayek's first two article publications. The journal in which Hayek published some of his first articles was closely associated with the Austrian School of Economics through its editorial direction. It underwent several name changes:

1892—1918: The journal was known as *Zeitschrift für Volkswirtschaft, Sozialpolitik und Verwaltung. Organ der Gesellschaft österreichischer Volkswirt.* ['Journal of Political Economy, Social Policy, and Administration. Publication of the Society of Austrian Political Economy'], and was published in Vienna by F. Tempsky.

1919—1920: Suspended publication.

1921—1927: It was known as *Zeitschrift für Volkswirtschaft und Sozialpolitik.* ['Journal of Political Economy and Social Policy'] and was published in Vienna and Leipzig by F. Deuticke.

After 1927, the journal was superseded by *Zeitschrift für Nationalökonomie.* ['Journal of National Economy']. See A—22, etc.

The heavily Austrian School of Economics-orientated editorial staff included:

1892—1918 Ernst von Plener (1841—1923)
1892—1914 Eugen von Böhm-Bawerk (1851—1914)
1892—1907 Karl Theodor von Inama-Sternegg (1843—1908)
1904—1916 Eugen von Philippovich (1858—1917)
1904—1918 Friedrich Freiherr von Wieser (1851—1926)
1911—1916 Robert Meyer (1855—1914)
1921—1927 R. Reisch (1866—?). Othmar Spann (1878—1950), and others.]

A—1b 'Diskontpolitik und Warenpreise.' *Der Österreichische Volkswirt* 17 (1, 2), (Vienna 1924).

['Discount Policy and Commodity Prices.']

A—2a 'Die Währungspolitik der Vereinigten Staaten seit der Überwindung der Krise von 1920.' *Zeitschrift für Volkswirtschaft und Sozialpolitik*. N. S. 5 (1925).

['The Monetary Policy in the United States Since Overcoming the Crisis of 1920.' Both this article and A—1a grew out of Hayek's post-graduate studies in America which he pursued from March 1923 to June 1924 at New York University. On the chronology of the Nobel Prize biography of Hayek: Official Announcement of the Royal Academy of Sciences, republished in the *Swedish Journal of Economics* 76 (December 1974): 469 ff. Also see Machlup (ed.) (1976), pp. 16—17, as well as the annotation in the present Hayek *Bibliography* on item A—64. Hayek's American academic sojourn took place while he was on a leave of absence from his Austrian civil service position (1921—1926) as a legal consultant (along with Ludwig von Mises) for carrying out the provisions of the Treaty of St. Germain; see A—145, p. 1 for Hayek's anecdote and background for his introduction to von Mises through von Wieser.]

A—2b 'Das amerikanische Bankwesen seit der Reform von 1914.' *Der Österreichische Volkswirt* 17 (29—33), (Vienna 1925).

['The American Banking System since the Reform of 1914.']

A—3a 'Bemerkungen zum Zurechnungsproblem.' *Jahrbücher für Nationalökonomie und Statistik* 124 (1926): 1—18.

['Comments on the Problem of Imputation.' On the valuation of producer goods. Compare Wilhelm Vleugel's *Die Lösung des wirtschaftlichen Zurechnungsproblems bei Böhm-Bawerk und Wieser*. Halle: Niemeyer (Königsberger Gelehrte Gesellschaft. Geisteswissenschaftliche Klasse, Schriften, vol. 7, Part 5), 1930.]

A—3b 'Die Bedeutung der Konjunkturforschung für das Wirtschaftsleben.' *Der Österreichische Volkswirt* 19 (2), (Vienna 1926).

['The Meaning of Business Cycle Research for Economic Life.']

A—4 'Friedrich Freiherr von Wieser.' *Jahrbücher für Nationalökonomie und Statistik* 125 (1926): 513—530.

[Commemorative article on the occasion of the death of Hayek's Austrian School of Economics mentor, von Wieser (1851—1926). Compare with Hayek's later article on von Wieser in *The International Encyclopaedia of the Social Sciences* (1968, 1972). Also see E—2 (1929) Hayek's German introduction and edition of von Wieser's Collected Writings. A—4 translated into English in an abridged form appears in *The Development of Economic Thought:*

Great Economists in Perspective. Edited by Henry William Spiegel. New York & London: John Wiley & Sons, Inc. 1952, 1961, pp. −567.]

A−5a 'Zur Problemstellung der Zinstheorie.' *Archiv für Sozialwissenschaften und Sozialpolitik* 58 (1927): 517−532.
['On the Setting of the Problem of Rent Theory.']

A−5b 'Konjunkturforschung in Österreich.' *Die Industrie* 32 (30), (Vienna 1927).
['Business Cycle Research in Austria.']

A−6 'Das intertemporale Gleichgewichtssystem der Preise und die Bewegungen des "Geldwertes".' *Weltwirtschaftliches Archiv* 28 (1928): 33−76.
['The Intertemporal Equilibrium System of Prices and the Movements of the "Value of Money".']

A−7a 'Einige Bemerkungen über das Verhältnis der Geldtheorie zur Konjunkturtheorie.' *Schriften des Vereins für Sozialpolitik* 173/2 (1928): 247−295. Also see same journal, vol. 175, for a discussion.
['Some Remarks on the Relationship between Monetary Theory and Business Cycle Theory.']
[See B−1 with annotation. The journal in which Hayek published this article was the publication of the influential *Verein für Sozialpolitik*, founded in 1872 by (among others) Gustav Schmoller (1838−1917). This organization for social reform did not express a monolithic unity of doctrine, but was, nevertheless, excoriated by its opponents as a union of 'Professorial Socialists' (*Katheder Sozialisten*). See the interesting group photograph of a meeting of the *Verein* at the University of Zurich, 11−13 September 1928, showing the wonderfully variegated grouping that includes Hayek, von Mises, Machlup, A. Rüstow, Hunold, Morgenstern, Strigl, and Sombart: in Albert Hunold, 'How Mises Changed My Mind.' *The Mont Pélèrin Quarterly* 3 (October 1961): 16−19. For background on the *Verein*, see Haney (1949), pp. 546, 820, 885. It was at the September 1928 meeting of the *Verein* that Hayek presented his paper, A−7a, which eventually grew into his *Geldtheorie* (1929).]

A−7b 'Diskussionsbemerkungen über "Kredit und Konjunktur."' *Schriften des Vereins für Sozialpolitik* 175, Verhandlungen 1928, (1928).
['Discussion Comments on "Credit and Business Cycle"' ... (Transactions 1928).]

A—8 'Theorie der Preistaxen.' *Közgazdasági Enciklopédia*, Budapest, 1929.

[In Hungarian-German printing.]

A—9a 'Gibt es einen "Widersinn des Sparens"? Eine Kritik der Krisentheorie von W. T. Foster und W. Catchings mit einigen Bemerkungen zur Lehre von den Beziehungen zwischen Geld und Kapital.' ['Is There a "Paradox of Saving"? A Critique of the Crisis-Theory of W. T. Foster and W. Catchings with some Remarks on the Theory of the Relationship between Money and Capital.'] *Zeitschrift für Nationalökonomie* 1, No. 3 (1929): 125—169; revised and enlarged edition, Vienna: Springer, 1931.

[English version: 'The Paradox of Saving.' *Economica* 11, No. 32 (May 1931). Reprinted in B—4 ('Appendix'). The English translation was done by Nicholas Kaldor and Georg Tugendhat.]

A—9b 'Wirkungen der Mietzinsbeschränkungen.' Munich: *Schriften des Vereins für Sozialpolitik* 182 (1930).

['The Repercussions of Rent Restrictions.' See P—1 for different treatments of the effects of rent control. A—9b formed the substance of Hayek's article in the Hayek—Friedman volume mentioned in P—1.]

A—9c 'Bemerkungen zur vorstehenden Erwiderung Prof. Emil Lederers.' *Zeitschrift für Nationalökonomie* 1 (5), (1930).

['Comments on the Preceding Reply of Prof. Emil Lederer.']

A—10 'Reflections on the Pure Theory of Money of Mr. J. M. Keynes.' *Economica* 11, No. 33 (August 1931—Part I): 270—295.

[See also A—11b.]

A—11a 'The Pure Theory of Money: A Rejoinder to Mr. Keynes.' *Economica* 11, No. 34 (November 1931): 398—403.

[In the same issue of *Economica*, pp. 387—397, Keynes' article appears: 'A Reply to Dr. Hayek.']

A—11b 'Reflections on the Pure Theory of Money of Mr. J. M. Keynes.' *Economica* 12 (February 1932—Part II): 22—44.

[See also A—10 and A—11a.]

A—11c 'Das Schicksal der Goldwährung.' *Der Deutsche Volkswirt* 6 (20), (1932).

['The Fate of the Gold Standard.' See P—8.]

A—11d 'Foreign Exchange Restrictions.' *The Economist* 6 (1932).

A—12 'Money and Capital: A Reply to Mr. Sraffa.' *Economic Journal* 42 (June 1932): 237—249.

A—13 'Kapitalaufzehrung.' *Weltwirtschaftliches Archiv* 36 (July 1932/
II): 86—108.
['Capital Consumption.']

A—14 'A Note on the Development of the Doctrine of "Forced Saving".'
Quarterly Journal of Economics 47 (November 1932): 123—133.
[Reprinted in B—4.]

A—15 'Gossen, Hermann Heinrich.' *Encyclopaedia of the Social Sciences.*
New York: Macmillan, 1932. vol. 7, p. 3.

A—16 'Macleod, Henry D.' *Encyclopaedia of the Social Sciences.* New
York: Macmillan, 1933. vol. 2, p. 30.
[Henry Dunning Macleod (1821—1902) was a Scottish economist
who wrote *The Theory and Practice of Banking*, 2 vols., (1856) and
The Theory of Credit, 2 vols., (1889—1891).]

A—17 'Norman, George W.' *Encyclopaedia of the Social Sciences.* New
York: Macmillan, 1933. vol. 2.

A—18 'Philippovich, Eugen von.' *Encyclopaedia of the Social Sciences.*
New York: Macmillan, 1934. vol. 12, p. 116.

A—19 'Saving.' *Encyclopaedia of the Social Sciences.* New York: Macmillan, 1934. vol. 13, pp. 548—552.
[Reprinted in revised form in B—4.]

A—20 'The Trend of Economic Thinking.' *Economica* 13 (May 1933):
121—137.
[Hayek's first inaugural lecture given at the University of London
about a year after he assumed the Tooke professorship, in which he
explained his general economic philosophy. See B—13, p. 254.]

A—21 Contribution to Gustav Clausing (ed.) *Der Stand und die nächste
Zukunft der Konjunkturforschung. Festschrift für Arthur Spiethoff.*
Munich: Duncker & Humblot, 1933.
[Translated into English in B—4 (chapter 6) as 'The Present State
and Immediate Prospects of the Study of Industrial Fluctuations.'
Arthur Spiethoff, (1873—1957), who is honoured in this *Festschrift*,
was born in 1873, studied under Schmoller, and devised a 'non-
monetary overinvestment theory' of the business cycle. See Haney
(1949), p. 673.]

A—22 'Über Neutrales Geld.' *Zeitschrift für Nationalökonomie* 4
(October 1933).
['Concerning Neutral Money.']

A—23 'Capital and Industrial Fluctuations.' *Econometrica* 2 (April
1934): 152—167.

A—24a 'On the Relationship between Investment and Output.' *Economic*

Journal 44 (1934): 207—231.

A—24b 'The Outlook for Interest Rates.' *The Economist* 7 (1934).

A—24c 'Stable Prices or Neutral Money.' *The Economist* 7 (1934).

A—25 'Carl Menger.' *Economica* N. S. 1 (November 1934): 393—420.
[This is an English translation of Hayek's Introduction to Menger's *Grundsätze* in E—7. Reprinted in *The Development of Economic Thought: Great Economists in Perspective*. Edited by Henry William Spiegel. New York and London: John Wiley & Sons, Inc. 1952, 527—553. Also reprinted in *Principles of Economics* by Carl Menger. Translated by James Dingwall and Bert F. Hoselitz. With an Introduction by F. A. Hayek. New York & London: New York University Press, 1981, pp. 11—36. See A—131a.]

A—26 'Preiserwartungen, Monetäre Störungen und Fehlinvestitionen.' *Nationalökonomisk Tidsskrift* 73, No. 3 (1935).
[Reprinted in a revised form in B—4 as 'Price Expectations, Monetary Disturbances and Malinvestments.' Originally delivered as a lecture on 7 December 1933 in the *Sozialökonomisk Samfund* in Copenhagen. First published in German and later in French in the *Revue de Science Économique*, Liège (October 1935).]

A—27a 'The Maintenance of Capital.' *Economica* N. S. 2 (1935): 241—276.
[Reprinted in B—4.]

A—27b 'A Regulated Gold Standard.' *The Economist* (11 May 1935).

A—28 'Spor miedzy szkola "Currency" i szkola "Banking".' *Ekonomista* 55 (Warsaw, 1935).

A—29 'Edwin Cannan' (Obituary). *Zeitschrift für Nationalökonomie* 6 (1935): 246—250.
[Cannan (1861—1935) is also celebrated by Hayek in A—72. Cannan associated himself at the London School of Economics with a group who developed liberal theory. This group included Lionel Robbins, Cannan's successor, and his colleague Sir Arnold Plant (see Plant, 1969), Sir Theodore Gregory (Athens), F. C. Benkam (Singapore), W. H. Hutt (South Africa), and F. W. Paish (Paris).]

A—30 'Technischer Fortschritt und Überkapazität.' *Österreichische Zeitschrift für Bankwesen* 1 (1936).
['Technical Progress and Overcapacity.']

A—31 'The Mythology of Capital.' *Quarterly Journal of Economics* 50 (1936): 199—228.
[Reprinted in William Fellner and Bernard F. Haley (eds.) *Readings in the Theory of Income Distribution*. Philadelphia: 1946.]

A—32 'Utility Analysis and Interest.' *Economic Journal* 46 (1936): 44—60.

A—33 'La situation monétaire internationale.' *Bulletin Périodique de la Société Belge d'Études et d'Expansion*, No. 103. (Brussels 1936). ['The International Monetary Situation.']

A—34 'Economics and Knowledge.' *Economica* N. S. 4 (February 1937): 33—54.

[Reprinted in B—7. Also reprinted in J. M. Buchanan and G. F. Thirlby (eds.) L. S. E. *Essays on Cost*. New York and London: New York University Press, 1981 as chapter 3. Originally presented as a presidential address to the London Economic Club, 10 November 1936.]

A—35 'Einleitung zu einer Kapitaltheorie.' *Zeitschrift für Nationalökonomie* 8 (1937): 1—9.

['Introduction to a Theory of Capital.']

A—36 'Das Goldproblem.' *Österreichische Zeitschrift für Bankwesen* 2 (1937).

['The Gold Problem.']

A—37a 'Investment that Raises the Demand for Capital.' *Review of Economic Statistics* 19 (November 1937).

[Reprinted in B—4.]

A—37b 'Freedom and the Economic System.' *Contemporary Review* (April 1938).

[Reprinted in enlarged form in P—2.]

A—38 'Economic Conditions of Inter-state Federation.' *New Commonwealth Quarterly* 5 (London 1939).

[Reprinted in B—7.]

A—39 'Pricing versus Rationing.' *The Banker* 51 (London, September 1939).

A—40 'The Economy of Capital.' *The Banker* 52 (London, October 1939).

A—41 'Mr. Keynes and War Costs.' *The Spectator* (London, 24 November 1939).

A—42 'Socialist Calculation: The Competitive "Solution".' *Economica* N. S. 7 (May 1940): 125—149.

[Reprinted in B—7.]

A—43 'The Counter-Revolution of Science.' Parts I—III. *Economica* N. S. 8 (February—August): 281—320.

[Reprinted in B—9.]

A—44 'Maintaining Capital Intact: A Reply [to Professor Pigou.]' *Economica* N. S. 8 (1941): 276—280.

A—45 'Planning, Science and Freedom.' *Nature* 148 (15 November 1941).

A—46 'Knowledge of Germany.' *The Spectator* (London, 26 December 1941).

A—47 'The Ricardo Effect.' *Economica* N. S. 9 (1942).
[Reprinted in B—7. See also in B—17, chapter 11: 'Three Elucidations of the Ricardo Effect,' and A—127.]

A—48 'Scientism and the Study of Society.' Part I: *Economica* N. S. 9 (1942). Part II: *Economica* 10 (1943). Part III: *Economica* 11 (1944).
[Reprinted in B—9.]

A—49 'A Comment on an Article by Mr. Kaldor: "Professor Hayek and the Concertina Effect".' *Economica* N. S. 9 (November 1942): 383—385.

A—50 'A Commodity Reserve Currency.' *Economic Journal* 53 (1943).
[Reprinted in B—7 as chapter 10. Also reprinted in part as a pamphlet, 'Material Relating to Proposals for an International Commodity Reserve Currency,' submitted to The International Monetary and Financial Conference at Bretton Woods, N. H. by the Committee for Economic Stability (1944). No. 380 of the F. A. Harper Archives at The Institute for Humane Studies.]

A—51 'The Facts of the Social Sciences.' *Ethics* 54 (October 1943).
[Reprinted in B—7.]

A—52 'The Geometrical Representation of Complementarity.' *Review of Economic Studies* 10 (1942—1943): 122—125.

A—53 'Gospodarka planowa a idea planowania prawa.' *Economista Polski* (London 1943).
[Cf. chapter 6 of B—6: 'Planning and the Rule of Law.']

A—54 Edited: 'John Rae and John Stuart Mill: A Correspondence.' *Economica* N. S. 10 (1943): 253—255.

A—55 'The Economic Position of South Tyrol.' In *Justice for South Tyrol*. London: 1943.
[Compare with P—3.]

A—56 'Richard von Strigl' (Obituary). *Economic Journal* 54 (1944): 284—286.
[Strigl, who died in 1944, was a 'Neo-Austrian' who developed the theory of saving and investment and analysed monopolistic competition theory.]

A—57 'Good and Bad Unemployment Policies.' *Sunday Times* (London, 30 April 1944).

A—58 'No Totalitarianism by the Back Door?' *Sunday Times* (London, 21 May 1944).

A—59 'The Use of Knowledge in Society.' *American Economic Review* 35 (September 1945): 519—530.
[Reprinted in B—7 and in a revised, abridged version as a pamphlet; Menlo Park, California: Institute for Humane Studies. (Reprint No. 5), no date (1971, 1975).]

A—60 'Time-Preference and Productivity: A Reconsideration.' *Economica* N. S. 12, No. 4 (February 1945): 22—25.

A—61 Edited: '"Notes on N. W. Senior's Political Economy" by John Stuart Mill.' *Economica* N. S. 12 (1945): 134—139.

A—62 'Nationalities and States in Central Europe.' *Central European Trade Review* 3 (London, 1945): 134—139.

A—63 'Notes on the Way.' *Time and Tide* (6 January 1945, 13 January 1945, 20 January 1945).

A—64 'Genius for Compromise.' *The Spectator* (London, 26 January 1945).

A—65 'Is There a German Nation?' *Time and Tide* (24 March 1945).

A—66 'The Future of Austria.' *The Spectator* (London, 6 April 1945).

A—67 'Tomorrow's World: Is it Going Left?' *The New York Magazine* (26 April 1945).

A—68 'State Boss Makes Slaves.' *Sunday Chronicle* (17 June 1945).

A—69 'A Plan for the Future of Germany.' *Sunday Review of Literature* (1945).

A—70 'Fuld Beskaeftigelse.' *Nationalökonomisk Tidsskrift* 84 (1946): 1—31.

A—71 'The London School of Economics 1895—1945.' *Economica* N. S. 13 (February 1946): 1—31.

A—72 'Socialism must face dangers of Statism.' *New Leader* (14 August 1946).

A—73 'Austria: Advance Post in Europe.' *The Commercial and Financial Chronicle* (28 November 1946).

A—74 'Probleme und Schwierigkeiten der englischen Wirtschaft.' *Schweizer Monatshefte* 27 (1947).
['Problems and Difficulties of the English Economy.']

A—75 'Full Employment Illusions.' *The Commercial and Financial Chronicle* (18 July 1947).

A—76 'This is Our Only Way.' *Evening Standard* (28 January 1947).

A—77 'Re-Nazification at Work.' *The Spectator* (London, 31 January 1947).

A—78 'Sound Advice.' *Time and Tide* (1 November 1947).

A—79 'Le plein emploi.' *Économie Appliquée* 1, No. 2—3, (Paris, ['Full Employment.']

A—80 'Der Mensch in der Planwirtschaft.' In Simon Moser (ed.) *Weltbild und Menschenbild*. Innsbruck and Vienna: 1948.
['Man in the Planned Economy.']

A—81 'Die politischen Folgen der Planwirtschaft.' *Die Industrie*, Zeitschrift der Vereinigung Österreicher Industrieller, No. 3 (Vienna, January 1948).
['The Political Effects of the Planned Economy.']

A—82 'Wesley Clair Mitchell 1874—1948' (Obituary). *Journal of the Royal Statistical Society* 111 (1948).
[Compare with Arthur F. Burns's commemoration of Mitchell in the *Twenty-ninth Report of The National Bureau of Economic Research*, New York: 1969; adapted Henry William Spiegel (ed.) *The Development of Economic Thought*, New York, 1952, 1961, pp. 414—442. Also note Hayek's personal association with Mitchell, as indicated in B—17, p. 3, note 3, during Hayek's stay in America during the early 1920s. Also note the correspondence between Wesley Mitchell and Hayek mentioned in Emil Kauder, *A History of Marginal Utility Theory*. Princeton University Press, 1965.]

A—83 'The Intellectuals and Socialism.' *The University of Chicago Law Review* 16 No. 3 (Spring 1949): 417—433. German translation in *Schweizer Monatshefte* 29 (1944—50); Norwegian translation (1951).
[Reprinted in B—13 and by the Institute for Humane Studies, 1971.]

A—84 'A Levy on Increasing Efficiency. The Economics of Development Charges.' *The Financial Times* (26—28 April 1949).

A—85 'Economics.' *Chambers' Encyclopaedia* 4 (Oxford 1950).

A—86 'Ricardo, David.' *Chambers' Encyclopaedia* 11 (Oxford 1950).

A—87 'Full Employment, Planning and Inflation.' *Institute of Public Affairs Review* 4(6) (Melbourne, Australia 1950).
[Reprinted as chapter 19 in B—13. Also in German (1951) and Spanish (1960).]

A—88 'Capitalism and the Proletariat.' *Farmand* 7, No. 56 (Oslo: 17 February 1951).

A—89 'Gleichheit und Gerechtigkeit.' *Jahresbericht der Züricher Volkswirtschaftlichen Gesellschaft* (1951).
['Equality and Justice.']

A—90 'Comte and Hegel.' *Measure* 2 (Chicago, July 1951).
[Reprinted in B—9]

A—91 'Comments on "The Economics and Politics of the Modern Corporation".' *The University of Chicago Law School, Conference Series* No. 8, (7 December 1951).

A—92 'Die Überlieferung der Ideale der Wirtschaftsfreiheit.' *Schweizer Monatshefte* 31, No. 6 (1951).
['The Transmission of the Ideals of Economic Freedom.' First in German (1951) and later in an English translation as 'The Ideals of Economic Freedom: A Liberal Inheritance,' in *The Owl* (London 1951), pp. 7—12. A 'corrected version' in English is reprinted as chapter 13 of B—13. Published in *The Freeman* 2 (28 July 1952): 729—731, as 'A Rebirth of Liberalism.' A remarkably similar overview of the various liberal currents that flowed into modern economic liberalism is given by Carlo Mötteli (a financial editor for *Neue Zücher Zeitung*) in *Swiss Review of World Affairs* 1, No. 8 (November 1951) and entitled 'The Regeneration of Liberalism,' reprinted in *The Mont Pélèrin Quarterly* 3 (October 1961): 29—30.]

A—93 'Worldwide Shortcomings of Wartime Planning.' *Commercial and Financial Chronicle* (18 April 1951).

A—94 'Die Ungerechtigkeit der Steuerprogression.' *Schweizer Monatshefte* 32 (November 1952).
['The Injustice of the Progressive Income Tax.' Cf. A—79 and A—73b of which this is a translation.]

A—95 'The Case Against Progressive Income Taxes.' *The Freeman* 4 (28 December 1953): 229—232.

A—96 'Leftist Foreign Correspondent.' *The Freeman* 3 (12 January 1953): 275.

A—97 'The Actonian Revival.' Review of *Lord Acton* by Gertrude Himmelfarb and *Acton's Political Philosophy* by G. E. Fasnacht. *The Freeman* 3 (23 March 1953): 461—462.

A—98 'Decline of the Rule of Law, Part I.' *The Freeman* 3 (20 April 1953): 518—520; Part II *The Freeman* 3 (4 May 1953): 561—563.

A—99 'Substitute for Foreign Aid.' *The Freeman* 3 (6 April 1953): 482—484.

A—100 'Entstehung und Verfall des Rechtsstaatsideales.' In: Albert Hunold (ed.) *Wirtschaft ohne Wunder*. Volkswirtschaftliche Studien für das Schweizerische Institut für Auslandsforschung. Zurich, 1953.
['The Rise and Fall of the Ideal of the Constitutional State.']

A—101 'Markwirtschaft und Wirtschaftspolitik.' *Ordo* 6 (February 1954): 3—18.
['Market Economy and Economic Policy.']

A—102 'Economic Myth.' *The Wall Street Journal* (4 February 1954).

A—103 'Capitalism: Myth v. Fact.' *University of Chicago Magazine* (May 1954).

A—104 'Wirtschaftsgeschichte und Politik.' *Ordo* 7 (March 1955).
['Economic History and Politics.' See E—10.]

A—105 'Degrees of Explanation.' *The British Journal for the Philosophy of Science* 6, No. 23 (1955): 209—225.
[Received by journal 11 November 1954. Hayek acknowledges indebtedness to Chester Barnand, Heinrich Klüver, Herbert Lamm, Michael Polanyi, Karl Popper, Warren Weaver and the members of a Faculty Seminar of the Committee of Social Thought in the University of Chicago 'for reading and commenting on an earlier draft of this paper.' Reprinted in revised form in B—13, chapter 1.]

A—106 'Towards a Theory of Economic Growth Discussion of Simon Kuznets' Paper.' In *National Policy for Economic Welfare at Home and Abroad*. New York: Columbia University Bicentennial Conference, 1955.

A—107 'Comments.' In Congress for Cultural Freedom (ed.) *Science and Freedom*. London: (Proceedings of the Hamburg Conference of the Congress for Cultural Freedom) 1955.
[Also printed in German.]

A—108 'Progressive Taxation Reconsidered.' In Mary Sennholz (ed.) *On Freedom and Free Enterprise: Essays in Honor of Ludwig von Mises*. Princeton: D. van Nostrand Co., 1956. Presented on the Occasion of the Fiftieth Anniversary of his [von Mises'] Doctorate, 26 February 1956.

A—109 'The Dilemma of Specialization.' In Leonard D. White (ed.) *The State of the Social Sciences*. Chicago: University of Chicago Press, 1956.
[Reprinted in B—13, chapter 8.]

A—110 'Über den "Sinn" sozialer Institutionen.' *Schweizer Monatshefte* 36 (October 1956).
['On the "Meaning" of Social Institutions.']

A—111 'Freedom & The Rule of Law.' (The Third Programme, BBC Radio; 1st of 2 talks.) *The Listener* (13 December 1956).

A—112 'Was ist und was heisst "sozial"?' In Albert Hunold (ed.) *Masse und Demokratie*. Zurich: 1957.
['What is "Social" — What Does It Mean?' Translated in an unauthorized English translation in A. Hunold (ed) *Freedom and Serfdom*. Dordrecht, 1961. The reprint in B—13, chapter 17, is a

revised version of the unauthorized English translation 'which in parts gravely misrepresented the meaning of the original.']

A—113 Review of *Mill and His Early Critics* by J. C. Rees. Leicester: University College of Leicester, 1956. In *Journal of Modern History* (June 1957): 54.

A—114 'Grundtatsachen des Fortschritts.' *Ordo* 9 (1957): 19—42. ['The Fundamental Facts of Progress.']

A—115 'Inflation Resulting from the Downward Inflexibility of Wages.' In: Committee for Economic Development (ed.) *Problems of United States Economic Development,* New York: 1958, vol. I, pp. 147—152. [Reprinted in B—13, chapter 21.]

A—116 'La Libertad, La Economia Planifacada y el Derecho.' *Temas Contemporaneos* (Buenos Aires) 3 (1958). ['Liberty, the Planned Economy, and the Law.']

A—117 'Das Inviduum im Wandel der Wirtschaftsordnung.' *Der Volkswirt* No. 51—52 (Frankfurt am Main 1958). ['The Individual and Change of Economic System.']

A—118 'The Creative Powers of a Free Civilization.' In Felix Morley (ed.) *Essays in Individuality.* Philadelphia: University of Pennsylvania Press, 1958.

A—119 'Freedom, Reason, and Tradition.' *Ethics* 68 (1958).

A—120 'Gleichheit, Wert und Verdienst.' *Ordo* 10 (1958): 5—29. ['Equality, Value, and Profit.']

A—121 'Attualità di un insegnamento,' In Angelo Dalle Molle (ed.) *Il Maestro dell' Economia di Domani* (Festschrift for Luigi Einaudi on his 85th Birthday). Verona, 1958, pp. 20—24. ['The Reality of a Teaching,' In *The Master of the Economics of the Future*, Luigi Einaudi (1874—1961), who is honoured in this Festschrift, was a classical liberal Italian economist and statesman. He was the first president of Italy and devised programmes for monetary stabilization. Einaudi is celebrated by Hayek, in an allusion, in A—72.]

A—122 'Liberalismus (1) Politischer Liberalismus.' *Handwörterbuch der Sozialwissenschaften* 6 (Stuttgart—Tübingen—Göttingen, 1959).

A—123 'Bernard Mandeville.' *Handwörterbuch der Sozialwissenschaften* 7 (Stuttgart—Tübingen—Göttingen, 1959).

A—124 'Unions, Inflation and profits.' In Philip D. Bradley (ed.) *The Public Stake in Union Power.* Charlottesville: University of Virginia Press, 1959. [Reprinted in B—13.]

A—125 'Freiheit und Unabhängigkeit.' *Schweizer Monatshefte* 39 (1959).
['Freedom and Independence.']

A—126 'Verantwortlichkeit und Freiheit.' In Albert Hunold (ed.) *Erziehung zur Freiheit.* Erlenbach-Zurich: E. Rentsch, 1959: pp. 147—170.

A—127 'Marktwirtschaft und Strukturpolitik.' *Dis Aussprache* 9 (1959). ['Market Economy and Structural Policy.']

A—128 'An Röpke.' In Welhelm Röpke, *Gegen die Brandung.* Zurich: E. Rentsch. 1959.
[On Röpke.']

A—129 'The Free Market Economy: The Most Efficient Way of Solving Economic Problems.' *Human Events* 16, No. 50 (16 December 1959).
[Reprinted in P—6]

A—130 'Inflation and Welfare State-ism.' *Commercial and Financial Chronicle* (19 March 1959).

A—131 'The Economics of Abundance.' In Henry Hazlitt (ed.) *The Critics of Keynesian Economics.* Princeton and London: Van Nostrand Co., 1960, pp. 126—130.

A—132 'The Social Environment.' In B. H. Bagdikian (ed.) *Man's Contracting World in an Expanding Universe.* Providence, R. I.: 1960.

A—133 'Freedom, Reason and Tradition.' *Proceedings of the 16th Annual Meeting:* The Western Conference of Prepaid Medical Service Plans (Winnipeg 1960).

A—134 'Progenitor of Scientism.' *National Review* (1960).

A—135 'Gobierno Democratico y Actividad Economica.' *Espejo* 1 (Mexico City, 1960).
['Democratic Government and Economic Activity.']

A—136 'The Corporation in a Democratic Society: In Whose Interest Ought it and Will It Be Run?' In M. Anshen and G. L. Bach (eds.) *Management and Corporations 1985.* New York: McGraw-Hill, 1960.
[Reprinted in B—13.]

A—137 'The "Non Sequitur" of the "Dependence Effect".' *The Southern Economic Journal* 27 (April 1961).
[Reprinted in B—13, chapter 23.]

A—138 'Freedom and Coercion: Some Comments and Mr. Hamowy's Criticism.' *New Individualist Review* 2, No. 2 (Summer 1961): 28—32.

A—139 'Die Ursachen der ständigen Gefährdung der Freiheit.' *Ordo* 12 (1961): 103—112.
['The Origins of the Constant Danger to Freedom.']

A—140 'How Much Education at Public Expense?' *Context* 1 (Chicago 1961).

A—141 'The Moral Element in Free Enterprise.' In National Association of Manufacturers (eds.) *The Spiritual and Moral Significance of Free Enterprise.* New York: 1962.
[Reprinted in B—13 as chapter 16. Originally delivered as an address to the 66th Congress of American Industry organized by the NAM (New York, 6 December 1961).]

A—142 'Rules, Perception and Intelligibility.' Proceedings of the British *Academy* 48 (1962), (London, 1963): 321—344.
[Reprinted as chapter 3 in B—13.]

A—143 'Wiener Schule.' *Handwörterbuch der Sozialwissenschaften* 12 (Stuttgart-Tübingen—Göttingen, 1962).
['The Vienna School.']

A—144 'The Uses of "Gresham's Law" as an Illustration of "Historical Theory".' *History and Theory* 1 (1962).
[Reprinted in B—13, chapter 24.]

A—145 'Alte Wahrheiten und neue Irrtümer.' In Internationales Institut der Sparkassen (ed.) *Das Sparwesen der Welt*, Proceedings of the 7th International Conference of Savings Banks (Amsterdam 1963).
['Old Truths and New Errors.' Reprinted in B—14; Italian translation in *Il Risparmio* 11 (Milan 1963).]

A—146 'Arten der Ordnung.' *Ordo* 14 (1963).
English version under the title 'Kinds of Order in Society.' *New Individualist Review* (University of Chicago) 3, No. 2 (Winter 1964): 3—12. [Reprinted in B—14.]
[The five volumes of *New Individualist Review* (1961—1968) in which 'Kinds of Order' appears have been published in one volume as *New Individualist Review*. Indianapolis: Liberty*Press*, 1981. Reprinted as pamphlet: Menlo Park, California: The Institute for Humane Studies (Studies in Social Theory No. 5), 1975. Hayek used this essay as the basis of the second chapter of vol. I of *Law, Legislation and Liberty* (B—15). Reprinted in German in B—14.]

A—147 'Recht, Gesetz und Wirtschaftsfreiheit.' In *Hundert Jahre Industrie und Handelskammer zu Dortmund 1863—1963.* Dortmund, 1963.
['Right, Law, and Economic Freedom.' Reprinted in B—14.]

A—148 Introduction to 'The Earlier Letters of John Stuart Mill.' In F. E. Mineka, (ed.) *John Stuart Mill*, vol. XII. Toronto: Toronto University Press and London: Routledge & Kegan Paul, 1963.

A—149 'The Legal and Political Philosophy of David Hume.' *Il Politico* 28, No. 4 (December 1963): 691—704.
[Lecture delivered for the Faculty of Law and Political Science of the University of Freiburg im Breisgau on 18 July 1963. Reprinted as chapter 7 of B—13. Also (in German) in B—14.]

A—150 'The Theory of Complex Phenomena.' In Mario A. Bunge (ed.) *The Critical Approach to Science and Philosophy: Essays in Honor of Karl R. Popper.* New York: The Free Press of Glencoe, Inc., 1964.
[Reprinted in B—13; see P—11c.]

A—151 Parts of 'Commerce, History of.' *Encyclopaedia Britannica*, VI. Chicago: 1964.

A—152 'Die Anschauungen der Mehrheit und die zeitgenössische Demokratie.' *Ordo* 15/16 (1965): 19—41.
['The Perception of the Majority and Contemporary Democracy.' Reprinted in B—14.]

A—153 'Kinds of Rationalism.' *The Economic Studies Quarterly* 15, No. 3 (Tokyo, 1965).
[Reprinted in B—13, chapter 5. Originally delivered as a lecture on 27 April 1964 at Rikkyo University, Tokyo. German translation in B—14.]

A—154 'Personal Recollections of Keynes and the "Keynesian Revolution".' *The Oriental Economist* 34 (Tokyo, January 1966).
[German translation in B—14. Reprinted in B—17.]

A—155 'The Misconception of Human Rights as Positive Claims.' *Farmand* Anniversary Issue II/12 (Oslo, 1966): 32—35.

A—156 'The Principles of a Liberal Social Order.' *Il Politico* 31, No. 4 (December 1966): 601—618.
[Paper submitted to The Tokyo Meeting of the Mont Pélerin Society, 5—10 September 1966. German translation in *Ordo* 18 (1967); also reprinted in B 14. Reprinted as chapter 11 of B—13 in a slightly altered version, deleting final poem linking spontaneous order to Lao-Tzu's Taoism of *wu-wei*. See Chiaki Mishiyama (1967) for a discussion of and reflection on Hayek's paper.]

A—157 'Dr. Bernard Mandeville.' *Proceedings of the British Academy* 52 (1966) (London 1967).
['Lecture on a Master Mind' delivered to the British Academy on 23 March 1966.

[Reprinted as chapter 15 of B—17. German translation B—14.]

A—158 'L'Étalon d'Or — Son Évolution.' *Revue d'Économie Politique* 76 (1966).

['The Gold Standard — Its Evolution.']

A—159 'Résultats de l'action des hommes mais non de leurs desseins.' In *Les Fondements Philosophiques des Systèmes Économiques*. Textes de Jacques Rueff et essais rédigés en son honneur. (Paris 1967).

[Translated in English in B—13 as 'The Results of Human Action but not of Human Design.' German translation in B—14.]

A—160 Remarks on 'Ernst Mach und das sozialwissenschaftliche Denken in Wien.' In Ernst Mach Institut (ed.) *Symposium aus Anlass des 50. Todestages von Ernst Mach.* (Freiburg im Breisgau, 1967).

[See B—10 for the influence of Mach (1838—1916) on Hayek. A—119 is part of a symposium commemorating the 50th anniversary of Mach's death: 'Ernst Mach and Social Science Thought in Vienna.']

A—161 'Rechtsordnung und Handelnsordnung.' In Eric Streissler (ed.) *Zur Einheit der Rechts-und Staatswissenschaften*, vol. 27. Karlsruhe, 1967.

['Legal Order and Commercial Order.' Reprinted in B—14.]

A—162 'The Constitution of A Liberal State.' *Il Politico* 32, No. 1 (September 1967): 455—461.

[German translation in *Ordo* 19 (1968) and in B—14.]

A—163 'Bruno Leoni, the Scholar.' *Il Politico* 33, No. 1 (March 1968): 21—25.

Also translated in the same journal as 'Bruno Leoni lo studioso.' (pp. 26—30). In Commemoration of Leoni's death (21 November 1967).

A—164 'Ordinamento giuridico e ordine sociale.' *Il Politico* 33, No. 4 (December 1968): 693—724.

A—165 'A Self-Generating Order for Society.' In John Nef (ed.) *Towards World Community*. The Hague, 1968.

A—166 Speech on the 70th Birthday of Leonard Reed. In *What's Past is Prologue*. New York: Foundation for Economic Education, 1968.

A—167 'Economic Thought VI: The Austrian School.' In *International Encyclopedia of the Social Sciences*. Edited by David L. Sills, New York: The Macmillan Co. & Free Press, 1968. 1972; vol. 4, pp. 458—462.

A—168 'Menger, Carl.' In *International Encyclopedia of the Social Sciences*. Edited by David L. Sills. New York: The Macmillan Company & Free Press, 1968, 1972; vol. 10, pp. 124—127.

A—169 'Wieser, Friedrich von.' In *International Encyclopedia of the Social Sciences*. Edited by David L. Sills. New York: The Macmillan Co. & The Free Press, 1968, 1972; vols, 15, 16, 17, pp. 549—550.

A—170 'Szientismus.' In W. Bernsdorf (ed.) *Wörterbuch der Soziologie*, 2nd edition (Stuttgart, 1969).
['Scientism.']

A—171 'Three Elucidations of the "Ricardo Effect".' *Journal of Political Economy* 77 (March—April 1969): 274—285.
[Reprinted in B—13 and (in German) in B—14.]

A—172 'The Primacy of the Abstract.' In Arthur Koestler and J. R. Smythe (eds.) *Beyond Reductionism — The Albach Symposium*. London, 1969.
[Reprinted in B—17.]

A—173 'Martwirtschaft oder Syndikalismus?' In *Protokoll des Wirtschaftstages der CDU/DSU* (Bonn 1969).
['Market Economy or Syndicalism?']

A—174 'Il sistema concorrenziale come strumento di conoscenza.' *L'industria* 1 (Turin, January—March 1970): 34—50.

A—175 'Principles or Expediency?' In *Toward Liberty: Essays in Honor of Ludwig von Mises on the Occasion of his 90th Birthday, 29 September 1971*. Sponsoring Committee F. A. von Hayek *et al*; F. A. Harper, Secretary. Menlo Park, California: Institute for Humane Studies, 1971, vol. I, pp. 29—45.

A—176 'Nature vs. Nurture Once Again.' A comment on C. D. Darlington, *The Evolution of Man and Society*, London, 1962 in *Encounter* (February 1971).
[Reprinted as chapter 19 in B—17.]

A—177 'Liberale und Konservative.' *Frankfurter Allgemeine Zeitung* (6 October 1971).

A—178 'The Outlook for the 1970s: Open or Repressed Inflation.' In Sudha R. Shenoy (ed.) *A Tiger by the Tail: The Keynesian Legacy of Inflation. A 40-Years' Running Commentary on Keynesianism*. London: Institute of Economic Affairs (Hobart Paperback No. 4), 1972.
[This actually appeared in a pamphlet format (P—11b) to which Hayek adds a new article, 'The Campaign Against Keynesian Inflation.' This article is also reprinted as chapter 13 of B—17.]

A—179 'Die Stellung von Mengers "Grundsätzen" in der Geschichte der

Volkswirtschaftslehre.' *Zeitschrift für Nationalökonomie* 32, No. 2 (Vienna, 1972.)
English version: 'The Place of Menger's *Grundsätze* in the History of Economic Thought.' In J. R. Hicks and W. Weber (eds.), *Carl Menger and the Austrian School of Economics.* Oxford, 1973, pp. 1–14. Reprinted as chapter 17 in B–17. Compare with E–7.
[The 1934 earlier and distinct biographical study entitled 'Carl Manger' found in E–7 was 'Written as an Introduction to the Reprint of Menger's *Grundsätze der Volkwirtschaftslehre* which constitutes the first of a series of four reprints embodying Menger's chief published contributions to Economic Science and which were published by the London School of Economics as Numbers 17 to 20 of its Series of Reprints of Scarce Works in Economics and Political Science.' An English translation of this earlier 'Carl Menger' Introduction can be found in Carl Menger, *Principles of Economics.* A translation of Menger's *Grundsätze* by James Digwall and Bert F. Hoselitz, with an Introduction ('Carl Menger') by F. A. Hayek, New York and London: New York University Press, 1981, pp. 11–36.

A–180 'The Illusion of a Just Incomes Policy.' *The Financial Times* (London, 19 April 1972).

A–181 'In Memoriam Ludwig von Mises 1881–1973.' *Zeitschrift für Nationalökonomie* 33 (Vienna 1973).

A–182 'Tribute to von Mises, Vienna Years.' *National Review* (Autumn 1973).

A–183 'Talk at the Mont Pélèrin.' *Newsletter of the Mont Pélèrin Society* 3 (Luxembourg 1973).

A–184 'Inflation: The Path to Unemployment.' Addendum 2 to Lord Robbins *et. al., Inflation: Causes, Consequences, Cures: Discourses on the Debate between the Monetary and the Trade Union Interpretations.* London: The Institute for Economic Affairs (IEA Readings, No. 14), 1974, pp. 115–120.
[Reprinted from *The Daily Telegraph* (London, 15 and 16 October 1974.]

A–185 'Inflation and Unemployment.' *New York Times* (15 November 1974).
[Reprinted from *The Daily Telegraph* (London).]

A–186 Hayek, F. A. 'Introduction' to *Catallaxy: The Science of Exchange.* Paper read at the first meeting of The Carl Menger Society (London, December 1974).
[Hayek did not continue his intention to complete this book. The

'Introduction' along with comment and discussion by Hayek, Lionel Robbins, and others is available in transcription at the Institute for Humane Studies.]

A—187 'The Pretence of Knowledge.' An Alfred Nobel Memorial Lecture, delivered 11 December 1974 at the Stockholm School of Economics. In *Les Prix Nobel en 1974*. Stockholm: Nobel Foundation, 1975.

[Reprinted in *Full Employment at Any Price* [P—13] . (Occasional Paper 45), Institute of Economic Affairs, London 1975. Also reprinted in *Unemployment and Monetary Policy: Government as Generator of the Business Cycle* with a foreward by Gerald O'Driscoll Jr. San Francisco: Cato Institute, 1979, pp. 23—36. This has also been reprinted as chapter 2 of B—17.]

A—188 'Freedom and Equality in Contemporary Society.' *PHP* 4 (The PHP Institute, Tokyo) (Tokyo 1975).

A—189 'Economics, Politics & Freedom: An Interview with F. A. Hayek.' Interview conducted by Tibor Machan in Salzburg, Austria. *Reason* 6 (February 1975): 4—12.

A—190 'Die Erhaltung des liberalen Gedankengutes.' In Friedrich A. Lutz (ed.) *Der Streit um die Gesellschaftsordnung* (Zurich 1975). ['The Preservation of the Liberal Ideal of Thought.']

A—191 TV interview on 'NBC Meet the Press.' Sunday, 22 June 1975. *Meet the Press* 19, No. 25 (22 June 1975) Washington D. C.: Merkle Press, Inc. 1975, 9 pp.

A—192 'The Courage of His Convictions.' In *Tribute to Mises 1881—1973*. The Session of the Mont Pélèrin Society at Brussels 1974 devoted to the Memory of Ludwig von Mises. Chislehurst, 1975.

A—193 'The Formation of the Open Society.' Address given by Professor Friedrich A. von Hayek at the University of Dallas Commencement Exercises, 18 May 1975. [Unpublished typescript, available at the Institute for Humane Studies.]

A—194 'Types of Mind.' *Encounter* 45 (September 1975). [This was revised and retitled 'Two Types of Mind' in chapter 4 of B—17.]

A—195 'Politicians Can't Be Trusted with Money.' [(Newspaper editor's title. Paper delivered in September at the Gold and Monetary Conference in Lausanne, Switzerland.) *The Daily Telegraph*. Part I (London, 30 September 1975); Part II 'Financial Power to the People' (newspaper editor's title, 1 October 1975).]

A—196 'A Discussion with Friedrich Hayek.' American Enterprise

Institute. *Domestic Affairs Studies* 39 (Washington, D. C. 1975).

A—197 'World Inflationary Recession.' Paper presented to the International Conference on World Economic Stabilization, 17—18 April 1975, co-sponsored by the First National Bank of Chicago and the University of Chicago. *First Chicago* Report 5/1975.

A—198 'The New Confusion about Planning.' *The Morgan Guaranty Survey* (January 1976): 4—13.

[German translation in *Die Industrie* 10 (1976).]

A—199 'Institutions May Fail, but Democracy Survives.' *U. S. News and World Report* (8 March 1976.)

A—200 'Adam Smith's Message in Today's Language.' *Daily Telegraph* (London, 9 March 1976).

[Reprinted as chapter 16 of B—17.]

A—201 'Il Problema della Moneta Oggi.' Academia Nationale dei Lincei. Atti de Convegni Rome (1976).

['The Problem of Money Today.']

A—202 'Adam Smith and the Open Society.' *Daily Telegraph* (London, 9 March 1976).

A—203 'Why We are Getting Poorer all the Time.' *Daily Telegraph* (London, 26 August 1976).

A—204 'Remembering My Cousin Ludwig Wittgenstein.' *Encounter* (August 1977).

A—205 'Die Illusion der sozialen Gerechtigkeit.' In *Schicksal? Grenzen der Machbarkeit. Ein Symposion.* Munich: Deutscher Taschenbuch Verlag, 1977.

['The Illusion of Social Justice.' Cf. B—16, vol. II of *Law, Legislation and Liberty: The Mirage of Social Justice* esp. chapter 9, also note chapter 5 of B—17: 'The Atavism of Social Justice.']

A—206 'Toward Free Market Money.' *Wall Street Journal* (19 August 1977).

A—207 'Persona Grata: Interview with Friedrich Hayek.' Interviewed by Albert Zlabinger, *World Research INK* 1, No. 12 (September 1977): 7—9. Also available as a 30-minute 16mm colour film, entitled 'Inside the Hayek Equation,' from World Research, Inc.; Campus Studies Division; 11722 Sorrento Valley Rd., San Diego, California 92121.

A—208 'An Interview with Friedrich Hayek.' by Richard Ebeling. *Libertarian Review* (September 1977): 10—16.

A—209 'Is There a Case for Private Property?' *Firing Line.* Columbia S. C.: Southern Educational Communications Association, 1977.

A—210 'Planning our Way to Serfdom.' *Reason* (Santa Barbara, California, March 1977).

A—211 'Coping with Ignorance.' Ludwig von Mises Memorial Lecture. *Imprimis* (Hillsdale College) 7 (July 1978) 6pp.
[Reprinted in Cheryl A. Yurchis (ed.) *Champions of Freedom.* Hillsdale, Michigan: Hillsdale College Press, (The Ludwig von Mises Lecture Series, vol. 5) 1979.]

A—212 'The Miscarriage of the Democratic Ideal.' *Encounter* (March 1978).
[A slightly revised version later appeared as chapter 16 of B—18.]

A—213 'Will the Democratic Ideal Prevail? In Arthur Seldon (ed.) *The Coming Confrontation: Will the Open Society Survive to 1989?* London: The Institute for Economic Affairs (Hobart Paperback No. 12), 1978, pp. 61—73.
[Revised version of an article which appeared in *Encounter* (March 1978).]

A—214 'Die Entthronung der Politik.' In *Überforderte Demokratie?* hrsg. von D. Frei, Sozialwissenschaftliche Studien des schweizerischen Instituts für Auslandsforschung. N. F. 7, Zurich 1978.
['The Dethronement of Politics' in *Has Democracy Overextended Itself?* See also chapter 18 of B—18: 'The Containment of Power and the Dethronement of Politics.']

A—215 'Can we still avoid inflation?' In Richard M. Ebeling (ed.) *The Austrian Theory of the Trade Cycle and Other Essays.* New York: Center for Libertarian Studies (Occasional Paper Series 8) 1978.

A—216 'Exploitation of Workers by Workers.' The last of three talks given by Professor F. A. Hayek under the title, 'The Market Economy' (Radio 3, BBC). The *Listener* (17 August 1978): 202—203.

A—217 'Powerful Reasons for Curbing Union Powers.' *The Times* (London, 10 October 1978).

A—218 'Notas sobre la Evolución de Sistemas de Reglas de Conducta.' *Teorema* 9, No. 1 (1979): 57—77.
['Notes on the Evolution of Systems of Rules of Conduct.' Spanish version of chapter 4 of B—13.]

A—219 'Towards a Free Market Monetary System.' *The Journal of Libertarian Studies* 3, No. 1 (1979): 1—8.
[A lecture delivered at the Gold and Monetary Conference, New Orleans, Louisiana (10 November 1977).]

A—220 'Darwinism.' *The Economist* (13 January 1979).

A—221 'There Will Have to be Changes: Managers Should Buy Back the

Workers.' *Daily Telegraph* (London, 30 January 1979).

A—222 'The Errors of Constructivism.' *Forbes* (10 December 1979).

A—223 'Freie Wahl der Währungen.' In J. Badura and O. Issing (eds.) *Geldpolitik*, Stuttgart and New York, 1980, pp. 136—146.
['Free Choice of Currency Standards.']

A—224 An Interview with F. A. Hayek.' Conducted by Richard E. Johns. *The American Economic Council Report* (May 1980).
[Reprinted in *IRI Insights* (publication of Investment Rarities, Inc.) 1 (November—December 1980): 6—12, 14—15. 32.]

A—225 'Midju-Modid.' *Frelsid* (Journal of the Freedom Association of Iceland) 1 (1980): 6—15.
['The Muddle of the Middle.']

A—226 'Dankadresse.' In Erich Hoppmann (ed.) *Friedrich A. von Hayek*. Baden-Baden: Nomos Verlagsgesellschaft. 1980. pp. 37—42.
[See Hoppmann (1980) in the Bibliography of Works Relating to Hayek.]

A—227 Review of Thomas Sowell's *Knowledge and Decisions* (New York: Basic Books, 1980) in *Reason* 13 (December 1981): 47—49.

A—228 'Recession as Inflation's Only Cure.' *Business Week* (15 December 1980).

A—229 'L'Hygiène de la démocratie.' French translation of the English text of a speech delivered 12 April 1980 at the Assemblée Nationale in Paris by Friedrich A. Hayek.
['The Health of Democracy.' In *Liberté économique et progrès social* (périodique d'information et de liaison des libéraux) No. 40 (December—January 1981): 20—23.]

A—230 'The Flaws in the Brandt Report.' *The Times* (London, 9 January 1981).

A—231 'Für Einen Neuen Liberalismus.' *Tivoles Tageszeitung* (14 February 1981).

A—232 'The Ethics of Liberty and Property.' Chapter 4 of a forthcoming book, *The Fatal Conceit*. Published in the proceedings of the Mont Pèlèrin Society 1982 General Meeting, 5—10 September, Berlin. Institut für Wirtschaftspolitik an der Universität zu Köln, 1982.

A—233 'Two Pages of Fiction on Socialist Calculation.' *Journal of Economic Affairs*, vol. 2, No. 3 (London, April 1983).

A—234 'The Austrian Critique of Keynes.' *The Economist* (11 June 1983).

A—235 'Friedrich Hayek on the Crisis.' *Encounter* (June 1983).

WORKS ABOUT OR RELEVANT TO HAYEK

Aaron, Raymond. 'La Définition Libérale de Libérté.' *Archiv europäischer Soziologen* II (1961). ['The Liberal Definition of Liberty.']

Agonito, Rosemary. 'Hayek Revisited: Mind as a Process of Classification.' In *Behaviourism: A Forum for Critical Discussions* 3, No. 2 (Spring 1975): 162–171.

Allen, Henry. 'Hayek, the Answer Man.' *The Washington Post* (2 December 1982), pp. C1, C17.

Arnold, G. L. 'The Faith of a Whig.' *Twentieth Century London* (August 1960).

Arnold, Roger A. 'The Efficiency Properties of Institutional Evolution: With Particular Reference to the Social–Philosophical Works of F. A. Hayek.' Virginia Polytechnic Institute and State University Ph. D. Dissertation, 1979. [Dissertation supervised by James M. Buchanan.]

——. 'Hayek and Institutional Evolution.' *The Journal of Libertarian Studies* 4, No. 4 (Fall 1980): 341–352.

Barry, Norman P. 'Austrian Economists on Money and Society.' *National Westminster Bank Quarterly Review* (May 1981): 20–31.

——. *An Introduction to Modern Political Theory.* London: MacMillan, 1981.

——. *Hayek's Social and Economic Philosophy.* London: Macmillan, 1979.

——. 'The Tradition of Spontaneous Order.' *Literature of Liberty* 5 (Summer 1982): 7–58. [A major section of this article deals with Hayek.]

Baumgarth, William P. 'The Political Philosophy of F. A. Hayek.' Harvard University Ph. D. Dissertation in Government, Cambridge, Mass., 1976.

—— 'Hayek and Political Order: The Rule of Law.' *The Journal of Libertarian Studies* 2, No. 1 (Winter 1978): 11–28.

Bay, Christian. 'Hayek's Liberalism: The Constitution of Perpetual Privilege.' *Political Science Review* 1 (Fall 1971): 93–124.

Beltran, L. *Economistas Modernos.* Barcelona: Terde, 1951. Chapter XI, pp. 113–125.

Bettelheim, Charles. 'Freiheit und Planwirtschaft.' In *Die Umschau. Internationale Revue*, Mainz, 1 (1946): 83–192. ['Freedom and the Planned Economy.']

Bianca, G. *Verso la Schiavitù. Replica a von Hayek*. Naples, 1979. ['(The Road) to Serfdom. Reply to von Hayek.']

Birner, Jack. 'Hayek's Research Program in Economics.' Ph. D. dissertation for Erasmus University in Rotterdam, no date (1982?). [In Dutch with a 36-page summary in English. The English summary is available at the Institute for Humane Studies, Menlo Park, California.]

Black, R. D., Collison Coats, A. W., and Goodwin, Craufurd D. W. (eds.) *The Marginal Revolution in Economics: Interpretation and Evaluation*. Durham, North Carolina: Duke University Press, 1973.

Böhm, Stephan B. 'Liberalism and Economics in the Hapsburg Monarchy,' 12 pp. Unpublished typescript. Paper presented to 'The History of Economics Society Conference,' Kress Library, Harvard University Graduate School of Business Administration, 16—19 June 1980. [Paper available at the Institute for Humane Studies]

Boland, L. A. 'Time in Economics vs. Economics in Time. The "Hayek Problem."' In *The Canadian Journal of Economics* (Canadian Economic Association) Toronto, 2, No. 2 (1978): 240—262.

Bosanquet, Nick. *After the New Right*. London: Heinemann Educational Books, 1983, pp. 30—46.

Bostaph, Samuel. 'The Methodological Debate between Carl Menger and the German Historical School.' *Atlantic Economic Journal* 6 (September 1978): 3—16.

Bradley, Jr, Robert. 'Market Socialism: A Subjectivist Evaluation.' *The Journal of Libertarian Studies* 5, No. 1 (Winter 1981): 23—40.

Brell, K. H. 'Zur Problematik der progressiven Einkommensbesteuerung. Eine Antikritik zu F. A. Hayeks "Ungerechtigkeit der Steuerprogression" und C. Fohls "Kritik der progressiven Einkommensbesteuerung".' Dissertation Karlsruhe (Berenz) 1957. ['On the Problematic of the Progressive Income Tax. A Counter-Critique to F. A. von Hayek's "The Injustice of the Progressive Income Tax" and C. Fohl's "Critique of the Progressive Income Tax".']

Brittan, Samuel. 'The True Limits of Insular Monetarism.' *The Fiancial Times* (London, 30 August 1979).

——. 'Hayek and the New Right'. *Encounter* 54 (January 1980): 30—46. Reprinted in revised version as chapter 3, 'Hayek, Freedom and Interest Groups.' In *Role and Limits of Governments: Essays in Political Economy*. Hounslow: Maurice Temple Smith, 1983.

Broadbeck, M. 'On the Philosophy of the Social Sciences.' *Philosophy of Science* 21, No. 2 (April 1959).

Brown, Pamela. 'Constitution or Competition? Alternative Views on

Monetary Reform.' *Literature of Liberty* 5 (Autumn 1982): 7—52. [A major section of this article surveys Hayek's proposals for the 'denationalization' of money. See Hayek, P—14, P—16a, and P—16b.]

Brozen, Yale M. 'The Antitrust Task Force Deconcentration Recommendation.' *Journal of Law & Economics* 13 (October 1970): 279—292.

Buchanan, James M. 'Cultural Evolution and Institutional Reform.' Unpublished manuscript.

——. *Cost and Choice*. Chicago: Markham Publishing Co., 1969.

——. *Freedom in Constitutional Contract*. College Station, Texas: Texas A & M University Press, 1979.

Buchanan, James M. and Thirlby G. F. (eds.) *L.S.E. Essays on Cost*. London: Weidenfeld & Nicolson, 1973. [Classic essays on cost from the London School of Economics, including Hayek.]

Buckley, Jr, William F. 'The Road to Serfdom: The Intellectuals and Socialism.' In Fritz Machlup (ed.) *Essays on Hayek*. New York: New York University Press, 1976, pp. 95—106.

Business Week. 'The Austrian School's Advice: "Hands Off!".' *Business Week* (3 August 1974).

Cabiatti, A. 'La Moneta Neutrale in un Libro de Dr. Hayek.' *Riforma Social* VLIII (1932).

Campbell, William F. 'Theory and History: The Methodology of Ludwig von Mises.' University of Minnesota MA thesis. Minneapolis, 1962.

Chambers, Raymond J. *Accounting, Evaluation and Economic Behavior*. Englewood Cliffs, New Jersey: Prentice-Hall, Inc., 1966. [Also see Thomas Cullom Taylor, Jr (1970).]

Congdon, Tim. 'Is the Provision of a Sound Currency a Necessary Function of the State?' *National Westminster Bank Quarterly Review*. (London, August 1981): 2—21. [Deals with the assorted problems of Hayek's (P—16b). See Norman P. Barry (May 1981).]

Conrad, O. 'Preise und Produktion: eine Auseinandersetzung mit Friedrich A. Hayek.' *Jahrbücher für Nationalokönomie und Statistik* 140 (1934).

Corbin, Peter D. (Principal Investigator, Research Coordinator, American Geographic Society.) 'Geoinflationary Variations in the U. S. Economy.' [Examination of the Austrian theory of inflation which emphasizes the spatio-temporal aspects of the inflationary process. Available at the Institute for Humane Studies.]

184   *Bibliography*

Crespigny, Anthony de. 'F. A. Hayek, Freedom for Progress.' in Anthony de Crespigny and Kenneth Minogue (eds.) *Contemporary Political Philosophers.* New York: Dodd, Mead and Co., 1975; London: Methuen, 1976, pp. 49—66.

Cunningham, Robert L. (ed.) *Liberty and the Rule of Law.* College Station, Texas: Texas A & M University Press, 1979. [A collection of 13 papers delivered at a conference in honour of F. A. Hayek, Jan. 14—18, 1976 in San Francisco. Co-sponsored by Liberty Fund, Inc. and the University of San Francisco.]

Davenport, John. 'An Unrepentant Old Whig.' *Fortune* (March 1960): 134—135, 192, 194, 197—198. [Outline of Hayek's Social Philosophy on the occasion of the publication of B—12.]

Davis, Kenneth. *Discretionary Justice: A Preliminary Inquiry.* Baton Rouge, Louisiana: Louisiana State University Press, 1969.

Delettres, J. M. *Les récentes théories des crises fondées sur les disparités des prix.* Paris: Pendone, 1941, pp. 195—276. ['Recent Theories of Economic Crises Based on Disparities in Prices.']

Diamond, Arthur M. 'F. A. Hayek on Constructivism and Ethics.' *The Journal of Libertarian Studies* 4, No. 4 (Fall 1980): 353—366.

Dietze, Gottfried. 'Hayek on The Rule of Law.' In Fritz Machlup (ed.) *Essays on Hayek.* New York: New York University Press, 1976, pp. 107—146.

——. 'From the Constitution of Liberty to its Deconstruction by Liberalist Dissipation, Disintegration, Disassociation, Disorder.' In Fritz Meyer (ed.) *Zur Verfassung der Freiheit. Festgabe für Friedrich von Hayek.* Stuttgart, New York: Gustav Fischer Verlag (*Ordo*, vol. 30), 1979, pp. 177—197.

Dolan, Edwin G. (ed.). *The Foundations of Modern Austrian Economics.* Kansas City: Sheed & Ward, Inc., 1976. [Exposition by several authors of the history, principles and applications of the Austrian School of Economics. Among the topics of interest are Israel M. Kirzner's 'On the Method of Austrian Economics' and 'The Theory of Capital'; Murray N. Rothbard's 'The Austrian Theory of Money,' and Gerald P. O'Driscoll Jr's and Sudha R. Shenoy's 'Inflation, Recession, and Stagflation.']

Dorn, J. A. 'Law and Liberty: A Comparison of Hayek and Bastiat.' Unpublished paper (October 1980), 50 pp. [Available at the Institute for Humane Studies.]

Dreyhaupt, K. F. and Siepmann U. 'Privater Wettbewerb im Geldwesen. Überlegungen zu einem Vorschlag von F. A. von Hayek.' *Ordo* 29

(1978). ['Private Competition in Monetary Affairs. Reflections on a Proposal by F. A. von Hayek.']

Durbin, E. F. M. 'Professor Hayek on Economic Planning and Political Liberty.' *Economic Journal* LV/220 (December 1945).

Dyer, P. W. and Hickman, R. H. 'American Conservatism and F. A. Hayek.' *Modern Age* 23, No. 4 (Fall 1979).

Eagley, Robert V. *The Structure of Classical Economic Theory*. New York: Oxford University Press, 1974.

Eastman, Max. Review of Hayek's *Capitalism and the Historians*. *The Freeman* 4 (22 February 1954): 385–387.

Eaton, Howard O. *The Austrian Philosophy of Value*. Norman, Okla.: The University of Oklahoma Press, 1930.

Ebeling, Richard. 'An Interview with Friedrich Hayek.' *Libertarian Review* (September 1977): 10–16.

—. 'Reflections on John Hick's "The Hayek Story".' Unpublished manuscript, no date; 23 pp.: Available from the Institute for Humane Studies, Menlo Park, California 94025.

—. 'Hayek on Inflation.' Unpublished Paper presented to the Carl Menger Society Conference entitled 'Hayek – An Introductory Course,' London, 6 December 1980.

Edelman, Gerald M. 'Through a Computer Darkly.' *Bulletin of The American Academy of Arts and Sciences*, vol. XXXVI, No. 1, (October 1982).

Ellis, Howard S. *German Monetary Theory, 1905–1933*. Cambridge, Mass: Harvard University Press, 1934.

Fabrini, L. 'La teoria del capitale e dell interesse di F. A. Hayek.' *Revista internazionale de scienze sociali*. Milano, Anno 58, Series 4, vol. 22 (1950): 250–256. ['The Theory of Capital and Interest of F. A. Hayek.']

Falconer, Robert T. 'Captial Intensity and the Real Wage: A Critical Evaluation of Hayek's Ricardo Effect.' Texas A & M Ph. D. Dissertation. College Station, Texas, 1971.

Fenizio, F. di, 'La "Via della Servitú" di F. A. Hayek.' *Giornale degli Economisti*, (January/February 1947).

Finer, H. *Road to Reaction*. London: Dobson, 1946. [Reprinted Boston, 1945. Westport, Connecticut: Greenwood Press, 1973.]

Fingleton, Eamonn. 'The Guru Who Came In From the Cold.' *NOW!* (30 January 1981) 39–41.

Flanagan, T. E. 'F. A. Hayek on Property and Justice.' Unpublished manuscript presented at the Theory of Property Summer Workshop at the University of Calgary, 7—14 July 1978.

Frankel, S. H. 'Hayek on Money.' Unpublished paper presented to The Carl Menger Society Conference on Hayek at University College, London, 28 October 1978. [This conference was structured around Hayek's newly published *New Studies in Philosophy, Politics, Economics and the History of Ideas*. In additon to Frankel, it featured Thomas Torrance, Hillel Steiner and Jeremy Shearmur.]

Fridriksson, Fridrik. 'Hayek á Íslandi 1940—1980.' *Frelsid* 3 (1981): 312—336. ['Hayek and Iceland, 1940—1980.']

——. *Friedrich A. Hayek*. Forthcoming book developed from Fridriksson's Virginia Polytechnic Institute M. A. thesis in economics.

Gambino, A. 'La Teoria Pura del Capitale e la Politica Bancaria.' *Giornale degli Economista*, 1947 reprinted in the author's *Problemi della Politica Creditizia*, Milano: Malfasi, 1948.

Garrigues, A. 'El individualismo verdadero y falso, segun Hayek.' *Moneda y credito, Revista de economie* 34 (Madrid, 1950): 3—14. ['Individualism: True and False, according to Hayek.']

Garrison, Roger W. 'The Austrian—Neoclassical Relation: A Study in Monetary Dynamics.' University of Virginia, Department of Economics, Ph. D. Dissertation, 1981.

Geddes, John M. 'New Vogue for Critic of Keynes.' *The New York Times* (7 May 1979).

Gerding, R. and Starbatty, J. 'Zur "Entnationalisierung des Geldes." Eine Zwischenbilanz.' Tübingen: Walter Eucken Institut (Vorträge und Aufsätze 78) (J. C. B. Mohr/Paul Siebeck), 1980. ['On the "Denationalisation of Money." An Interim Statement.']

Gilbert, J. C. 'Professor Heyk's Contribution to Trade Cycle Theory.' *Economic Essays in Commemoration of the Dundee School of Economics, 1931—1955*. pp. 51—62.

Glasner, David. 'Friedrich Hayek: An Appreciation.' *Intercollegiate Review* 7 (Summer 1971): 251—255.

Good, D. F. 'The Great Depression and Austrian Growth after 1873.' *The Economic History Review* 31 (1978).

Gordon, Scott. 'The Political Economy of F. A. Hayek.' *Canadian Journal of Economics* 14 (1981): 470—487.

Graf, Hans-Georg. *'Muster-Voraussagen' und 'Erklärungen des Prinzips' bei F. A. von Hayek*. Tübingen: Walter Eucken Institut (Vorträge und Aufsätze 65) (J. C. B. Mohr/P. Siebeck.), 1978. [' "Pattern-Prediction" and "Clarification of Principle" in F. A. von Hayek.']

——. 'Nicht-nomologische Theorie bei Komplexen Sachverhalten.' *Ordo*, Jahrbuch für die Ordnung von Wirtschaft und Gesellschaft 26

(1975): 298–308. ['Non-nomological Theory in Complex Phenomena.']

Graham, F. D. 'Keynes vs. Hayek on a Commodity Reserve Currency.' *The Economic Journal* 54 (1944): 422–429.

Grant, James. 'Hayek: The Road to Stockholm.' *The Alternative: An American Spectator* 8, No. 8 (May 1975): 10–12.

Gray, John N. 'F. A. Hayek on Liberty and Tradition.' *The Journal of Libertarian Studies* 4 (Spring 1980): 119–137.

——. 'Hayek on Liberty, Rights and Justice.' *Ethics: Special Issue on Rights*, 82, No. 1, (October 1981): pp. 73–84.

——. 'Hayek on Spontaneous Order.' Unpublished paper presented to The Carl Menger Society Conference on Hayek, London, 30 October 1982.

——. 'F. A. Hayek and the Rebirth of Classical Liberalism.' *Literature of Liberty*, vol. V, No. 4, (Winter 1982): pp. 19–66.

——. 'Hayek as a Conservative.' *The Salisbury Review* (Summer 1983).

Grinder, Walter E. Review of two books: *Macro-Economic Thinking & The Market Economy* by Ludwig M. Lachmann; and *A Tiger by the Tail: The Keynesian Legacy of Inflation*. In *Libertarian Review* (November 1974): 4–5.

——. Review of 4 books: F. A. Hayek's *The Counter-Revolution of Science; Individualism and Economic Order; Studies in Philosophy, Politics and Economics*; and Ludwig M. Lachmann's *The Legacy of Max Weber*. In *Libertarian Review* 4, No. 4 (April 1975): 4–5.

——. 'In Pursuit of the Subjective Paradigm' and 'Austrian Economics in the Present Crisis of Economic Thought.' In *Capital, Expectations and the Market Process* by Ludwig M. Lachmann. Edited by Walter E. Grinder. Kansas City: Sheed, Andrews & McMeel, Inc. 1977.

——. 'The Austrian Theory of the Business Cycle: Reflections on Some Socio-Economic Effects.' Unpublished paper presented at The Symposium on Austrian Economics, University of Hartford, 22–28 June 1975. [Available at the Institute for Humane Studies, Menlo Park, California 94025.]

Gross, N. T. *The Industrial Revolution in the Hapsburg Monarchy, 1750–1914*. Fontana Economic History of Europe, vol. 4, Part 1. London, 1973.

Haberler, G. *Prosperity and Depression*. 3rd edition, Geneva: 1941, pp. 48–58, 481–491.

Haberler, Gottfried. 'Mises' Private Seminar: Reminiscences.' *The Mont Pèlerin Quarterly* 3 (October 1961): 20–21. [See also an expanded version in *Wirtschaftspolitische Blätter* (Journal of Political Economy,

Vienna) 28, 4 (1981). A Festschrift issue on the Centenary of Ludwig von Mises' birth (1881–1981).]

Hagel III, John. 'From Laissez Faire to *Zwangswirtschaft*: The Dynamics of Interventionism.' Unpublished paper presented to the Symposium on Austrian Economics. University of Hartford, June 22–28, 1975, 37 pp. [Available at the Institute for Humane Studies.]

Hamowy, Ronald. 'Hayek's Conception of Freedom: A Critique.' *New Individualist Review* 1, No. 1 (April 1961): 28–31.

—. 'Freedom and The Rule of Law in F. A. Hayek.' *Il Politico* 36, No. 2 (June 1971): 349–377.

—. 'Law and the Liberal Society: F. A. Hayek's *Constitution of Liberty*.' *Journal of Libertarian Studies* 2, No. 4 (1978): 287–297.

Hampshire, Stuart. *Thought and Action*. London: Chatto and Windam, 1970.

—. 'On Having a Reason.' In G. A. Vesey (ed.) *Human Values*. Royal Institute of Philosophy Lectures, vol. II, 1976–1979: Harvester Press, 1976. Chapter 5.

Haney, Lewis H. *History of Economic Thought*. New York: Macmillan, 1949, 4th edition. [See especially pp. 607–634 ('Fully Developed Subjectivism: The Austrian School.') and pp. 811–831 ('Economic Thought in Germany and Austria, from 1870 to World War II.']

Hansen, A. H. and Tout, H. 'Investment and Saving in Business Cycle Theory.' *Econometrica*, I/3 (1933).

Harris, R. 'On Hayek.' *Swinton Journal* (1970).

Harrod, R. *Money*. London: St. Martin's Press, 1969.

—. 'Professor Hayek on Individualism.' In R. Harrod (ed.) *Economic Essays*, 2nd edition. London and New York: 1972. pp. 293–301.

Hart, H. L. A. *The Concept of Law*. Oxford: Clarendon Press, 1961.

Hartwell, Ronald Max. 'Capitalism and the Historians.' In Fritz Machlup (ed.) *Essays on Hayek*. New York: New York University Press, 1976, pp. 73–94.

Hawtrey, Ralph G. *Capital and Employment*. London, 1937, especially chapter 8: Professor Hayek's *Prices and Production*.'

—. 'The Trade Cycle and Capital Intensity.' *Economica* N. S. 7 (February 1940): 1–15. [Hawtrey was an economist connected with the British Treasury from 1919 to 1937. He 'developed a purely monetary theory of the business cycle on a macro-economic concept of equilibrium.' See citation under Sennholz.]

—. 'Professor Hayek's Pure Theory of Capital.' *Economic Journal* (Royal Economic Society) 51 (London 1941): 281–290.

——. 'Professor Hayek's "Prices and Production".' In *Capital and Employment*, 2nd edition. London: Longmans, Green & Co., 1952, pp. 233–267.

Heimann, E. 'Professor Hayek on German Socialism.' *The American Economic Review.* 35 (1945): 935–937. [Compare with B. Hoselitz.]

Hicks, J. R. 'Maintaining Capital Intact: A Further Suggestion.' *Economica* 9 (1942): 174–179.

——. 'The Hayek Story.' In *Critical Essays in Monetary Theory*. (Oxford University Press: 1967. [See Richard M. Ebeling citation.]

Hicks, J. R. and Weber, W. *Carl Menger and the Austrian School of Economics*. Oxford: Oxford University Press, 1973.

Hoppmann, Erich (ed.) *Friedrich A. von Hayek. Vorträge und Ansprachen auf der Festveranstaltung der Freiburger Wirtschaftswissenschaftlichen Fakultät zum 80. Geburtstag von Friedrich A. von Hayek*. Baden-Baden: Nomos Verlagsgesellschaft, 1980. [Festschrift with bibliography on F. A. Hayek's 80th birthday presented by the Faculty of Economics of the University of Freiburg. Contributors include: Erich Hoppmann, Bernhard Stoeckle, Karl Brandt, Christian Watrin, Hans Otto Lenel, and Klaus Peter Krause. Hayek's 'Dankadresse,' pp. 37–42, surveys highlights in Hayek's intellectual career and writings from the vantage point of his 80th year. The Hoppmann-edited Festschrift honouring Hayek also lists the contributors to the earlier 1979 *Ordo* Festschrift for Hayek, edited by Fritz Meyer, *et. al.* (p. 53), and contains valuable updatings on bibliography by and about Hayek (pp. 55–60.)]

Hoselitz, B. F. 'Professor Hayek on German Socialism.' *The American Economic Review* 35 (1945): 926–934. [Compare with E. Heimann.]

Housinden, Daniel M. *Capital, Profits, and Prices: An Essay in The Philosophy of Economics*. New York: Columbia University Press, 1981.

Howey, Richard S. *The Rise of the Marginal Utility School: 1870–1889*. Lawrence, Kansas: The University of Kansas Press, 1960.

Hoy, Calvin M. 'Hayek's Philosophy of Liberty.' Columbia University Ph. D. Dissertation. New York, 1982.

Hummel, Jeffrey Roger. 'Problems with Austrian Business Cycle Theory.' *Reason Papers* No. 5 (Winter, 1979): 41–53.

Hunt, Lester. 'Toward a Natural History of Morality.' Unpublished essay.

Hutchinson, T. W. *The Politics and Philosophy of Economics: Marxians,*

Keynesians and Austrians. New York and London: New York University Press, 1981.

Institute of Public Affairs Review. *F. A. Hayek Issue*, vol. 30, No. 4 (Melbourne, December 1976).

Janik, Allan and Toulmin, Stephen. *Wittgenstein's Vienna.* New York: Simon and Schuster, 1973. [Important along with Carl Schorske's volume on *Fin-de-siècle Vienna* for the cultural-historical context in which Hayek and his cousin Wittgenstein lived. See A—143.]

Johnson, Hans Chr. Garmann. 'Velferdssatat of Rettsstat — Konflikt eller Harmoni?' Garman Johnsen in *Ideer of Frihet*, No. 1, Bergen: 1982.

Johnson, Frank. 'The Facts of Hayek.' *Sunday Telegraph Magazine* (London, no date, [1975?]): 30—34. [Profile and biographical sketch along with photographs of F. A. Hayek.]

Johnston, William. *The Austrian Mind: An Intellectual and Social History, 1848—1938.* Berkeley, Los Angeles, London: University of California Press, 1972.

Johr, W. A. 'Note on Professor Hayek's "True Theory of Unemployment."' *Kyklos* 30, No. 4 (1970): 713—723.

Jones, Harry W. 'The Rule of Law and the Welfare State.' *Columbia Law Review* 58, No. 2 (February 1958).

Kaldor, N. 'Prof. Hayek and the Concertina Effect.' In *Economica* N. S. 9 (1942): 148—176; reprinted in: Kaldor, *Essays on Economic Stability and Growth.* London: Duckworth, 1960.

Kasp, M. E. *Die geldliche Wechsellagenlehre. Darstellung und Kritik der geldlichen Wechsellagentheorien von Hawtrey, Wicksell und Hayek.* Jena: Fischer, 1939. ['Monetary (Exchange) Models. Representation and Critique of the Monetary (Exchange) Theories of Hawtrey, Wicksell and Hayek.']

Kauder, Emil. 'Intellectual and Political Roots of the Older Austrian School.' *Zeitschrift für Nationalökonomie* 17 (1957): 411—425.

—. *A History of Marginal Utility Theory.* Princeton: Princeton University Press, 1965.

Keizai, S. 'Theories and Thoughts of Prof. Hayek.' *The World Economy.* Tokyo, 1964.

Keynes, J. M. 'A Reply to Dr. Hayek.' *Economica* 12 (November 1931): 387—397. [Cf. Hayek: A—10, A—11a, A—11b.]

Kirzner, Israel M. *The Economic Point of View: An Essay in The History of Economic Thought.* Princeton: Van Nostrand, 1960.

—. 'Divergent Approaches in Libertarian Economic Thought.' *The*

Intercollegiate Review 3 (January—February 1967): 101—108.

—. *Competition and Entrepreneurship*. Chicago and London: The University of Chicago Press, 1973.

—. 'Hayek, Knowledge and Market Processes.' Paper delivered at The Allied Social Science Association meetings in Dallas, Texas. New York: Xerox, 1975.

—. *Perception, Opportunity and Profit. Studies in the Theory of Entrepreneurship*. Chicago and London: University of Chicago Press, 1979. Chapter 2.

—. 'Entrepreneurship, Choice, and Freedom.' In *Verfassung der Freiheit: Festgabe für Friedrich A. von Hayek zur Vollendung seines achtzigsten Lebensjahres*. Edited by Fritz W. Meyer, *et. al.* Stuttgart, New York: Gustav Fischer Verlag (*Ordo* 30) 1979, pp. 245—256.

Knight, F. H. 'Professor Hayek and the Theory of Investment.' *The Economic Journal* 45 (1935): 77—94.

Klein, Daniel. 'F. A. Hayek, Lectures in Retrospect on J. M. Keynes.' *Market Process*, Center for the Study of Market Processes, vol. 1, No. 2 (Summer 1983).

Koslowski, Peter F. 'The Ethics of Capitalism.' In S. Pejovich (ed.) *Philosophical and Economic Foundations of Capitalism*. Toronto: 1983.

Kristol, Irving. 'Capitalism, Socialism and Nihilism.' In *Two Cheers for Capitalism*. New York, 1978. Chapter 7.

Lachmann, Ludwig M. *Macro-economic Thinking and the Market Economy: An Essay on the Neglect of the Micro-Foundations and Its Consequences*. London: The Institute of Economic Affairs (Hobart Paper 56), 1973, 56 pp. Reprinted, Menlo Park, California: Institute for Humane Studies (Studies in Economics, No. 6), 1978. [See also Lachmann's essay 'Toward a Critique of Macroeconomics.' pp. 152—159, in Edwin G. Dolan (ed.) *The Foundations of Modern Austrian Economics*.]

—. 'Methodological Individualism in The Market Economy.' In *Roads to Freedom: Essays in Honour of Friedrich A. von Hayek*. Edited by Erich Streissler *et. al.* London: Routledge & Kegan Paul, 1969. [This essay is also reprinted in *Capital, Expectations...*]

—. 'Reflections on Hayekian Capital Theory.' Paper delivered at The Allied Social Science Association meetings in Dallas, Texas. New York: Xerox, 1975.

—. *Capital, Expectations, and the Market Process: Essays on The Theory of the Market Economy*. Edited with an Introduction by

Walter E. Grinder. Kansas City: Sheed Andrews & McMeel, Inc.; 1977. [See in this volume especially Walter E. Grinder's Introduction 'In Pursuit of the Subjective Paradigm' (pp. 3–24) and his 'Austrian Economics in the Present Crisis of Economic Thought' (pp. 25–41). Noteworthy among Lachmann's articles in this volume are: 'The Significance of The Austrian School of Economics in The History of Ideas' (pp. 45–64), and 'A Reconsideration of the Austrian Theory of Industrial Fluctuations,' (pp. 267–286). The Appendix contains a useful Bibliography of 'The Writings of Ludwig M. Lachmann, ' (pp. 338–340.)]

——. 'From Mises to Shackle: An Essay on Austrian Economics and the Kaleidic Society.' *Journal of Economic Literature* 14 (March 1976): 54–62.

——. 'Austrian Economics under Fire: The Hayek–Sraffa Duel in Retrospect,' 18 pp. [Available at the Institute for Humane Studies.]

——. 'Austrian Economics: An Interview with Ludwig Lachmann.' Interviewed by Richard Ebeling. *Institute Scholar* (Publication of the Institute for Humane Studies) 2, No. 2 (February 1982): 6–9. [The Interview contains interesting facts about Hayek, The London School of Economics, and the Austrian approach to money and inflation.]

——. 'Ludwig von Mises and The Extension of Subjectivism.' In *Method, Process, and Austrian Economics: Essays in Honour of Ludwig von Mises*. Edited by Israel M. Kirzner. Lexington, Massachusetts & Toronto: Lexington Books, D. C. Heath and Company, 1982, pp. 31–40.

Lakatos, I. 'Popper on Demarcation and Induction.' In P. A. Schilpp (ed.) *The Philosophy of Karl Popper*. LaSalle, Illinois; 1973, pp. 241–273.

Lavoie, Don. 'A Critique of the Standard Account of the Socialist Calculation Debate.' *The Journal of Libertarian Studies* 5, No. 1 (Winter 1981): 4–87.

——. 'The Market as a Procedure for the Discovery and Convergence of Inarticulate Knowledge.' Paper presented at The Liberty Fund Conference on Thomas Sowell's *Knowledge and Decisions*. Savannah, Georgia; April 1982. [See *Literature of Liberty* 5 (Summer 1982): 60, for a summary of Lavoie's paper.]

——. 'Rivalry and Central Planning: A Reexamination of the Debate over Economic Calculation under Socialism.' Ph. D. Dissertation, New York University, 1982.

Leduc, G. 'En relisant von Hayek.' *Revue d'Économie Politique* 86 (1976): 491–494. ['Rereading von Hayek.']

Leoni, Bruno. *Freedom and the Law.* Princeton, New Jersey: D. Van Nostrand, 1961.

Lepage, Henri. 'Hayek ou l'économie politique de la liberté.' ['Hayek or The Political Economy of Liberty']. Part 6 of *Demain le libéralism* ['Tomorrow Liberalism']. Paris: Le Livre de Poche (8358L), Collection *Pluriel*, 1980, pp. 409–453. [Lepage, author of the influential *Tomorrow, Capitalism*, surveys the scholarly achievements of Hayek, covering the Austrian School of Economics, Hayek's theory of the business cycle, his rivalry with Keynes, the value of liberty, the Road to Serfdom, and Hayek's 'Grand Synthesis' (*Law, Legislation and Liberty*). The article is sprinkled by anecdotes culled from a long interview with Hayek in February 1979.]

Letwin, Shirley Robin. 'The Achievements of Friedrich A. Hayek.' In Fritz Machlup (ed.) *Essays on Hayek*. New York: New York University Press, 1976, pp. 147–162.

Leube, Kurt R. 'Friedrich A. von Hayek – Nobelpreis für Wirtschaftswissenschaften.' (University of Salzburg Research Papers, 1974). ['Friedrich A. von Hayek – Nobel Prize for Economic Science.']

——. 'F. A. von Hayek. Zu seinem 75. Geburtstag.' *Salzburger Nachrichten* (1975). ['F. A. von Hayek. On His 75th Birthday.']

——. 'Inflationstheorie bei Hayek und Keynes.' (Paper prepared for a Seminar at the University of Salzburg, 1975). ['Inflation Theory in Hayek and Keynes.']

——. 'Vorwort und Bibliographie zur Wiederauflage F. A. Hayek: *Geldtheorie und Konjunkturtheorie*. Salzburg, 1975. ['Foreword and Bibliography to the Second (German) Edition of F. A. Hayek, *Geltheorie*,' (B–1).]

——. 'Ausgewählte Bibliographie zur Wiederauflage F. A. Hayek: *Preise und Produktion*.' Vienna, 1975. ['Selected Bibliography to the Second (German) Edition of F. A. Hayek's *Prices and Production*,' (B–2).]

——. 'Hayek's Perception of the "Rules of Law".' *The Intercollegiate Review* (Winter 1976/1977).

——. 'Bibliographischer Anhang.' In F. A. Hayek, *Geldtheorie und Konjunkturtheorie*. Salzburg: 2. erw. Aufl., 1976, pp. 148–160. [Kurt Leube was from 1969–1977 Hayek's Research Assistant and associate at the University of Salzburg. He currently is Managing Coeditor with Albert Zlabinger of The International Carl Menger Library,

194 *Bibliography*

Phiosophia-Verlag, and is working on a life of Eugen von Böhm-Bawerk. He has written and lectured extensively on Hayek and The Austrian School of Economics. The 'Bibliographical Appendix' in this entry on the German reprinting of Hayek's *Geldtheorie* (B—1), is but one of an extensive number of scholarly and bibliographic contributions by Leube on Hayek. In subesequent editions of the present *Bibliography* we will cite the extensive writings by Leube.]

——. 'Bibliographisches Nachwort zur Wiederauflage F. A. Hayek: *Individualismus und wirtschaftliche Ordnung.*' (Salzburg 1977). ['Bibliographical Afterword to the Second (German) Edition of F. A. Hayek: (B—7).']

——. 'Böhm-Bawerk, Wieser und Hayek.' (Unpublished paper presented in Bonn, 1977.)

——. 'Wer sind die "Austrians".' *Wirtschaftspolitische Blätter*, 1978. ['Who Are the "Austrians".']

——. 'Ökonom und Philosoph: Zum 80. Geburtstag des grossen Österreichers Friedrich A. von Hayek.' *Die Industrie* 19 (1979). ['Economist and Philosopher: On the 80th Birthday of the great Austrian Friedrich A. von Hayek.']

——. 'F. A. Hayek — Zum 80. Geburtstag.' *Zeitschrift für das gesamte Kreditwesen*. Frankfurt am Main 1979. ['F. A. Hayek — On his 80th Birthday.']

——. 'Hayek und die österr. Schule der Nationalökonomie.' *Bayern Kurier* (Munich 1979). ['Hayek and the Austrian School of Economics.']

Liggio, Leonard P. 'Hayek — An Overview.' Unpublished paper presented to The Carl Menger Society Conference entitled 'Hayek — An Introductory Course,' London, 6 December 1980. [See also contributions at this conference by Pirie, Ebeling, Steele, Graham Smith, and Shearmur. The edited papers, are available through the Institute for Humane Studies.]

Lippincott, Benjamin E. (ed.) *On the Economic Theory of Socialism.* New York: Augustus M. Kelley, 1970.

Loenen, J. H. M. M. 'The Concept of Freedom in Berlin and Others: An Attempt at Clarification.' *The Journal of Value Inquiry* 10 (Winter 1976): 279—285.

Lutz, Friedrich A. 'Professor Hayek's Theory of Interest.' *Economica* 10 (1943): 302—310.

——. 'On Neutral Money.' In *Roads to Freedom: Essays in Honour of Friedrich A. von Hayek*. Edited by Erich Streissler *et. al.* London: Routledge & Kegan Paul, 1969, pp. 105—116.

Lynch, Thomas E. 'Toward a Rational Political Philosophy: An Essay on the Origins of Hayek's Liberal Radicalism.' B. A. Honours Thesis for The Degree in Political Economy. Williamstown, Massachusetts; Williams College, January 1981, 72 pp. [Available at the Institute for Humane Studies, Menlo Park, California 94025.]

McClain, Stephen Michael. 'The Political Thought of the Austrian School of Economics.' The Johns Hopkins University Ph. D. Dissertation. Baltimore, 1979. [McClain's premiss is that 'the Austrian School, through the writings of Ludwig von Mises and Friedrich von Hayek, explicitly and comprehensively fashioned a political theory for capitalism.' Chapters on Hayek cover his political thought, concept of liberty, limits of knowledge and the spontaneous order, the rule of law, and constitutionalism.]

Macfie, A. L. *Theories of the Trade Cycle*. London: MacMillan, 1934. [Deals with Hayek's *Geldtheorie und Konjunkturtheorie* (B−1) and *Preise und Produktion* (B−2) on pp. 45−87.]

Machlup, Fritz. 'Liberalism and the Choice of Freedoms' In *Roads to Freedom: Essays in Honour of Friedrich A. von Hayek*. Edited by Erich Streissler *et. al.*: London: Routledge & Kegan Paul, 1969, pp. 117−146. [Machlup has been a close personal and intellectual friend of Hayek's since the early 1920s.]

—. 'Friedrich von Hayek's Contribution to Economics.' *The Swedish Journal of Economics* 76 (December 1974): 498−531. [Reprinted in revised, updated form as 'Hayek's Contribution to Economics' in Machlup's *Essays on Hayek* (1976).]

— (ed.). 'Hayek's Contribution to Economics.' In *Essays on Hayek* with a Foreword by M. Friedman. New York: New York University Press, 1976, pp. 13−59. [Contains the proceedings of a special regional meeting of the Mont Pélèrin Society (August 24−28, 1975) held at Hillsdale College (Michigan). Contributors to this quasi-Festschrift include Fritz Machlup, William F. Buckley, Jr, Gottfried Dietze, Ronald Max Hartwell, Shirley Robbin Letwin, George C. Roche III, and Arthur Shenfield. This volume contains 'Excerpts of The Official Announcement of the (Swedish) Royal Academy of Sciences' (p. xv, ff) pertaining to Hayek's Nobel Prize in Economics. Also included is Hayek's brief banquet speech reprinted from the Nobel Foundation's volume *Les Prix Nobel 1974*, pp. 38−39.]

—. 'Friedrich von Hayek on Scientific and Scientistic Attitudes.' *The Swedish Journal of Economics* 76 (1974). [Reprinted in Machlup,

Methodology of Economics and Other Social Sciences. New York and London, 1978, pp. 513—519.]

——. *Würdigung der Werke von Friedrich August von Hayek.* Tübingen: Walter Eucken Institut (Vorträge und Aufsätze, Heft 62), 1977, pp. 63—75.
['Assessment of the Works of Friedrich August von Hayek.']

Mackie, J. L. *Ethics: Inventing Right and Wrong.* London: Penguin Books, 1977. pp. 83—102.

Maling, Charles E. 'Austrian Business Cycle Theory and Its Implications.' *Reason Papers* No. 2 (Fall 1975): 65—90.

Mantoux, E. *L'Epargne Forcée Monétaire.* Lyon: Borc & Riou, 1941, pp. 52—62, 151—161, 191—200.

Marget, Arthur W. 'Review of Friedrich A. Hayek, *Prices and Production* and *Preise und Produktion.*' *Journal of Political Economy* 40 (April 1932): 261—266.

Marrama, V. 'Teoria e Politica della Piena Occupazione.' In *La Teoria Hayekiana dell' Effetto di Ricardo,* Rome: Ediz. Ital., 1948, chapter VII, pp. 129—144.

Matis, H. *Österreichs Wirtschaft 1848—1913.* ['Austria's Economy, 1848—1913.'] Berlin, 1972.

——. "Sozioökonomische Aspekte des Liberalismus in Österreich 1848—1918.' ['Socio-economic Aspects of Liberalism in Austria, 1848—1918.'] In H.-U. Wehler (ed.) *Sozialgeschichte Heute.* Göttingen: 1974.

May, Arthur. *Vienna in the Age of Franz Josef.* Norman: University of Oklahoma Press, 1966. [See especially chapter 3, 'The Kingdom of Learning.' and chapter 7, 'Science and Scholarship.']

Melis, R. 'Rettifiche al neutralismo economico.' *Il Politico* 16 (1951) 275—284.
['Alterations in Economic Neutrality.']

Meyer, Fritz W. *et al.* (eds) *Zur Verfassung der Freiheit: Festgabe für Friedrich A. von Hayek zur Vollendung seines achtzigsten Lebensjahres.* Stuttgart, New York: Gustav Fischer Verlag. (*Ordo:* Jahrbuch für die Ordnung von Wirtschaft und Gesellschaft, vol. 30), 1979. ['On the Constitution of Liberty: A Gift for Friedrich A. von Hayek on the Completion of his 80th Year.' This Festschift honouring Hayek contains contributions from Karl Popper, Chiaki Nishiyama, George J. Stigler, Ludwig M. Lachmann, Charles K. Rowley, Arthur Seldon, Christian Watrin, Israel Kirzner, James M. Buchanan, Milton Friedman, and others.]

Milgate, M. 'On the Origin of the Notion of "Intertemporal Equilibrium".' *Economica* 46 (Fall 1979). [Cf. Hayek, A–6.]

Miller, David. 'Review of *Law, Legislation and Liberty*, vol. II: The Mirage of Social Justice.' *British Journal of Law and Society* 4 (Summer 1977): 142–145.

Miller, Eugene F. 'Hayek's Critique of Reason.' *Modern Age* 20, No. 4 (Fall 1976): 383–394.

—. 'The Cognitive Basis of Hayek's Political Thought.' In Robert L. Cunningham *Liberty and the Rule of Law*. College Station and London: Texas A & M University Press, 1979, pp. 242–267.

Miller, Robert. 'Hayek, the Inter-War Years and the Gold Standard.' Unpublished paper presented to The Carl Menger Society, 10 June 1978.

Minard, Lawrence. 'Wave of the Past? Or Wave of the Future?' *Forbes* (1 October 1979): 45–50, 52. [Profile on Hayek with painting of Hayek featured in the cover of this issue of *Forbes*. This painting is now at the Heritage Foundation in Washington, D. C.]

Mises, Ludwig von. *Bureaucracy*. New Haven: Yale University Press, 1944.

—' *Human Action*. Chicago: Henry Regnery, 1966.

—. *The Historical Setting of the Austrian School*. New Rochelle, New York, 1969.

—. *The Theory of Money and Credit*. Irvington-on-Hudson, New York: Foundation for Economic Education, 1971; Indianapolis: Liberty *Classics*, 1981. [Foreword by Murray N. Rothbard, (1981); Preface by Lionel Robbins (1934)]

—. *On the Manipulation of Money and Credit*. Dobbs Ferry, New York: Free Market Books, 1978.

Molsberger, G. 'Grundsätzliches über Freiheit, Ordnung und Wettbewerb.' In *Ordo*, Jahrbuch 24 (1973): 315–325. ['Basic Principle of Freedom, Order and Competition.']

Morrell, Stephen O. 'In Search of a New Monetary Order. An Open Discussion on Aspects of a Freely Competitive Monetary Arrangement.' *Institute Scholar* (Publication of the Institute for Humane Studies) 1, No. 2, (1980): 1–2.

Morris, M. W. 'The Political Thought of F. A. Hayek.' *Political Studies* 2 (1972): 169–184.

Moss, Lawrence S. (ed.). *The Economics of Ludwig von Mises: Toward a Critical Reappraisal*. Kansas City: Sheed and Ward, Inc., 1976. [This volume resulted from the Symposium on the Economics of

Ludwig von Mises, Atlanta, Georgia, 5 November 1974 to assess the recently deceased Mises' (29 September 1881–10 October 1973) contributions to economic and social thought. Among the interesting essays included in this volume are Fritz Machlup's 'The Monetary Economics of Ludwig von Mises' and Israel M. Kirzner's 'Ludwig von Mises and Economic Calculation under Socialism.' Since Hayek's life and writings are intimately connected with those of von Mises, this volume offers a valuable research tool in Fritz Machlup's two *Appendices* on Mises: 'Chronology' and 'Major Translated Writings of Ludwig von Mises.']

Murray, A. H. 'Professor Hayek's Philosophy.' *Economica* 12 (August 1945): 149–162.

Nagel, E. 'The Logic of Social Science.' *The Journal of Philosophy*, XLXI (1951). Reprinted in the author's *Logic Without Metaphysics*, Glenco, Ill.: Free Press, 1956, pp. 361–368.

Nawroth, E. E. *Die Sozial- und Wirtschaftsphilosophie des Neoliberalismus.* Heidelberg: Kerle and Lowen: Nauwelaerts, 1961. ['The Social and Economic Philosophy of Neoliberalism.']

Nishiyama, Chiaki. 'The Theory of Self-Love. An Essay on the Methodology of the Social Sciences, and Especially of Economics, with Special Reference to Bernard Mandeville.' University of Chicago Ph.D. Dissertation, 1960.
[Nishiyama's dissertation was done under Hayek's supervision. From 1950–1962 Hayek was professor of social and moral science in the Committee of Social Thought headed by John U. Nef at the University of Chicago. 1960 also saw the publication of Hayek's B–12.]

——. 'Hayek's Theory of Sensory Order and the Methodology of the Social Sciences.' *The Journal of Applied Sociology* 7 (Tokyo 1964).

——. 'Revival of the Philosophy of Economics: A Critique of Hayek's System of Liberty.' *The Economics Studies Quarterly* 15, No. 2. (Tokyo 1965).

——. 'Arguments for the Principles of Liberty and the Philosophy of Science.' *Il Politico* 32 (June 1967): 336–347.
[Commentary on and response to Hayek, A–115.]

——. 'Anti-Rationalism or Critical Rationalism.' In *Zur Verfassung der Freiheit: Festgabe für Friedrich A. von Hayek zur Vollendung seines achtzigsten Lebensjahres.* Edited by Fritz W. Meyer *et al.* Stuttgart, New York: Gustav Fischer Verlag (*Ordo* 30) 1979, pp. 21–42.

——. *Human Capitalism.* A Presidential Lecture delivered at the 1981

Stockholm Regional Meeting of the Mont Pélèrin Society, 30 August 1981. Hoover Institution, Stanford University, 1982, 33pp.

North, Gary. 'Hayek's Evolutionism.' In *The Dominion Covenant: Genesis.* Tyler, Texas: Institute for Christian Economics, 1982, pp. 326–342.

Nozick, Robert. *Anarchy, State, and Utopia.* New York: Basic Books, 1974.

——. 'On Austrian Methodology.' *Synthese* 36 (1977): 353–392.

Oakeshott, Michael. *Rationalism in Politics.* London: Methuen, 1962.

O'Driscoll, Jr, Gerald P. 'Hayek and Keynes: A Retrospective Assessment.' Iowa State University Department of Economics Staff Paper No. 20. Ames, Iowa: Xerox, 1975. [Paper prepared for the Symposium on Austrian Economics, University of Hartford, 22–28 June 1975.]

——. 'Comments on Professor Machlup's Paper.' Unpublished manuscript presented at a special regional meeting of the Mont Pélèrin Society, held 24–28 August 1975, at Hillsdale College in Hillsdale, Michigan. [The quasi-Festschrift volume (*Essays on Hayek.* Edited by Fritz Machlup. New York: New York University Press, 1975) was a product of the Hillsdale Mont Pélèrin meeting and included the important Fritz Machlup bibliographical essay (in revised form) to which Prof. O'Driscoll alludes in his title. O'Driscoll's comments in this unpublished manuscript assess Hayek's contributions to economic and social theory.]

——. 'Spontaneous Order and the Coordination of Economic Activities.' *The Journal of Libertarian Studies*, 1, No. 2 (Spring 1977): 137–151.

——. *Economics as a Coordination Problem: The Contributions of Friedrich A. Hayek* with a foreword by F. A. Hayek. Kansas City: Sheed Andrews & McMeel, 1977.

——. 'Frank A. Fetter and "Austrian" Business Cycle Theory.' *History of Political Economy* 12, 4 (1980): 542–557.

O'Driscoll, Gerald P. and Rizzo, Mario J. 'What is Austrian Economics?' Presented at The American Economic Association meetings in Denver, October 1980, 70 pp. [A revised and enlarged version will be forthcoming as a book: Oxford: Basil Blackwell, 1983, to be entitled *The Economics of Time and Ignorance.*]

O'Neill, John. (ed.) *Modes of Individualism and Collectivism.* London: Heinemann, 1973. [A wide-ranging anthology of articles, including Hayek's 'Scientism and the Study of Society' (A–46), sections from Karl Popper's *The Poverty of Historicism* (1961). etc. The

O'Neill anthology presents the methodological debate in the social sciences over scientism and the confrontation between methodological individualism and its opponents. Contains a valuable bibliography on these issues, pp. 339—346. See also Jeffrey Paul (1974).]

Ordo Jahrbuch. *Hayek Festschrift*, vol. 30, Fischer Verlag, 1979.

Palmer, G. G. D. 'The Rate of Interest in the Trade Cycle Theories of Prof. Hayek.' *The South African Journal of Economics* 23 (1955): 1—18.

Pasour, Jr, E. C. 'Cost and Choice — Austrians vs. Conventional Views.' *The Journal of Libertarian Studies* (Winter 1978): 327—336.

Paul, Jeffrey Elliott. 'Individualism, Holism, and Human: An Investigation into Social Scientific Methodology.' Brandeis University (Department of Philosophy) Ph.D. Dissertation [74—16, 832] 1974. [See also John O'Neill (ed.) 1973).]

Peel, J. D. Y. *Herbert Spencer: The Evolution of a Sociologist.* London: Heinemann, 1971.

Pigou, A. C. 'Maintaining Capital Intact, on F. A. von Hayek: The Pure Theory of Capital.' *Economica* 8 (1941): 271—275.

Pirie, Madsen. 'Hayek — An Introduction.' Unpublished paper presented to The Carl Menger Society Conference entitled 'Hayek — An Introductory Course,' London, 6 December 1980.

Plant, Sir Arnold. 'A Tribute to Hayek — The Rational Persuader.' *Economic Age* 2, No. 2 (January—February, 1970): 4—8.

Polanyi, Michael. 'The Determinants of Social Action.' In *Roads to Freedom: Essays in Honour of Friedrich A. von Hayek.* Edited by Erich Streissler *et. al.* London: Routledge & Kegan Paul, 1969, pp. 145—179. [A paper on the polycentric self-regulating processes of the spontaneous order vs. central planning. Polanyi originally presented the present essay at the University of Chicago in 1950, the year in which Hayek joined the Committee on Social Thought at the University of Chicago. See also Polanyi's *The Logic of Liberty.* London and Chicago, 1951.]

Prebisch, Raúl. 'The Ideas of Friedrich von Hayek.' *Cepal Review* No. 15 (December, 1981).

Quine, W. V. *Ontological Relativity.* New York, 1969.

Raico, Ralph. 'A Libertarian Maestro.' *The Alternative: An American Spectator* 8, No. 8 (May 1975): 21—23. [Analysis of Hayek.]

Ranulf, Sv. 'On the Survival Chances of Democracy.' Aarhus (Universitetsforlaget). Copenhagen: Munksgaard, 1948.

Raz, Joseph. 'The Rule of Law and Its Virtues.' *Law Quarterly Review*

93 (April 1977): 185—211. [Reprinted in Cunningham (1979), pp. 3—21.]

Reekie, W. Duncan. *Industry, Prices and Markets.* Oxford: Philip Allan Publishers, Ltd. 1979. American Publisher, John Wiley, 1979.

Rees, J. C. 'Hayek on Liberty.' *Philosophy* (1961).

Rhees, Rush. *Without Answers.* London: Routledge & Kegan Paul, 1969.

Rizzo, Mario J. *Time, Uncertainty and Equilibrium — Explorations on Austrian Themes.* Lexington, Mass.: Heath and Co., 1979.

Robbins, Lionel. 'Hayek on Liberty.' *Economica* (February 1961): 66—81. [Cf. following version of this article.]

——. 'Hayek on Liberty.' *Economics and Politics.* London: Macmillan, 1963. [Cf. preceding version of this article.]

——. *Autobiography of an Economist.* London: Macmillan & Co., 1971.

Roberts, Paul Craig. *Alienation in the Soviet Economy.* Albuquerque: University of New Mexico Press, 1971.

Robertson, David J. 'Why I Am a Conservative.' Unpublished paper presented to The Carl Menger Society, 11 March 1978. [A critique of Hayek's 'Why I am not a Conservative.']

Roche III, George C. 'The Relevance of Friedrich A. Hayek.' In Fritz Machlup (ed.) *Essays on Hayek.* New York: New York University Press, 1976, 1—12.

Rothbard, Murray N. *Man, Economy and State.* Princeton, N. J.: D. Van Nostrand, 1962.

——. 'The Case for a 100 Percent Gold Dollar.' In Leland B. Yeager (ed.) *In Search of Monetary Constitution.* Cambridge, Mass.: Harvard University Press, 1962, pp. 94—136.

——. 'Money, The State and Modern Mercantilism.' *Modern Age* (Summer 1963): 279—289.

——. 'Von Mises, Ludwig.' In *International Encyclopaedia of the Social Sciences.* Edited by David L. Sills. New York: The Macmillan Company & The Free Press, 1968, 1972, vol. 15, 16, 17, pp. 379—382.

——. 'Conservatives Gratified by Nobel Prize to Von Hayek.' *Human Events* (16 November 1974).

——. *America's Great Depression.* Kansas City: Sheed & Ward, 1975.

——. 'The Austrian Theory of Money.' In Edwin G. Dolan (ed.) *The Foundations of Modern Austrian Economics.* Kansas City: Sheed & Ward, 1976, pp. 160—184.

——. 'The New Deal and The International Monetary System.' In *Watershed of Empire: Essays on New Deal Foreign Policy.* Edited by

Leonard P. Liggio and James J. Martin. With a Preface by Felix Morley. Colorado Springs: Ralph Myles, Publisher, 1976, pp. 19–64.

——. 'Inflation and the Business Cycle: The Collapse of the Keynesian Paradigm.' In *For a New Liberty*. New York: Collier Macmillan, 1978, pp. 171–193.

——. *What Has Government Done to Our Money?* Novato, California: Libertarian Publishers, 1978.

——. 'F. A. Hayek and the Concept of Coercion.' *Ordo* 31 (Stuttgart, New York: Gustav Fischer Verlag, 1980), pp. 43–50. [See following citation.]

——. 'F. A. Hayek and the Concept of Coercion.' In *The Ethics of Liberty*. Atlantic Highlands, N. J.: Humanities Press 1981, Chapter 28. [See preceding citation for original publication of this essay.]

——. 'The Laissez-Faire Radical: A Quest for the Historical Mises.' *The Journal of Libertarian Studies* 5, No. 3 (Summer 1981): 237–254.

Roy, Subroto. 'On Liberty and Economic Growth: Preface to a Philosophy for India.' Cambridge University Ph.D. Dissertation, 1982.

Rudner, R. S. 'Philosophy and Social Science.' *Philosophy of Science* XXI/2 (April 1954).

Rueff, Jacques. 'Laudatio: Un Message pour le siècle.' In Erich Streissler *et al.* (eds.) *Roads to Freedom: Essays in Honour of Friedrich A. von Hayek*. London: Routledge & Kegan Paul, 1969, pp. 1–3. [Tribute to Hayek's intellectual achievements: 'Laudatio: a Message for the Age,' presented for the Hayek 70th birthday Festschrift.]

Rupp, Hanns Heinrich. 'Zweikammersystem und Bundesverfassungsgericht. Bemerkungen zu einem verfassungspolitischen Reformvorschlag F. A. von Hayeks.' In *Zur Verfassung der Freiheit: Festgabe für Friedrich A. von Hayek zur Vollendung seines achtzigsten Lebensjahres*. Stuttgart, New York: Gustav Fischer Verlag, 1979, pp. 95–104. ['A Two-Chamber System and the Federal Constitutional Court – Notes on a Proposition of F. A. von Hayek for a Constitutional Reform.']

Ryle, Gilbert. 'Knowing How and Knowing That.' *Proceedings of the Aristotelian Society* 46, (1945/1946): 1–16.

Sabrin, Murray and Corbin, Peter B. (American Geographical Society.) 'Geographical Implications of Austrian Trade-Cycle Theory: An Analysis of the U.S. Economy, 1947–1972.' A Preliminary Report to the Fred C. Koch Foundation. Wichita, Kansas (February 1976), 68 pp. [Empirical studies testing Austrian trade-cycle theory, accompanied by computer graphic print-out. See Corbin. Available at the Institute for Humane Studies.]

Sacristan, A. 'Friedrich August von Hayek o el intento de romper con la neoclassica.' In *Comercio Esterior* 25 (1975), pp. 193—195. ['Friedrich August von Hayek on the Intention of Breaking with Neoclassicism.']

Sampson, Geoffrey. 'Nozick vs. Hayek; Retrospective vs. Anticipant Liberalism.' Unpublished paper presented to The Carl Menger Society Conference on Nozick, 27 October 1979.

Sarduski, W. 'The Political Doctrine of Neoliberalism and the Problem of Democracy.' *Panstwo i Prawo* 3 (1978): 90—100.

Saulnier, R. J. *Contemporary Monetary Theory: Studies on Some Recent Theories of Money, Prices and Production.* New York: Columbia University Press, 1938 and London: King, 1938.

Schorske, Carl E. *Fin-de-siècle Vienna, Politics and Culture.* New York: Basic Books, 1980. [See also Allan Janik and Stephen Toulmin, *Wittgenstein's Vienna* (1973); Arthur May, *Vienna in the Age of Franz Josef* (1966); and William Johnston, *The Austrian Mind: An Intellectual and Social History, 1848—1938.* Berkeley, Los Angeles, London: University of California Press, 1972.]

Schuller, A. 'Konkurrenz der Währungen als geldwirtschaftliches Ordnungsprinzip.' In *Wirtschaftspolitische Chronik* (Institut für Wirtschaftspolitik an der Universität Köln) 26 (1977): 23—50. ['Concurrent Monetary Standards as an Ordering Principle of Monetary Economics.']

Schumpeter, Joseph. *Capitalism, Socialism and Democracy.* London: Unwin, 1974. New York: Harper and Row, 1950.

——. *History of Economic Analysis.* Edited from manuscript by Elizabeth Boody Schumpeter. New York: Oxford University Press, 1954, 1966.

Scott, K. J. 'Methodological and Epistemological Individualism.' *The British Journal of the Philosophy of Science* 2 (1960/1961).

Seldon, Arthur. 'Hayek on Liberty and Liberalism.' *Contemporary Review* 200 (1961): 399—406.

—— (ed.). 'Philosophy' *Agenda for a Free Society: Essays on Hayek's The Constitution of Liberty.* London: Published for the Institute of Economic Affairs by Hutchinson, 1961.

Seligman, Ben B. *Main Currents in Modern Economics: Economic Thought Since 1870.* New York: The Free Press of Glencoe, 1962.

Sennholz, Hans F. 'Chicago Monetary Tradition in the Light of

Austrian Theory.' *Reason* 3, No. 7 (October 1971): 24—30.

Shackle, G. L. S. *Epistemics and Economics: A Critique of Economic Doctrines*. Cambridge: Cambridge University Press, 1972, 1976.

Shackle, G. L. S. 'F. A. Hayek, 1899 — .' In D. P. O'Brian and John R. Presley (eds.) *Pioneers of Modern Economics in Britain*. London: Macmillan. New York: Barnes & Noble.

Shearmur, Jeremy. 'Hayek, Smith (and Hume).' Unpublished manuscript of paper presented at one-day Conference on Hayek at University College, London, 28 October 1978, and sponsored by The Carl Menger Society.

——. 'Libertarianism and Conservatism in the Work of F. A. von Hayek.' Unpublished manuscript; lecture originally presented to The Carl Menger Society in London, 1976.

——. 'Menger, Hayek & Methodological Individualism.' Unpublished paper presented to The Carl Menger Society, 11 February 1978.

——. 'Abstract Institutions in an Open Society.' In H. Berghel *et al.* (eds.) *Wittgenstein, The Vienna Circle and Critical Materialism*. Vienna: Hölder-Richler-Tempsky, 1979, pp. 349—354.

——. 'Hayek and the Invisible Hand.' Unpublished paper presented to the Seminar for Austro-German Philosophy at Carl Menger joint conference on Austrian Philosophy and Austrian Politics, London, 26 April 1980.

——. 'Hayek on Politics.' Unpublished paper presented to The Carl Menger Society conference entitled 'Hayek — An Introductory Course,' London, 6 December 1980.

——. 'Hayek on Law,' Unpublished paper presented to The Carl Menger Society Conference on Hayek, London, 30 October 1982.

——. *Adam Smith's Second Thoughts*. (Pamphlet). London: Adam Smith Club, 1982.

——. 'The Austrian Connection: F. A. Hayek and the Thought of Carl Menger.' In B. Smith and W. Grassl (eds.) *Austrian Philosophy and Austrian Politics*. Munich: Philosophia Verlag, forthcoming (1982—1983).

Shenfield, Arthur. 'Scientism and the Study of Society.' In Fritz Machlup (ed.) *Essays on Hayek*. New York: New York University Press, 1976, 61—72.

——. 'Friedrich A. Hayek: Nobel Prizewinner.' In Fritz Machlup (ed.) *Essays on Hayek*. New York: New York University Press, 1976, pp. 171—176.

——. 'The New Thought of F. A. Hayek.' *Modern Age* 20 (Winter 1976): 54—61.

Shenoy, Sudha R. 'Introduction: The Debate, 1931—71, ' in F. A. Hayek, *A Tiger by the Tail: The Keynesian Legacy of Inflation.* Compiled and Introduced by Sudha Shenoy. London: The Institute of Economic Affairs, 1972, pp. 1—12.

Shibata, K. *A Dynamic Theory of World Capitalism*, 2nd edition. Kyoto: Sanwa Shobo, September 1954.

Silverman, Paul. 'Law and Economics in Interwar Vienna: Kelsen, Mises, and the Geistkreis.' University of Chicago Dissertation.

—. 'Science and Liberalism in Interwar Vienna: The Mises and Vienna Circles.' Paper prepared for the Liberty Fund Seminar on Austrian Economics and its Historical and Philosophical Background, Graz, Austria. 28—31 July 1980, 53 pp. Available at the Institute for Humane Studies, Menlo Park, California 94025. [This Conference had contributions by Israel Kirzner, Ludwig Lachmann, Carl Schorske and others.]

Simson, W. von 'Zu F. A. Hayeks verfassungsrechtlichen Ideen.' *Der Staat, Zeitschrift für Staatslehre, Öffentliches Recht und Verfassungsgeschichte.* Berlin 18, No. 3, (1979): 403—421. ['On F. A. Hayek's Ideas of Constitutional Justice.']

Somers, H. M. *Public Finance and National Income.* Philadelphia: Blakiston, 1949, pp. 93—101.

Smith, Graham. 'Hayek on Law.' Unpublished paper presented to The Carl Menger Society conference entitled 'Hayek — An Introductory Course,' London, 6 December 1980.

Smithies, A. 'Professor Hayek on the Pure Theory of Capital.' *American Economic Review*, XXXI/4, (December 1941).

Sowell, Thomas. *Knowledge and Decisions.* New York: Basic Books, 1980.

Spadero, Louis M. (ed.) *New Directions in Austrian Economics.* Kansas City: Sheed Andrews & McMeel, 1978.

Spencer, Roger W. 'Inflation, Unemployment and Hayek.' *Review* (Federal Reserve Bank of St. Louis.) 57 (1975): 6—10.

Spiegel, Henry William. *The Growth of Economic Thought.* Chapter 23: 'The Austrian School Accent on Utility.' [Also note Spiegel's valuable annotated *Bibliography*.]

Sraffa, Piero. 'Dr. Hayek on Money and Capital [on F. A. von Hayek's *Prices and Production*] London 1931.' *The Economic Journal* 42 (1932): 42—53, 249—251.

Stadler, M. 'Vollbeschäftigung um jeden Preis?' *Wirtschaft und Gesellschaft* 3 (1978); ['Full Employment at any Price?']

Steedman, Ian. 'On some Concepts of Rationality in Economics.'

No date, 27 pp. [Deals with Hayek's notion of economic rationality and cites Hayek's A—34 and A—46. Available at the Institute for Humane Studies.]

Steele, David Ramsey. 'Spontaneous Order and Traditionalism in Hayek.' Expanded version of a paper delivered to The Colloquium on Austrian Philosophy and Austrian Politics, organized jointly by The Seminar for Austro-German Philosophy and The Carl Menger Society, at the Institute of Comtemporary Arts, London, 26—27 April 1980, 75 pp. (Available at the Institute for Humane Studies.)

——. 'Hayek on Socialism.' Unpublished paper presented to The Carl Menger Society Conference entitled 'Hayek — An Introductory Course,' London, 6 December 1980.

——. 'Posing The Problem: The Impossibility of Economic Calculation under Socialism.' *The Journal of Libertarian Studies.* 5, No. 1 (Winter 1981): 7—22.

Steiner, Hillel. 'Hayek and Liberty.' Unpublished paper presented to The Carl Menger Society Conference on Hayek, 28 October 1978.

Stewart, William P. 'Methodological Individualism: A Commentary on F. A. von Hayek.' Unpublished paper presented at the First Libertarian Scholars Conference. New York, 23—24 September 1972.

Stigler, George J. 'The Development of Utility Theory.' *Journal of Political Economy* 58 (1950): 307—327, 372—396.

Streeten, P. 'Principles and Problems of a Liberal Order of the Economy.' *Weltwirtschaftliches Archiv* 104 (1970): 1—5.

Streissler, Erich *et. al.* (eds.) *Roads to Freedom: Essays in Honour of Friedrich A. von Hayek.* London: Routledge & Kegan Paul, 1969. [This Festschrift of 'honourary essays' presented to Hayek on his 70th birthday includes essays by Streissler, Jacques Rueff, Peter T. Bauer, James M. Buchanan, Gottfried Haberler, George N. Halm, Ludwig M. Lachmann, Friedrich A. Lutz, Fritz Machlup, Frank W. Paish, Michael Polanyi, Karl R. Popper, Günter Schmölders, and Gordon Tulloch. This Festschrift also contains the first extensive Hayek bibliography, pp. 309—315, composed in the early months of 1969. Streissler's own contributions in *Road to Freedom* include a useful 'Introduction' to Hayek's life and writings and the essay 'Hayek on Growth: A Reconsideration on His Early Theoretical Work,' pp. 245—285.]

——. (ed.) 'Bibliography of the Writings of Friedrich A. von Hayek.' *Roads to Freedom: Essays in Honour of Friedrich A. von Hayek.* London: Routledge & Kegan Paul, 1969, pp. 309—315. [This bibliography is the earliest of the extensive Hayek bibliographies, presented as part of a Festschrift to Hayek on his 70th birthday. See previous citation.]

Streissler, Erich and Watrin, Christian (eds.) with the collaboration of Monika Streissler. *Zur Theorie marktwirtschaftlicher Ordnungen.* Tübingen: J. C. B. Mohr (Paul Siebeck), 1980. ['On the Theory of Market Economic Orders.' Twelve articles and 9 commentaries on the philosophical, evolution-theoretical, economic and social dimensions of market-economic thought.]

Swan, George Steven. 'The Libertarian Future: Biologically Impossible?' *Individual Liberty* (Newsletter of The Society for Individual Liberty) 12 (November 1981): 4—5. [Commentary on Hayek's P—19.]

Taylor, Fred M. 'The Guidance of Production in a Socialist State.' Benjamin E. Lippincott (ed.) *On The Economic Theory of Socialism.* New York: Augustus M. Kelley, 1970.

Taylor, Jr., Thomas Cullom. 'Accounting Theory in the Light of Austrian Economic Analysis.' The Louisiana State University and Agricultural and Mechanical College. (Accounting) Ph. D. Dissertation, [70—18, 565], 1970.

Taylor, Thomas C. *The Fundamentals of Austrian Economics.* London: Published by the Adam Smith Institute in association with The Carl Menger Society. 1980. 2nd edition. (First published by the Cato Institute.)

Torrance, J. 'The Emergence of Sociology in Austria, 1885—1935.' *Archives Européennes de Sociologie* 17 (1976).

Torrence, Thoams. 'Hayek's Critique of Social Injustice.' Unpublished paper presented to The Carl Menger Society Conference on Hayek, 28 October 1978.

Tsiang, S. Ch. 'The Variations of Real Wages and Profit Margins in Relation to the Trade Cycle.' Dissertation. London: Pittman, 1947.

Ullmann-Margalit, Edna. 'Invisible Hand Explanations.' *Synthese* 30 (1978): 263—281. [See Vernon (1979) and Barry (1982).]

Vaughn, Karen I. 'Does It Matter That Costs are Subjective?' *Southern Economic Journal* (Summer 1980): 702—715.

Vernon, R. 'The Great Society' and the 'Open Society': Liberalism in Hayek and Popper.' *Canadian Journal of Political Science* 9 (June 1976).

——. 'Unintended Consequences.' *Political Theory* 7 (1979): 57—74.

Viner, Jacob. 'Hayek on Freedom and Coercion.' *Southern Economic Journal* 27 (January 1961): 230—236.

Walter Eucken Institut (Mohr, J. C. B. & Siebeck, P.). 'Bibliographie der Schriften von F. A. Hayek.' In *Freiburger Studien, Gesammelte Aufsätze, Wirtschaftswissenschaftliche und wirtschaftsrechtliche Untersuchungen* 5, Tübingen: Walter Eucken Institut, 1969, pp. 279–284.

Weber, Wilhelm. 'Wirtschaftswissenschaft und Wirtschaftspolitik in Österreich, 1848–1948.' ['Economic Science and Economics Policy in Austria, 1848–1948.'] In Hans Mayer (ed.) *Hundert Jahre österreichischer Wirtschaftsentwicklung, 1848–1948*. Vienna: Springer, 1949, pp. 624–678.

Weiler, Gershon. *Mauthner's Critique of Language.* Cambridge: Cambridge University Press, 1970. [Also see Janik & Toulmin, *Wittgenstein's Vienna*.]

Weimer, W. B. and Palerma, D. S. (eds.) *Cognition and Symbolic Processes*, vol. II. New York: 1978.

Welinder, C. 'Hayek och "Ricardo-effekten".' In *Ekonomisk Tidsskrift* (Uppsala och Stockholm) 42 (1940): 33–39. ['Hayek on the "Ricardo-Effect."']

White, Lawrence H. 'Mises, Hayek, Hahn and The Market Process: Comment on Littlechild.' In *Method, Process, and Austrian Economics: Essays in Honour of Ludwig von Mises*. Edited by Israel M. Kirzner. Lexington, Mass. Toronto: Lexington Books, D. C. Heath and Company, 1982, pp. 103–110.

Widmer, Kingsley. 'Utopia and Liberty: Some Contemporary Issues Within Their Tradition.' *Literature of Liberty* 4, No. 4 (Winter 1981): 5–62, especially pp. 8–10, with notes.

Wien-Claudi, F. *Austrian Theories of Capital, Interest and the Trade Cycle*. London: Nott, 1936.

Wieser, Friedrich Freiherr von. 'The Austrian School and the Theory of Value.' *Economic Journal* (England) (1891).

——. 'The Theory of Value (A Reply to Professor Macvane).' *Annals of the American Academy of Political and Social Science* (1891).

——. *Social Economics*. Translated by A. Ford Himrichs. With a Preface by Wesley Clair Mitchell. New York: Adolphis Co., 1927. Reprinted New York: Augustus M. Kelley, 1967. [In his preface, Mitchell refers to von Wieser's recent death (July 23, 1926) and to von Wieser's 'pupil and friend, Dr. Friedrich A. von Hayek.' The translator, Himrichs, states: 'Dr. Friedrich A. von Hayek, a pupil and close friend of von Wieser, has read the proofs and submitted many suggestions.']

Wilde, Olga. 'Bibliographie der wissenschaftlichen Veröffentlichungen von Friedrich von Hayek.' In *Friedrich A. von Hayek*, edited by Erich Hoppmann. Baden-Baden: Nomos Verlagsgesellschaft, 1980, pp. 55–56. ['Bibliography of the Scholarly Publications of Friedrich A. von Hayek.']

Wilhelm, Morris M. 'The Political Philosophy of Friedrich A. Hayek.' Columbia University Ph. D. Dissertation in Political Science, New York, 1969. An article based on this, in condensed form, appears as 'The Political Thought of Friedrich A. Hayek,' in *Political Studies* 20, No. 2 (June 1972): 169–184.

Willgerodt, H. 'Liberalismus zwischen Spontanität und Gestaltung. Zu v. Hayek's gesammelten Aufsätzen.' In *Zeitschrift für Wirtschafts- und Sozialwissenschaften*. Berlin 92, No. 4, (1972): 461–465. ['Liberalism between Spontaneity and Organization. On von Hayek's Collected Articles.' Refers to B–14.]

Wilson, T. 'Captial Theory and the Trade Cycle.' *Review of Economic Studies*, VII (June 1940).

Winch, Peter. 'Nature and Convention.' *Proceedings of the Aristotelian Society* 60 (1959–1960): 231–252. Reprinted as chapter 3 of Winch's *Ethics and Action*. London: Routledge & Kegan Paul, 1976.

Winterberger, G. 'Friedrich August von Hayek – Zum Achtzigsten Geburtstag des grossen Nationalökonomen, Staats- und Rechtsphilosophen.' *Schweizer Monatshefte* 5 (1979): 359–363. [Friedrich August von Hayek: On the 80th Birthday of the Great Economist, Social Scientist, and Moral Philosopher.']

Wootton, B. *Freedom Under Planning*. London: Allen & Unwin, 1946.

Worsthorne, Peregrine. 'F. A. Hayek: Next Construction for the Giant.' In *Prophets of Freedom and Enterprise*. Edited by Michael Ivens. London: Kogan Page Ltd., for Aims of Industry, 1975, pp. 70–80.

Zöller, Michael. 'Handeln in Ungewissheit. F. A. von Hayek's Grundlegung einer freiheitlichen Sozialphilosophie.' ['Acting under Uncertainty. F. A. von Hayek's Foundation of a Liberal Social Philosophy.'] In *Zur Verfassung der Freiheit: Festgabe für Friedrich A. von Hayek zur Vollendung seines achtzigsten Lebensjahres*. Stuttgart, New York: Gustav Fischer Verlag (*Ordo* 30), 1979, pp. 117–129.

Notes

CHAPTER 1

1. F. A. Hayek, [B−10], *The Sensory Order*, London: Routledge & Kegan Paul, 1952, pp. 4−5. *The Sensory Order* has not in fact gone wholly ignored by psychologists. For a useful symposium on it, see W. B. Weimer and D. S. Palermo, eds., *Cognition and Symbolic Processes*, vol. II, New York, 1978. Also 'Hayek Revisited: Mind as a Process of Classification' by Rosemary Agnitto in *Behaviorism: a Forum for Critical Discussion*, 3/2, Nevada (Spring 1975): 162−71. Neglect of Hayek's contributions to psychology by professional psychologists may in part be due to his drawing on a tradition of psychology − the neo-Kantian tradition of Helmholtz and Wundt − which fell on hard times when behavioural and psychoanalytical approaches came to dominate the theoretical investigation of mental life.

2. Hayek, [B−10], *Sensory Order*, p. 5, para. 1.12. At times, Hayek goes so far as almost to relativize any distinction between appearance and reality. When he adopts such a position, he breaks with a decisive element in Kantian critical philosophy, for which the distinction between how things seem to us and how they are in themselves must be fundamental. On other occasions, Hayek affirms strongly his commitment to conjectural realism of a Popperian sort. In *Sensory Order* pp. 173 he says:

If the classification of events in the external world effected by our senses proves not to be a 'true' classification, i.e., not one which enables us adequately to describe the regularities in this world, and if the properties which our senses attribute to these events are not objective properties of these individual events, but merely attributes defining the classes to which our senses assign them, this means that we cannot regard the phenomenal world in any sense as more 'real' than the constructions of science: we must assume the existence of an objective world (or better, of an objective order of the events which we experience in their phenomenal order) towards the recognition of which the phenomenal order is merely a first approximation. The task of science is thus to try and approach ever more closely towards a reproduction of this objective order — a task which it can perform only by replacing the sensory order of events by a new and different classification.

I wish to thank Professor W. W. Bartley III, Hayek's biographer, for drawing my attention to this important statement.

3. Ibid., p. 171, para. 8.24.

4. Ibid., p. 42, para. 2.15.

5. Ibid., p. 165, para. 8.2.

6. Ibid., p. 193, para. 8.93, and his [B—12], *The Constitution of Liberty*, London: Routledge & Kegan Paul, 1960, pp. 13, 438. See Mach's influence on Hayek by consulting the Bibliography: B—10 and A—119.

7. Hayek, [B—10], *Sensory Order*, pp. 178—9, para. 8.45. Hayek's affirmation of a practical dualism in the theory of the mind may well have been influenced by von Mises, who adopts a very similar standpoint in several of his writings.

8. Ibid., p. 194, para. 8.97.

9. Ibid.

10. See W. V. Quine, *Ontological Relativity*, New York: Columbia University Press, 1969. Unlike Hayek, Quine sees compelling reasons for postulating a realm of abstract entities, including numbers, but, like Hayek, he admits no ontological gulf between body and mind. Hayek's objection to the neutral monism defended by William James, Bertrand Russell and John Dewey seems to be on the grounds of its psychologistic features as it is stated by these writers: see [B—10], *Sensory Order*, p. 176, para. 8.38. Neutral monism need not have these features, however, and perhaps Hayek's system need not exclude it.

11. See Hayek's interesting discussion of differences of method as between natural and social sciences in [E—5], the collection which he edited: *Collectivist Economic Planning*, London: Routledge &

Kegan Paul, 1956 (originally published 1935), pp. 10–11. Hayek withdraws from the strong methodological dualism about natural and social science adopted here and in many of his earlier writings, explicitly in the Preface to his [B–13], *Studies in Philosophy, Politics and Economics*, London: Routledge & Kegan Paul, 1967, p. viii, where he asserts that through Popper's work 'the difference between the two groups of disciplines has thereby been greatly narrowed.' For an important discussion of Popper's demarcation criterion for science, see I. Lakatos, 'Popper on Demarcation and Induction', in P. A. Schilpp, ed., *The Philosophy of Karl Popper*, La Salle, Illinois: Open Court K. R. 1974, pp. 241–73.

12. See F. A. Hayek, 'Kinds of Rationalism' in his [B–13], *Studies*, pp. 82–95, and his [B–15] *Law, Legislation and Liberty*, vol. I, London: Routledge & Kegan Paul, 1973, p. 29.

13. Karl R. Popper 'Replies to my critics', Schlipp, ed., *The Philosophy of Karl Popper*, pp. 1059–60.

14. J. W. N. Watkins 'The Unity of Popper's thought', Schlipp, ed., *The Philosophy of Karl Popper*, pp. 401–2.

15. Hayek, [B–10], *Sensory Order*, p. 176, para. 8.39.

16. Hayek acknowledges the affinities between his conception of evolving tradition and Popper's idea of 'world three' in the first volume of his forthcoming trilogy, *The Fatal Conceit: the Intellectual Error of Socialism*, which I have been privileged to see in manuscript. Earlier, Hayek had cited Popper's idea of a world of abstract entities with approval in [B–18], *Law, Legislation and Liberty*, vol. III, London: Routledge & Kegan Paul, 1979, p. 157.

17. See Hayek's reminiscences, [A–204], 'Remembering My Cousin Ludwig Wittgenstein', *Encounter* (August 1977).

18. I owe to Professor Hayek this information regarding his interest in Mauthner's work. Wittgenstein's reference to Mauthner occurs in para. 4.0031 of his *Tractatus Logico-Philosophicus*, London: Routledge & Kegan Paul, 1861. The only book-length study of Mauthner's philosophy in English is that of Gershon Weiler, *Mauthner's Critique of Language*, Cambridge: Cambridge University Press, 1970. Also see Allen Janik and Stephen Toulmin, *Wittgenstein's Vienna*, New York: Simon & Schuster, 1973, pp. 121–33, 178–82.

19. In attributing a pragmatist aspect to Hayek's Kantianism, I do not mean to ascribe to Hayek any of the doctrines of modern pragmatism, but rather to note the sense in which for Hayek action

or practice has primacy in the generation of knowledge. For Hayek, in some contrast with Kant, knowledge emanates from practical life in the sense that it is ultimately embodied in judgements and dispositions to act.

20. In his [B–13], *Studies*, p. 24, speaking of 'the erroneous belief that if we look only long enough, or at a sufficient number of instances of natural events, a pattern will always reveal itself', Hayek remarks that 'in those cases the theorizing has been done already by our senses.'

21. See Gilbert Ryle, 'Knowing How and Knowing That', *Proceedings of the Aristotelian Society*, 46 (1945–6): 1–16.

22. See Michael Polanyi, *The Tacit Dimension*, London: Routledge & Kegan Paul, 1967.

23. Michael Oakeshott, 'Rational Conduct', in *Rationalism in Politics*, London: Methuen, 1962, pp. 97–100.

24. Hayek, [B–13], *Studies*, p. 44, note 4.

25. Quoted by T. W. Hutchinson, *The Politics and Philosophy of Economics*, Oxford: Basil Blackwell, 1981, p. 214.

26. Norman P. Barry, *Hayek's Social and Economic Philosophy*, London: Macmillan, 1979, p. 41.

27. Ibid., p. 40. Barry has since modified his view that Hayek's work embodies conflicting methodological commitments. See his 'Restating the Liberal Order: Hayek's Philosophical Economics' in J. R. Shackleton and E. Lorksley, eds., *Twelve Contemporary Economists*, London: Macmillan, 1983.

28. Hayek, [B–17], *New Studies in Philosophy, Politics, Economics and the History of Ideas*, London: Routledge & Kegan Paul, 1978, pp. 51–2.

29. Hayek, [B–13], *Studies*, p. viii.

30. Ibid., p. 6: 'while this possibilty [of falsification] always exists, its likelihood in the case of a well-confirmed hypothesis is so small that we often disregard it in practice.'

31. Ibid., p. 16.

32. Hayek, [B–17], *New Studies*, p. 45, note 14.

33. Hayek, [B–13], *Studies*, London: Routledge & Kegan Paul, 1967, pp. 60–2.

34. Hayek, [B–16], *Law Legislation and Liberty*, vol. II, London: Routledge & Kegan Paul, 1976, p. 25.

35. I have in mind, of course, Popper's important criticism of holistic social engineering in Karl R. Popper, *The Poverty of Historicism*, London: Routledge & Kegan Paul, 1972, pp. 83–93.

CHAPTER 2

1. Hayek, [B—5], *Law, Legislation and Liberty*, vol. I, London: Routledge & Kegan Paul, 1973, p. 17.
2. Descartes may not always have committed the errors Hayek finds in him or his disciples. See on this Stuart Hampshire, 'On Having a Reason', chapter 5 of G. A. Vesey, ed., *Human Values*, Royal Institute of Philosophy Lectures, vol. II, 1976—7, Harvester Press, 1976, where on p. 88 Hampshire speaks in Hayekian fashion of 'a Cartesian error, which was not consistently Descartes', and which consists of assuming a necessary connection between thought on the one side and consciousness and explicitness on the other...'
3. Hayek, [B—13], *Studies in Philosophy, Politics and Economics*, London: Routledge & Kegan Paul, 1967, p. 73. On Hayek's view of spontaneous order, see Norman P. Barry, 'The Tradition of Spontaneous Order', *Literature of Liberty* 5 (Summer 1982), 7—58.
4. Hayek, [B—13], *Studies*, pp. 71—2.
5. Hayek, [B—15], *Law, Legislation and Liberty*, vol. I, p. 13.
6. Hayek, [B—17], *New Studies in Philosophy, Politics, Economics and the History of Ideas*, London: Routledge & Kegan Paul, 1978, p. 253.
7. Hayek, [B—13], *Studies*, p. 76 'The problems of how galaxies or solar systems are formed and what is their resulting structure is much more like the problems which the social sciences have to face than the problems of mechanics...' See also [B—16], *Law, Legislation, and Liberty*, vol. II, London: Routledge & Kegan Paul, 1976, pp. 39—40.
8. Hayek, [B—17], *New Studies*, p. 250.
9. On Spencer, See J. D. Y. Peel, *Herbert Spencer: the Evolution of a Sociologist*, London: Heinemann, 1971.
10. See Hayek, [B—18], *Law Legislation and Liberty*, vol. III, London: Routledge & Kegan Paul, 1979, pp. 153—5.
11. See Peter Winch, 'Nature and Convention', *Proceedings of the Aristotelian Society*, 60 (1959—60): 231—52, reprinted as chapter 3 of Winch's *Ethics and Action*, London: Routledge & Kegan Paul, 1976. In some of his writings published after *The Open Society and Its Enemies*, Popper comes closer to a Hayekian position. In his 'Towards a Rational Theory of Tradition', in particular, perhaps in response to Oakeshott's writings, he effectively abandons the

Sophistic dichotomy of nature and convention entailed in his earlier writings. See Popper's *Conjectures and Refutations*, London: Routledge & Kegan Paul, 1963, for this study.

12. Hayek, [B—10], *The Sensory Order*, London: Routledge & Kegan Paul, 1952, p. 180; and [B—15], *Law Legislation and Liberty*, vol. I, London: Routledge & Kegan Paul, 1973. p. 39.

13. The best source for Hume's criticism of moral rationalism remains his *Treatise of Human Nature*, especially Book III, Part I.

14. I refer particularly to volume 1 of his forthcoming trilogy, *The Fatal Conceit: the Intellectual Error of Socialism*, where Hayek addresses most explicitly the similarities and differences between biological and cultural evolution.

15. Thus in 'Rules, Perception and Intelligibility' [A—142, reprinted as chapter 3 in B—13, *Studies*], Hayek links rules of action with rules of perception as follows:

...the capacity of the child to understand various meanings of sentences expressed by the appropriate grammatical structure provides the most conspicuous example of the capacity of rule-perception. Rules which we cannot state thus do not govern only our actions. They also govern our perceptions, and particularly our perceptions of other people's actions. The child who speaks grammatically without knowing the rules of grammar not only understands all the shades of meaning expressed by others through following the rules of grammar, but may also be able to correct a grammatical mistake in the speech of others. (*Studies*, p. 45)

16. See Robert Nozick, *Anarchy, State and Utopia*, New York: Basic Books, 1974, pp. 18—22, for an illuminating account of invisible-hand explanations.

17. See Carl Menger, *Principles of Economics*, trans., J. Dinguwall and B. F. Hoselitz, intro. by F. A. Hayek, New York and London: New York University Press, 1981, chapter 8.

18. See Hayek's [B—13], *Studies*, chapter 4.

19. The connections between the utility of a code of conduct and its impact on the growth of human numbers are explored in his as yet unpublished writings, particularly the first volume of *The Fatal Conceit*.

20. See Hayek, [B—13], *Studies*, p. 61: '...if "to have meaning" is to have a place in an order which we share with other people, this

order itself cannot have meaning because it cannot have a place in itself.'

21. Personal communication to the author.

22. See Hayek, [B–12], *The Constitution of Liberty*, London: Routledge & Kegan Paul, 1960, p. 160.

23. On the calculation debate, see *The Journal of Libertarian Studies* 5 (Winter 1981), especially the historical paper by Don Lavoie, 'A Critique of the Standard Account of the Socialist Calculation Debate', pp. 41–87.

24. All the preceding three quotations occur on pp. 80–1 of Hayek, [B–7], *Individualism and Economic Order*, London: Routledge & Kegan Paul, 1976.

25. Ibid., p. 50.

26. Isreal M. Kirzner, *Competition and Entrepreneurship*, Chicago and London: University of Chicago Press, 1973, p. 68.

27. Joseph Schumpeter, *Capitalism, Socialism and Democracy*, London: Unwin, 1974, chapter XVI.

28. See Paul Craig Roberts, *Alienation in the Soviet Economy*, Albuquerque: University of New Mexico Press, 1971.

29. See R. D. Laing, *The Politics of the Family*, for a useful account of this research.

30. Walter Block, *Defending the Undefendable*, New York: Fleet Press.

31. L. von Mises, *Human Activities*, Chicago: Henry Regnery, 1966, Part One.

32. Gary S. Becker, *The Economic Approach to Human Behavior*, Chicago: University of Chicago Press, 1976, p. 5.

33. Ibid., p. 7.

34. Henri Le Page, *Tomorrow, Capitalism*, La Salle and London: Open Court, 1978, p. 176.

35. Becker, *Economic Approach*, p. 294.

36. See D. H. Hodgson, *Consequences of Utilitarianism*, Oxford: Clarendon Press, 1967.

37. Joseph Schumpeter, *Capitalism, Socialism and Democracy*, London: Unwin, 1974, chapters 11–14.

38. Peter Unwin, *The Idea of a Social Science*, London: Routledge & Kegan Paul, 1958.

39. Robert Nozick, *Anarchy, State and Utopia*, New York: Basic Books, 1974, pp. 21–2.

CHAPTER 3

1. Hayek, [B—12], *The Constitution of Liberty*, London: Routledge & Kegan Paul, 1960, pp. 35—6.
2. Hayek, [B—13], *Studies in Philosophy, Politics and Economics*, London: Routledge & Kegan Paul, 1967, p. 38.
3. Hayek, [B—13], *Studies*, p. 113. Hayek acknowledges earlier in his Hume essay (p. 109, note 5: 'My attention was first directed to these parts of Hume's works many years ago by Professor Sir Arnold Plant, whose development of the Humean theory of property we are still eagerly awaiting.') Hayek is alluding to his discussions with Sir Arnold in the early 1930s at the London School of Economics, where Hayek had migrated to take up the Tooke Professorship. See Sir Arnold Plant, 'A Tribute to Hayek — The Rational Persuader', *Economic Age* 2, (January—February 1970): 4—8, especially p. 5: 'I myself had returned to LSE in the middle of 1930 after six years at the University of Cape Town, where I had developed a special interest in the scope of and functions of property and ownership, both private and public. It was a delight to find Hayek as well seized of the economic significance of the ramifications of property law as I was myself. I recall his excitement when I called his attention to the profound discussion of these matters in David Hume's *Enquiry Concerning the Principles of Morals*: section III, Of Justice, and my own gratitude to him for his influence on my own thinking about so-called intellectual and industrial property law.' The entirety of Sir Arnold's article should be consulted for the light it sheds on LSE during the thirties as a seedbed for transmitting Austrian economics. (One visitor described LSE as '*ein Vorort von Wien*' — a suburb of Vienna; p. 6). See also Hayek's important inaugural lecture delivered at LSE on 1 March 1933, [A—20], 'The Trend of Economic Thinking', (*Economica* 13 (May 1933), 121—37) and his revealing article [A—71] on the history of 'The London School of Economics, 1895—1945', *Economica* N.S. 13 (February 1946), 1—13. During the 1940s Hayek was also editor of LSE's journal, *Economica*.
4. H. L. A. Hart, *The Concept of Law*, Oxford: Clarendon Press, 1961.
5. See, especially, Henry Sidgwick's masterpiece, *The Methods of Ethics*, in which Sidgwick defends an indirect form of utilitarian morality.
6. For Hayek's criticism of the standard variety of utilitarian theory,

see especially [B—16], *Law, Legislation and Liberty*, vol. II, London: Routledge & Kegan Paul, 1976, pp. 17—23.

7. See Hayek, [B—13], *Studies*, p. 173: 'An optimal policy in a catallaxy may aim, and ought to aim, at increasing the chances of any member of society taken at random of having a high income, or, what amounts to the same thing, the chance that, whatever his share in total income may be, the real equivalent of this share will be as large as we know how to make it.'

8. See Hayek, [B—16], *Law, Legislation and Liberty*, vol. II, p. xiii, for his endorsement of some aspects of Rawls's theory.

9. See Ronald Hamowy, 'Law and the Liberal Society: F. A. Hayek's *Constitution of Liberty*', *Journal of Libertarian Studies* 2, no. 4 (Winter 1978): 287—97; J. Raz, 'The Rule of Law and Its Virtue', in *Liberty and the Rule of Law*, ed. R. L. Cunningham, Texas A & M University Press, 1979, pp. 3—21; and John N. Gray, 'F. A. Hayek on Liberty and Tradition', *Journal of Libertarian Studies* 4, (Spring 1980): 119—37.

10. See note 9 above.

11. Ibid.

12. Hayek, [B—13], *Studies*, p. 168 ff.

13. Hayek, [B—13], *Studies*, pp. 116—7.

14. Raz, 'Rule of Law', p. 19.

15. Hamowy, 'Law and the Liberal Society', pp. 291—2.

16. I draw heavily here on the account of universalization given in J. L. Mackie's *Ethics: Inventing Right and Wrong*, London: Penguin Books, 1977, pp. 83—102.

17. Hayek, [B—13], *Studies*, p. 168.

18. Ibid., pp. 116—17: 'What Kant had to say about this [justice] seems to derive directly from Hume.'

19. See R. M. Hare, *Moral Thinking*, Oxford: Clarendon Press, 1981.

20. Hayek, [B—13], *Studies*, p. 168.

21. Ibid., p. 166.

22. Ibid., p. 163.

23. See Hamowy, 'Law and the Liberal Society'.

24. Hamowy is surely right that Hayek's account of coercion is faulty. On this see Murray N. Rothbard, *The Ethics of Liberty*, Atlantic Highlands, N.J.: Humanities Press, 1981, chapter 28, 'F. A. Hayek and the Concept of Coercion'.

25. See J. L. Mackie, *Ethics*, p. 88: 'This...thesis is well formulated by Hobbes: "That a man...be contented with so much liberty

against other men, as he would allow other men against himself."
Hobbes equates this with the Golden Rule of the New Testament...'

26. Bruno Leoni, *Freedom and the Law*, Princeton, New Jersey: D. Van Nostrand, 1961, pp. 21–2.

27. See Hayek, [B–18], *Law, Legislation and Liberty* vol. III, London: Routledge & Kegan Paul, 1978, chapter 17.

28. See James M. Buchanan, 'Cultural Evolution and Institutional Reform' (unpubl.). I am most grateful to Professor Buchanan for allowing me to read this paper.

29. James Buchanan, *Freedom in Constitutional Contract*, College Station: Texas A & M University Press, 1977, pp. 25–30.

30. Robert Nozick, *Anarchy, State, and Utopia*, New York: Basic Books, 1974, pp. 18–22. For a most penetrating discussion of some related aspects of social explanation, see Nozick's 'On Austrian Methodology', *Synthese* 36 (1977): 353–92. See also Edna Ullmann-Margalit's 'Invisible Hand Explanations', *Synthese* 30 (1978): 263–91. I am indebted to Professor Lester Hunt both for directing me to Ms. Ullmann-Margalit's article and for showing me his unpublished paper, 'Toward a Natural History of Morality', in which some of Ullmann-Margalit's work is pushed further. See also Norman P. Barry, 'The Tradition of Spontaneous Order', *Literature of Liberty* 5 (Summer 1982): 7–58, as well as Richard Vernon, 'Unintended Consequences', *Political Theory* 7 (1979): 57–74.

31. The insatiability of senescence-related basic needs is noted by Hayek in [B–12], *Constitution of Liberty*, pp. 208–30.

32. See ibid., chapter 6.

33. See Nozick, *Anarchy, State and Utopia*, pp. 160–4.

34. John Rawls, *A Theory of Justice*, Cambridge, Mass: Belnap Press of the Harvard University Press, 1971.

35. A. M. Honoré, 'Social Justice' in R. S. Summers, ed., *Essays in Legal Philosophy*, Oxford: Clarendon Press, 1968.

36. Nozick, *Anarchy, State and Utopia*, chapter 7.

37. Ibid., chapter 10.

38. Hayek, [B–18], *Law, Legislation and Liberty*, vol. III, pp. 146–7.

CHAPTER 4

1. Hayek, [B–13], *Studies in Philosophy, Politics and Economics*, London: Routledge & Kegan Paul, 1967.

2. Ibid., p. 35.

3. Hayek, [B—9], *The Counter-Revolution of Science*, London: J. M. Dent and Sons Ltd., Everyman Library, 1972, chapter 3.

4. Hayek, [B—13], *Studies*, p. 26.

5. Ibid., p. 36. See also p. 18: 'Where our predictions are thus limited to some general and perhaps only negative attributes of what is likely to happen, we evidently also shall have little power to control developments.' And on p. 19: 'The wise legislator or statesman will probably attempt to cultivate rather than to control the forces of the social process.'

6. Hayek, [B—16], *Law, Legislation and Liberty*, vol II, London: Routledge & Kegan Paul, 1976, p. 157, note 25.

7. Michael Oakeshott, *Rationalism in Politics*, London: Methuen, 1962, p. 4.

8. Rush Rhees, *Without Answers*, London: Routledge & Kegan Paul, 1969, p. 49.

9. Hayek, [B—2], *Prices and Production*, London: Routledge & Kegan Paul, 1967, pp. 3—4.

10. On this see Gerald P. O'Driscoll Jr, *Economics as a Coordination Problem: The Contributions of F. A. Hayek*, foreword by F. A. Hayek, Kansas City: Sheel Andrews and McMeel, 1977, pp. 48—9.

11. Hayek, [P—16b], *Denationalisation of Money*, 2nd edition, London: Institute of Economic Affairs, 1978, p. 52.

12. Ibid.

13. Hayek, [B—12], *The Constitution of Liberty*, London: Routledge & Kegan Paul, 1960, pp. 520—1, note 2.

14. G. L. S. Shackle, *Epistemics and Economics: A Critique of Economic Doctrines*, Cambridge: Cambridge University Press, 1976. Shackle's most explicit critique of Hayek may be found in his paper on Hayek in D. P. O'Brien and J. R. Besley, *Pioneers of Modern Economics in Britain*, London: MacMillan, 1983.

15. See Shackle's section on Keynes in *Epistemics and Economics*.

16. I am grateful to Professor Hayek for discussion on the possibility of secondary deflation in the context of stabilization policy. Responsibility for my interpretation of his views remains mine. Hayek advocates a 'big bang' monetary contraction in [P—16b] *Denationalisation of Money*, chapter XXII.

17. See Hayek, [P—16b], *Denationalisation of Money*, 2nd edition, pp. 128—9, for a complete answer to these criticisms.

CHAPTER 5

1. John Stuart Mill, *The Spirit of the Age*, introduced by F. A. Hayek, Chicago: University of Chicago Press, 1942, p. xxxiii.

2. See G. Himmelfarb, ed., *John Stuart Mill on Politics and Culture*, Garden City, New York: Anchor Books, Doubleday, 1962, for Mill's reviews of Tocqueville.

3. J. S. Mill, *Utilitarianism, On Liberty and Considerations on Representative Government*, London: J. M. Dent and Sons Ltd, Everyman Library, 1972, p. 4.

4. For an account of moral thought and practical reasoning that has much in common with Hayek's and with Mill's, see R. M. Hare, *Moral Thinking: Its Levels, Method and Point*, Oxford: Clarendon Press, 1981.

5. John Gray, *Mill on Liberty: A Defence*, London: Routledge & Kegan Paul (International Library of Philosophy), 1983.

6. Thomas Sowell, *Knowledge and Decisions*, New York: Basic Books, 1980, p. 107.

7. See Hayek, [B—12], *Constitution of Liberty*, London: Routledge & Kegan Paul, 1960, p. 146, for an explicit criticism of Mill; and Hayek's 'Individualism, True and False', in [B—7], for his recognition that abstract individualism destroys liberty.

8. John Stuart Mill, *Principles of Political Economy*, Book II, chapter I: 'Of Property', first paragraph, in *Collected Works of John Stuart Mill*, Toronto: Toronto University Press.

9. Herbert Spencer, *An Autiobiography*, vol. II, London: Williams and Norgate, 1904, pp. 88—89.

10. John Stuart Mill, 'Dr. Whewell on Moral Philosophy' in Mill's *Essays on Ethics, Religion and Society*, ed., J. M. Robson, in *Collected Works of J. S. Mill*, vol. X, Toronto: Toronto University Press, 1969, p. 181.

11. John Stuart Mill, *Later Letters 1840—1873*, ed., F. E. Mineka and D. N. Windley, vol. IV, *Collected Works*, vol. XVII, Toronto, Toronto University Press, 1922, p. 188.

12. D. G. Brown, 'Mill's Act Utilitarianism', *Philosophical Quarterly*, 24 (1974), 67.

13. John Rawls, 'Two Concepts of Rules', *Philosophical Review*, 64 (1955), 3—32.

14. J. J. C. Smart in *Utilitarianism: For and Against*, Cambridge:

Cambridge University Press, 1973, 'Outline of a System of Utilitarian Ethics', section 2, pp. 9—12.

15. Henry Sidgwick, *The Ethics of T. H. Green, Herbert Spencer and J. Martineau*, London: Macmillan, 1902, pp. 135—312.
16. Ibid., p. 183.
17. Ibid., p. 185.
18. See the Everyman edition of *Utilitarianism, Liberty and Representative Government*, London: Dent, 1972, pp. 397—413, for some valuable selections from J. S. Mill's *Auguste Comte and Positivism*, in which his criticisms of Comte are particularly striking.
19. H. Sidgwick, 'The Relations of Ethics with Sociology', *Miscellaneous Essays and Addresses*, London: Macmillan, 1904. Sidgwick also has an extremely interesting paper on 'The Theory of Evolution in its Application to Practice' in *Mind*, vol. 1, No. 1 (1876).
20. I use the word 'proposal' advisedly so as to stress the normative character of Popper's falsificationism, which he himself stressed from the start, but which subsequent critics (e.g. Lakatos, 'Popper on Demarcation and Induction', P. A. Schilpps, ed., *Library of Living Philosophers*, Illinois: Open Court K. R., 1974) have not always fully acknowledged. See *Logic of Scientific Discovery*, London: Hutchinson, 1959, pp. 50—6, for a criticism of naturalistic approaches to the problem of scientific method.
21. See L. Kolakowski, *The Alienation of Reason: a history of positivist thought*, Garden City, New York: Doubleday, 1968, where the legend of Popper's positivism is still alive. It is ironical that the greatest living scourge of positivism should continue to be described as a positivist.
22. I have in mind, particularly, Popper's associate W. W. Bartley III. See for example, W. W. Bartley III and M. Bunge, 1964, *The Critical Approach to Science and Philosophy*, 'Rationality versus the Theory of Rationality', p. 19ff.
23. See R. Nozick, *Anarchy, State and Utopia*, pp. 312—17.
24. It has been argued that, in so far as any criticism of comprehensively critical rationalism only reinforces it by demonstrating its criticizability, the theory is self-validating and *therefore* self-defeating. See on this, J. W. N. Watkins, 'Comprehensively Critical Rationalism', *Philosophy*, 1969. Bartley has replied to this criticism. A most useful general statement of Bartley's development of Popper's theory of rationality may be found in *Philosophia*, vol. 11, nos. 1—2 (February 1982), 121—221. I am indebted to Professor Bartley for conversations

on these questions and for letting me have copies of a number of his unpublished papers on the theory of rationality, of which one — 'Non-justificationism: Popper versus Wittgenstein' (Invited Lecture, International Wittgenstein Symposium, Kirchberg am Wechsel, Austria, August 1982) — is particularly relevant to the assessment of Hayek's rationality theory.

CHAPTER 6

1. That inflationary credit policies will stimulate the economy only in so far as they are not expected is not, of course, a new insight, since it is to be found in Hume's economic writings, if not earlier, but it is to Hayek that we owe the systematic statement of this insight.

2. I owe this point to Neera Badhwar.

3. Hayek [B—17], *New Studies in Philosophy, Politics, Economics and the History of Ideas*, London: Routledge & Kegan Paul, 1978, p. 250.

4. Hayek [B—15], *Law, Legislation and Liberty*, vol. 1, London: Routledge & Kegan Paul, 1973, p. 36.

5. Ibid., pp. 36—7.

6. See James Buchanan and Gordon Tullock, *The Calculus of Consent*, Michigan: University of Michigan Press, 1962.

7. Hayek [B—6], *The Road to Serfdom*, London: George Routledge & Sons, 1944, chapter 10.

8. David Friedman, *The Machinery of Freedom*, New York: Harper and Row, 1973, pp. 213—17.

9. I owe this historical fact to Sir Isaiah Berlin.

10. For Rothbard's criticisms of Hayek, see *The Ethics of Liberty*, Atlantic Highlands, N.J.: Humanities Press, chapter 28.

11. See Hayek [B—16], *Law, Legislation and Liberty*, vol. II, London: Routledge & Kegan Paul, 1976, pp. 23—4.

12. Ibid., p. 36.

13. Hayek [B—18], *Law, Legislation and Liberty*, vol. III, p. 192, note 5.

14. Ronald Hamowy, 'The Hayekian Model of Government in an Open Society', *Journal of Libertarian Studies*, vol. VI, no. 2, (Spring 1982), 141.

15. A general philosophical argument for the permanence of some measure of social chaos has been put beautifully by Shackle in

in *Epistemics and Economics*, Cambridge: Cambridge University Press, 1976, p. 239:

Rationalism, the belief that conduct can be understood as part of the determinate order and process of Nature, into which it is assimilated in virtue of the fact that men choose what is best for them in their circumstances, is a paradox. For it claims to confer upon man freedom to choose, yet to be able to predict what they will choose ...for the sake of prereconciliation of choices, and also for its own unfathomable possibilities, the future must be assumed away. Thus the value-construct describes free, prereconciled, determinate choices in a timeless system. Beauty, clarity and unity are achieved by a set of axioms as economic as those of classical physical dynamics. Can the real flux of history, personal and public, be appropriately understood in terms of this conception? The contrast is such that we have difficulty in achieving any mental collation of the two ideas. Macbeth's despair expresses more nearly the impact of the torrent of events.

16. See James Buchanan, *Freedom in Constitutional Contracts*, College Station, Texas: Texas A & M University Press, 1979.
17. See John Gray, 'F. A. Hayek on Liberty and Tradition', *Journal of Libertarian Studies* 4, (Spring 1980), 119—37.
18. See Michael Oakeshott, *Human Conduct*, Oxford: Oxford University Press, 1975, for a profound evocation of the historicity of human individuality.
19. See Hayek, [B—7], *Individualism and Economic Order*, London: George Routledge & Sons, 1948, chapter 1.
20. For Irving Kristol's critique of Hayekian liberalism, see his 'Capitalism, Socialism and Nihilism', in *Two Cheers for Capitalism*, New York: Basic Books, 1978, chapter 7.
21. See Joseph Schumpeter, *Capitalism, Socialism and Democracy*, London: Unwin, 1974, chapter 13.
22. Hayek [B—16], *Law, Legislation and Liberty*, vol. II, p. 147.
23. Hayek discusses unviable moralities ibid., in chapter 11.
24. Polanyi's account of moral inversion may be found in his *Personal Knowledge*, Chicago: University of Chicago Press, 1958, pp. 233—5.
25. Hayek [B—18], *Law, Legislation and Liberty*, vol. III, pp. 165—6.
26. Michael Oakeshott, *On History*, Oxford: Basil Blackwell, 1983, pp. 102—106.

27. James Buchanan, *The Limits of Liberty: between Anarchy & Leviathan*: Chicago and London, University of Chicago Press, 1975.

28. I am grateful to Professor Gary Becker for illuminating discussion on these points.

Index

Ackerman, B. 98
action:
    freedom of 62, 98
    rules of 15, 23, 29, 33—4, 43
        51—2, 54, 109, 215n.
Acton, Lord 50, 96, 102
Aristotelianism 131
    epistemology 117
    in science 6
Austrian School of Economics
        16—19, 34, 55
    trade cycle 84—6, 88—9, 93

Badhwar, N. 223n.
Barry, Norman P. 18—19, 213n.,
        214n.
Becker, Gary 45—6, 47—9, 51—3,
        82—3, 139
Bell, Daniel 50, 131
Bentham, Jeremy 42, 59, 106—7
bicameralism 69—72, 125—8
Block, Walter 44
Brown, D. G. 106
Buchanan, James 70—1, 120, 122,
        128—9, 139
Burke, Edmund 1, 42

calculation 50—2, 216n.; see also
        social order
capital theory 17, 86
capitalism, see market economy
catallaxy 35, 82, 91, 92, 94,
        122, 131; see also economic
        theory
Collectivist Economic Planning
        18—19
conservatism vii, 13, 118, 122,
        129—30
    moral 44
    neoconservatives 131—2, 134
Constitution of Liberty, The 9, 15,
        57, 72, 216n., 219n., 221n.

constructivism, see rationalism:
        constructivist; social order:
        constructivism
convention, social:
    and free society 50, 88, 99—10,
        118
    and individuality 99—101
    see also moral philosophy; rules
Counter-Revolution of Science,
        The 17
culture, evolution of 31—4, 41—55,
        77—8, 108—10, 111, 115,
        118—19, 122, 130
    and mind 27
    and morality 133—9
    and rules 29
    see also tradition

democracy, majoritarian 71—2
Denationalisation of Money 90—1,
        220n.
Descartes, René 24—5, 27, 30, 113,
        214n.
Distribution, see justice: social
        distribution
dualism 9—10, 12, 19, 112—13,
        211n., 212n.
Dworkin, R. M. 98

economic theory 2—3, 17—20, 28,
        79—90, 116—17
    classical 16, 82, 83—4
    market exchanges 31—2
    microeconomics 86—7, 116
    public planning 36, 38—40, 80,
        82—3
    spontaneous order 31—2, 34—40,
        82, 94
    see also catallaxy; equilibrium;
        Mill, J. S.; Mises, L. von;
        resources, allocation of; trade
        cycle; value

'Economics and Knowledge' 17—18, 83
empiricism 6, 11, 19
  in economics 17—18
entrepreneur, role of 37—8, 82
epistemology:
  evolutionary theory 11, 24,
    110—14, 117, 119, 134—7, 139
  Hayek's contribution vii—viii, 3—4,
    5—8, 9, 12, 21—4, 110, 116
  and market institutions 40—1,
    75, 113
  see also falsifiability; Kant, I.;
    knowledge; Mill, J. S.;
    Polanyi, Michael; Popper,
    Karl; Wittgenstein, L. von
equilibrium, concept of 18, 31, 36—7,
    83—4, 92—4

falsifiability 10, 12, 19—20, 110—11,
    112, 213n., 222n.
*Fatal Concept: The Intellectual Error
  of Socialism, The* 212n., 215n.
Ferguson, Adam 50, 131
freedom, individual, *see* liberty
Friedman, David 121
Friedman, Milton 88—90, 117.
functionalism, *see* social order:
  functionalism

government, limitation of 2;
  see also interventionism;
    statism

Hamowy, Ronald 62—3, 67, 125—6
Hare, R. M. 63, 65—6, 97
Hart, H. L. A. 59
Helmholtz, H. 210n.
Hobbes, Thomas 31, 71, 100, 121, 124
Hodgson, D. H. 50
Honoré, A. M. 76
Hume, David 13, 33, 42, 110—11, 130,
    217n., 223n.
  empiricism 6
  and justice 7—8, 58—61, 65—6, 76
  and morality 31, 58—60. 96—7
Hutchinson, T. W. 18—19

individualism vii
  libertarian 129—30
  methodological 52—3, 54—5
Individualism and Economic Order
    36—7
'Individualism, True and False' 221n.

individuality 43, 99—101, 129—30
  Romantic conception 42, 95, 101
interventionism:
  economic 64, 82—3, 88—93, 120—1
  and liberty 98—9, 124, 127—8
  and social order 112—13, 138
  see also statism

judgement 101
  and knowledge 14, 24
justice:
  Hayek on 7—8, 60—1, 62—6,
    68—71, 76, 97—8, 107, 128
  social distributive 72—5, 105,
    131—3
  see also Hume, David; Kant, I.;
    Mill, J. S.; rules; welfare, general

Kant, I. 1, 13, 210n.
  epistemology 4—6, 11—12, 13—15,
    21, 23, 117
  influence on Hayek 4—8, 10, 13,
    60, 96—7, 107, 117—18,
    212—13n.
  and law and justice 7—8, 62—3,
    65—6, 69
  limits of reason 5, 24—5
Keynesianism 87—90, 92—3, 116—17
Kirzner, Israel 37
knowledge:
  fragmented 28, 37, 82—3
  practical 13—15, 21, 25, 28, 30,
    36—40, 41—2, 134—5, 139—40,
    213n.
  primacy of practical 34, 79, 117,
    119
  theoretical 14—15, 30, 34—5, 37,
    39, 79, 81—2, 88—9, 135
  see also epistemology; rules
Kristol, Irving 50, 131

Lakatos, I. 20
Lamarck, J. B. de 108—9
language 13
  and rules 34
  and spontaneous order 29, 31—2,
    56
law, rule of 2, 7, 56—61, 72, 80, 113,
    118
  natural 7, 58—9, 68
  objectivity of 68
  and spontaneous order 29, 31—2, 35,
    56, 70—1, 76—8, 124—5, 126—7

see also justice; Kant I.; liberty;
  positivism
Law, Legislation and Liberty 24,
  27—8, 69, 72, 119—20, 123,
  132, 217—18n.
Le Page, Henri 48
'Legal and Political Philosophy of
  David Hume, The' 58
Leoni, Bruno 69
liberalism, classical 13, 95—6, 103,
  120, 131
  Hayek's restatement of vii, 1—2,
    129—30, 140
liberty 13, 15—16, 113—14, 118,
  133—4
  equal liberty 98—9
  and evolution 103
  and individuality 100—1
  limitation of 98—9
  priority of 2, 61
  protection of 125—9
  and rule of law 61—71, 72, 76—8,
    113, 125
  and spontaneous order 119—20.
    121—5
  see also convention; law;
    Mill, J. S.; property
Locke, John 1, 7, 76

Mach, Ernst:
  influence on Hayek 4, 8—10
  positivism 6, 9—10
Mackie, J. L. 218n.
Maistre, Josef de 122
Mandeville, Bernard 29, 33, 44, 132
market economy:
  Hayek's support for 2, 28—9,
    82, 90—4, 103, 113, 116—17,
    131—5
  pricing 38—40, 85—7, 89
  and social justice 74—5, 131—3
  and spontaneous order 31—9,
    41, 50—1, 70, 86, 94
  see also equilibrium
Marx, Karl vii, 102
  economic theory 16, 74
Mauthner, Fritz 13
Menger, Carl 16—17, 19, 33—4, 54
Mill, J. S. vii, 95—103, 112
  economics 3, 16, 74, 95, 102
  and epistemology 3
  and liberty 13, 98—101, 105, 125

and morality 59, 96—8, 100,
  104—7
nationalism 102
social justice 95, 102, 105
see also reason, human;
  utilitarianism
mind viii, 5, 8—12, 21—5, 211n.
  autonomy of 24
  and cultural evolution 11, 27,
    30, 136—7
  see also epistemology; rules
Mises, L. von 41, 46, 54, 84, 102
  on economics 17—18
  influence on Hayek 4, 16—17,
    19, 36, 39, 86, 89, 211n.
monetarism 88—91
money 17, 29, 54, 90—1
  catallaxy 91, 94
  and market forces 91—2, 93
  non-neutrality of 85—6
  quantity theory 86—7, 89
Moore, G. E. 103—4
moral philosophy 42, 44—5, 50,
  56, 100, 114, 129—32
  and evolution 56—9, 107—8, 118,
    138—9
  and free market economy 131—4,
    138—9
  and neoconservative argument 132,
    134
  and radical argument 132—4
  relativism 56—8
  and spontaneous order 29, 31,
    56, 58
  and utilitarianism 59—61, 65,
    96—8, 103—7
  see also Hume, David; Mill, J. S.;
    rules; Spencer, Herbert

*New Studies in Philosophy,
  Politics, Economics and the
  History of Ideas* 21, 29, 119
'Notes on the Evolution of
  Systems of Rules of Conduct' 34
Nozick, Robert 7, 33, 40, 54, 72,
  74, 76—7, 115

Oakeshott, Michael 67, 214—15n.
  epistemology 14, 114
  social theory 53, 81, 130, 138
ontology, monism of Hayek 9—10,
  211n.

perception, theory of:
   Hayek 9, 12, 14, 22—3, 29
   rules of 14, 23, 29, 33—4, 43,
      51—2, 54, 109, 215n.
   see also Popper, K.; reductionism
philosophy, social:
   Hayek's contribution to
      vii—viii, 1, 3, 12—13, 20—1,
      24—6, 28, 41—55, 112, 129—40
   Kant, influence of 7, 24—5
   and spontaneous order 119
   see also Popper, K.; social order;
      tradition
Pierce, C. S. 110, 137
Plant, Sir Arnold 217n.
Plato, and philosophy of mind 30
Polanyi, Michael:
   epistemology 14—16, 114
   influence on Hayek 4, 102, 133,
      138
   and social order 28, 33, 35
politics 61—2
   and constructivism 81—2
Popper, K. 110—15, 210n., 212n.,
      214—15n., 222n.
   epistemology 8, 10—12, 24,
      110—12, 114, 134—7
   and free society 13, 113
   influence on Hayek 4, 10—13,
      19—20
   and perception 11—12, 14
   social philosophy 12, 16, 20—1,
      25, 29, 81—2, 112—13, 213n.
positivism 6, 8—10, 222n.
   legal 68, 71—2
pragmatism 13—14, 137, 212—13n.
Prices and Production 86—7
'Principles of a Liberal Social Order'
      62—3
property, rights to 61, 67—8, 76—8,
      134—5
psychology, philosophical vii—viii,
      3, 210n.

Quine, W. V. 10

rationalism vii—viii, 10, 23, 25, 59,
      112—16, 130, 132, 139
   constructivist 10, 27—30, 31, 94,
      113, 140
   critical, 10, 222n.
Rawls, John 7, 60, 63, 75, 98, 106
Raz, J. 62—3

Reagan, Ronald 94
reason, Human:
   limits of vii—viii, 4, 30, 113—15,
      130
   Mill on 97
   see also Kant, I.; rationalism
reductionism:
   in perception 9, 10
   in social theory 53—5
religion and social order 32, 47, 50—1
resources, allocation of 36, 38, 41, 69,
      76, 83, 85—6, 102
Rhees, Rush 81—2
rights 121
   and law 7, 61—2
   moral 7, 62, 68
   natural 7, 68, 127
Road to Serfdom, The 72, 121
Roberts, Paul Craig 39—40
Rothbard, Murray 122
rules:
   hierarchy of 23
   and justice 62—7, 97—8
   and knowledge 13—15, 21—5
   meta-conscious 22—3, 46, 115
   and morality 60—1, 106, 114
   selection of 23, 44—7, 51—2, 54
   and social order 29—30, 33—4,
      41—8, 51—2, 54
   see also action; perception;
      utilitarianism
Ryle, Gilbert 14, 15

Schumpeter, Joseph 38, 50—1, 131
science:
   Hayek on 5—6, 79, 211n., 212n.
   methodology 10, 17—21, 110—12,
      211n.
   and spontaneous order 35
   see also social science
Sensory Order, The 3—4, 5, 9, 11—13,
      22, 210—11n.
Shackle, G. L. S. 92—3, 128, 223—4n.
Sidgwick, Henry 59, 106—8
Smart, J. J. C. 106
Smith, Adam 1, 50, 82, 124—5, 127,
      131
social order 24—6, 98
   and constructivism 27—30, 31, 42,
      49, 51, 81—2, 112—13, 122,
      133, 139—40
   economic approach 45—51, 55,
      82, 139

and evolution 31—4, 41—55, 57,
    77—8, 103, 134—5, 138—9
and functionalism 45—6, 137—8
and invisible hand thesis 33—4, 54,
    118, 120—1
planning 25, 28, 35--6, 80—1, 113,
    122, 124
spontaneous 23, 26, 27—30, 31—4,
    35, 54—5, 92, 118—25, 139
see also calculation; economic
    theory; knowledge; practical;
    Polanyi, Michael; reductionism;
    rules; traditions
social science 3, 139
    constructivism in 81—2, 113
    new research programme vi,
        139—40
    and public policy 80—3, 89—91,
        116—18
    and theory 79—80
    see also subjectivism
socialism 122
    and economic theory 36, 38—40,
        41, 82, 102—3
    and epistemology viii
Sowell, Thomas 100
Spencer, Herbert 29, 98, 103—10
    and evolution 107—10
    and morality 103—7
statism, rise of 120—1, 124;
    see also interventionism
*Studies in Philosophy, Politics and
    Economics* 19—20, 23, 28, 57—9,
    65—6, 79—81, 212n., 214n.,
    215—16n.
subjectivism in social studies 17—20
Sumner, W. G. 33

Thatcher, Margaret 94
'Theory of Complex Phenomena, The'
    80

totalitarianism 74, 121, 124
trade cycle, theory of 84—6, 88—9,
    92—3
traditions:
    as bearer of knowledge 12, 25, 34
    cultural 41—3, 48—50, 55, 77—8,
        109, 129—30, 134
    in free society 100—1, 113
    see also culture, evolution of
Tulloch, Gordon 120

universalizability, test of 7—8, 60,
    62—8, 96—8, 127
utilitarianism 42, 53
    act-utilitarianism 50
    indirect 59—61, 65, 96—7, 104—5,
        107, 109
    preference-utilitarianism 60
    rational 107
    rule-utilitarianism 56
    see also moral philosophy

value, subjective theory of 16—17, 92
Virginia School of public choice
    theorists 120—1

Watkins, J. W. N. 11—12
welfare, general 78, 124
    and justice 60—1, 65—6, 97
Wicksell, Knut 86
Wieser, F. von 16, 89
will, freedom of 9
Winch, Peter 29, 53
Wittgenstein, L.:
    epistemology 8, 14—15, 21, 23—4,
        114—15
    influence on Hayek 4, 13—15
    and judgement 24
    and social theory 25, 29—30, 50,
        53
Wundt, W. 210n.